BEST REVENGE

How the Theater Saved My Life and Has Been Killing Me Ever Since

STEPHEN FIFE

Co-Starring

Joseph Chaikin and Sholem Asch

And Featuring Appearances by

Sam Shepard, Joseph Papp, John Guare, James Woods, Peter Brook, F. Murray Abraham, Groucho Marx, Dustin Hoffman, Samuel Beckett, Mary Tyler Moore, The Ghost of Tennessee Williams, Franz Kafka, Dracula, Mulder & Scully, Mom, Dad, Keats, My Ex-Wife and Several Ex-Girlfriends, The Agent for the Agent of Neil Simon, Blanche DuBois, The Voice of Dr. Martin Luther King, Vincent van Gogh, Al Jolson, Buechner, The Jews of Atlanta, Humus Guy, Goldie Hawn's Psychic, Blake, Several Actors You've Never Heard Of, My Soon-To-Be Ex-Girlfriend, My Brothers, My Ex-Dog, The Agent for the Agent for the Agent of John Malkovich, And a Cast of a Thousand Creditors

Cune

Best Revenge:
How the Theater Saved My Life
and Has Been Killing Me Ever Since
Cune Press, Seattle, 2004
© 2004 by Stephen Fife
All Rights Reserved

Credits:
Flyer for *God of Vengeance* by Andy Suggs, Art Director,
Carroll / White Advertising, Atlanta
"The Boomerang and the Jewish Dentist" by Stephen Fife first appeared in
American Theatre Magazine, November 1999 (page 206)
Playscript for *God of Vengeance* by Sholem Asch and Adapted by Stephen Fife
(page 209) © Stephen Fife 1992, 1998
Tributes to Joe Chaikin (page 201-205) are © the authors 2003
These tributes first appeared in the *Village Voice* in July 2003
Arthur Miller tribute to Joe Chaikin (page 204) © Arthur Miller 2003
Reprinted by permission of International Creative Management, Inc.
Sam Shepard tribute to Joe Chaikin (page 205) © Sam Shepard 2003
Author photo on flap © Beverly Hall 2002

Library of Congress Cataloging-in-Publication Data

Fife, Stephen.
    Best revenge : how the theatre saved my life and has been killing me ever
since / by Stephen Fife ; co-starring Joseph Chaikin and Sholem Asch and featuring
appearances by Sam Shepard ... [et al.].
        p. cm.
    ISBN 1-885942-10-9 — ISBN 1-885942-24-9 (pbk.)
    1. Fife, Stephen. 2. Dramatists, American—20th century—Biography.
3. Theater—United States—History—20th century. I. Chaikin, Joseph, 1935-
II. Asch, Sholem, 1880-1957. III. Shepard, Sam, 1943- IV. Title.
    PS3556.I42149Z464 2004
    812'.6—dc22   2003017598

Copies of *Best Revenge* can be purchased from your local independent
bookstore, from www.cunepress.com, or by calling 1-800-445-8032.

Cune Press,
PO Box 31024,
Seattle, WA 98103
Ph (206) 789-7055
Fax (206) 782-1330
www.cunepress.com

TABLE OF CONTENTS

■ *"Muss es sein? Es muss sein."*—Goethe, *Faust*

(Okay, I admit it: Beethoven said this, not Goethe. But Goethe sounds way cooler, don't you think? And *Faust* is about a deal with the devil, which theater has certainly been for me. Then again, Faust had loads of money and babes, while I'm sitting here in the buff on Saturday night eating day-old Chinese. So yeah, Beethoven said it. He had a really torrid affair with his young cousin, right? But was it a girl or a boy cousin? Damn.)

This book is dedicated to Joe Chaikin, who died after I finished writing this volume. Your spirit lives on, Joe, wherever daring theater is being made. In the same vein, here's to the playwrights, actors, designers, producers, stage managers, technical staff, running crews, literary managers, playreaders, managing directors, box office personnel, house managers, ushers, envelope-stuffers, and all others who are trying to keep the Hopeless Invalid from expiring ... Not to worry. Your patient will soon rise from his sickbed and give you a swift kick in the Downstage Area.

Thanks to Steve Winer, Jill Bossert, and Phil Cates for their manuscript notes. Thanks to Jane Rollins for the joke. Thanks to Sarah Redwine at Carroll / White Advertising in Atlanta for taking time out from her busy schedule to help secure permission to reproduce the production postcard (designed by Art Director Andy Suggs) from the 7 Stages / Jewish Theatre of the South Production of *God of Vengeance*.

Special thanks to Holly for giving me permission to use certain e-mails she sent me in October 1998. I tip my metaphorical hat. That took guts.

Also, certain names have been changed to protect the innocent (or to placate those who swore they would never speak to me again and / or would kick my ass if I used their real names). To F. Murray and everyone else: see the Beethoven quote above. Ask Ah-nald to translate.

GLOSSARY
(LINGO YOU NEED TO KNOW)

alte kochers—Old guys; or, what seventy-five-year-old Jews call seventy-six-year-old Jews.

improvs—Acting exercises, often performed in the service of exploring themes and characters in the written script. A great compliment to the writer, a playwright's delight. (Or is it really the actors' way of saying, "Our words are better than yours?" Hmm.)

kreplach—A Jewish dumpling. Here's a joke: A mom is disturbed to find her baby son is terrified of *kreplach*. She patiently shows him how *kreplach* are made, first mixing the dough, then rolling out a four-cornered pastry, then putting in filling. After each stage, the baby smiles back at her. "See, there's nothing to be afraid of," she says, folding over the corners. "Aaaah!" the baby cries out when she's finished, *"kreplach!!!!"*

landsmen—"When Eastern European Jews first arrived in the United States, they sought to maintain Old Country ties. To express their feelings for their compatriots, people from their own *shtetl*, they borrowed the term *landsman* from the German immigrants' term *landsmann*."—*All-Purpose Yiddish* by Ira Steingroot.

lit-crit—Literally "Literary Criticism." But anyone who has gone to graduate school, or who has a friend who uses the word "semiotics" in a sentence, knows what I'm talking about.

Litvaks—"The Litvaks settled in the Baltic states and Belorussia, took their name from the Yiddish for Lithuania, whose capital, Vilna, was known as the Jerusalem of the North. [They] esteemed study, learning, strict observance of the Torah, logic, reason, and skepticism."—*All-Purpose Yiddish*.

meshuggeneh—Derived from the Hebrew word for "crazy." Ira Steingroot denotes this usage as specifically feminine, but I've always heard it applied equally to men and women. (Not that women may not be a bit crazier, but for the purposes of appearing neutral and above-it-all, like some kind of freakin' Oliver Wendell Holmes, I'm gonna say that it's entirely equal and, like, sexless. Okay? I mean, I don't know, call me crazy ...)

5

NEA—National Endowment for the Arts. They used to give money to writers until they found out that we spent it on things that we needed, like food and rent. (Horrors!) Now they give it to our parents (theater institutions) to hold for us until we're dead.

New York Times **review**—What playwrights will kill their mothers for.

Leni Riefenstahl—Hitler's personal filmmaker. A hot number, she revolutionized the art of propaganda, photographed African tribesmen for *National Geographic,* and walked away from a helicopter crash at age ninety-nine with only scratches. Currently biding her time until the next Reich.

Second Night—What comes after Opening Night. Otherwise referred to as (a) "working off the hangover" or (b) "trying to remember what happened to your underwear."

shlag—Yiddish for whipped cream. It's what rich people put on their dessert, because when you're rich, life can never be too sweet.

shtetl—A town or city in Eastern Europe. Where the Jews of Manhattan's upper West Side really come from, as opposed to France or Haagen Dasz or some place like that.

John Simon—Theaterspeak for a species of shark found mostly in uptown performing spaces, often with a blonde ingenue in his mouth.

Yiddishkeit—"The totality of the Jewish heritage that is loved and passed on from generation to generation ... Religious observance may be part, but *Yiddishkeit* encompasses a world view, an ethos, and a sensibility."—*All-Purpose Yiddish.*

Chapter One

A Brief History of Chopped Liver

THE REHEARSAL WAS ALREADY in progress when I arrived. The actors were splayed across the floor in some kind of stretching exercise, twisting their bodies into various kinds of painful-looking contortions, and nobody was even aware that I had walked into the room.

My heart sank. I had done many such exercises myself years ago when I was an actor, but I was a playwright now—okay, the adapter in this case, but the playwright was dead, and who the hell knows what an adapter does anyway?—and I had wanted to be among the first there that morning, to mingle and feel a part of the company, to greet the actors and feel that great flush of pleasure that comes from everyone saying how "great your play is," how much they "love it," how they "can't wait to get started." It's really the purest form of playwright (or adapter) pleasure, before all the negative elements start creeping in ... as they always do, all too quickly.

But I had missed it, despite flying all night, taking three planes from Los Angeles, changing first in Chicago, then in Greenville, North Carolina. Arriving unmet at the Atlanta airport ("What am I, chopped liver?" I had asked. "You got it!" was the gist of the unspoken reply.), I had rented a car and managed to decipher my own hastily-scribbled driving directions to the point that I only got lost a few times on my way to the ivy-covered stone building in the funky section of the city known as Little Five Points.

It was eighty-four degrees in October, I had not slept all night, and I was already starting to burn up with a flu I had felt myself coming down with as I ran desperately through LAX to catch my flight (the travel service listed departure as 11:45 PM; at the airport I found it actually left at 11:30). I squeezed my eyes shut, having a sudden memory of an incident at around 7:00 AM on the Greenville leg of my flight, when I had spilled a large plastic cup of orange juice all over the dark suit of an impeccably-dressed Japanese businessman. Poor guy. I really thought for a moment that he was going to strangle me.

"Have a good flight?"

I opened my eyes, and a small man in his early sixties was standing in front of me. He had watery-blue eyes and thinning gray hair and a winningly self-amused smile. He was also one of the three or four people I most admired in the theater, perhaps in the world.

"Yeah, Joe, it was fine. Sorry I'm late."

"No problem. We are waiting for you to begin," Joe Chaikin said, in the clipped speech rhythm caused by his aphasia, the result of a stroke he suffered in the middle of his third open-heart surgery.

Then Joe turned to the actors and the various members of the two theater companies—7 Stages and the Jewish Theatre of the South—who were here for the first rehearsal of this joint production of Sholem Asch's Yiddish classic, *God of Vengeance.*

"Everybody—this is the playwright," Joe said.

I heard a sudden gush of "It's great," "We love your play," and "Can't wait to get started" from all around me, and I let that wave of pleasure roll over me, until of course someone had to chime in, "Isn't he the adapter?"

(Actually, he / she referred to me as the "adap*tater*," but I'm not going to start off making southern jokes, except to say that this sounded like a genetically-altered potato.)

Joe shrugged, he couldn't care less. He gathered the actors around a table and proceeded with the first read-through of the script. I sat nearby, smiling, alternately shivering and burning with fever.

And yes, I did excuse myself afterward and hightail it out of there. I'm as paranoid as any Jewish mother or artistic director, haunted even as I sat there by nightmares of infecting the entire company and closing down the show with whatever foul illness I had brought with me from the land of palm trees, air-kisses, and endlessly-recycled plotlines.

Speaking of which—when the call first came from Atlanta, I was in the midst of conniving the end of the world.

More specifically, I was writing a treatment for a screenplay about a face-off between the US and China that leads to the beginning of World War III. There were assassinations galore, the assumption of power by the first female president, plenty of gut-wrenching power plays, plenty of hot steamy sex in and around the oval office ... Not to mention an enterprising young female reporter from North Bohunk and a grizzled veteran from the *Washington Post*, who join forces (the erotic thing between them is "there but unspoken") and manage (at the eleventh hour) to expose the devious plot (which ends up being about money and power) on nationwide TV just before the planes are about to fly from the Chinese warships. (Yikes!)

I was writing this for a small film company that was co-headed by my best friend at the time, Michael, a fellow playwright from the Columbia MFA program, and a guy who had already had some successes on film and TV. The thing was, I had *thought* Michael was my best friend, but now I was beginning to wonder. He had suggested the realm of material that his company was looking for ("Big budget! Action! With big parts for big actors!"), but had recently responded to my recounting of the world's demise with a spate of confusing notes. ("Make it bigger! And more realistic!") He had also begun to hint that not only his name, but also that of his film company partner, would appear on the script (perhaps also the guy who got them coffee). And then there was a little issue about my not getting paid—anything—until the script was sold to a studio. Which, I was starting to realize, could very well be never. (Double Yikes!)

Then again, I was in the midst of a take-no-prisoners divorce settlement with my ex, and an ongoing conflict with the new woman in my life, Holly, my (her words) "life partner." These were only contributing to my end-of-the-world frame of mind. So when a call came from Mira Hirsch, artistic director of the Jewish Theater of the South ("The what?" I asked, laughing), I was very receptive.

"You don't know what I've gone through to track you down!" she said, also laughing. "You're a hard person to find!"

(Was I really? I had spent many years being one of the easier people in the world to find—living with, then married to, the same woman for sixteen years, living all that time on New York City's upper West Side, never with enough money to go anywhere . . .)

It turned out that Mira had tried to locate me through the Jewish Repertory Theater, the NYC company that had originally commissioned and produced my adaptation of *God of Vengeance* in 1992. Mira told me how unhelpful JRT's artistic director, Ran Avni, had been. It didn't surprise me. If there was nothing in it for Ran, then Ran wouldn't even make a pretense of lifting a finger. Mira had then stumbled upon Barbara Hogenson, a literary agent who had just dumped me a month or so before (Jan. 1998). And Barbara—who still represented my "life partner" Holly—had given her my number.

Mira said that Joseph Chaikin, all-around theater icon and Sam Shepard's best buddy, wanted to direct *God of Vengeance*, but had been unable to find an adaptation he liked. I was the last hope. Would I please send a copy of my version ASAP?

I put a script in the mail later that day, but I felt like I already knew what was going to happen. In true Hollywood fashion, I had gone to see a psychic a month earlier. My basic purpose had been to get her take on whether or not I should dump my current divorce lawyer, who had badly screwed up my case, but who was also family (my second cousin). The psychic, who had 8 × 10 glossies of Goldie Hawn all around (her presiding spirit?), had nothing substantial to say about attorneys. But she had told me in a wise and knowing voice that "a classic Jewish story which you are associated with will be performed in the south."

"What the hell?" I had thought at the time. Here I'm paying Miss Goldie all this money to give me some useful advice while my life is falling apart, and she's talking Tevye in Dixieland. At best it seemed like a bad idea. At worst it seemed a lot worse.

For a moment I had had this image of my family forebear Al Jolson in blackface, down on bended knee, singing "Swanee." That was some messed-up karma, no doubt about it. What if it had fallen on me, his many-times-removed nephew on my "Mammy" side, to purge it, all these years later?

But no, this wasn't going around schools and community clubs in darkest Mississippi, explaining, "What Is A Jew? And Why Should You Not Hate Us?" (Believe me, I'd had jobs like that.) This was a good thing. A great thing. The chance to work with an idol of mine, a man I really admired, to have one of those longtime theater dreams come true, when so many others had been dashed, laughed at, burned at the stake.

But what if it didn't happen? I mean, the first thing Miss Goldie had told me was that I was going to have a big acting career. Well, my so-called acting career (which included playing a gay St. Peter in some misbegotten religious pageant) had come to an ignominious close almost twenty-five years earlier. The chances of reviving it now were pretty much zero. So what if she was wrong about this too?

"I love your version of the play. So spare, so pared down, so poetic. I read many, many versions. Yours is the best."

These words filtered down to me from a great distance, they were a soft gentle rain falling from the highest point of heaven, drifting through a stratosphere of form-letter rejections, unreturned phone calls, and casual dismissals from agents, until they fell on the parched ground of my unfulfilled dreams and thwarted ambitions.

But could I be hearing right? Was I just making this up?

No, there was Joe Chaikin, sitting across from me at the Pad Thai restaurant in NYC, looking very spare and pared down himself, with his older sister Shami beside him—as sturdy and solid and imposing as Joe was frail and poetic. It was just two months after I had mailed in my script, and here I was, discussing a production for this coming October (hooray for Miss Goldie!). It was such an odd feeling, having wishes come true for a change. I decided to push it.

"Did you read the Donald Margulies version?" I asked.

Joe nodded. "No good," he said.

Okay. Well. This day was now officially a national holiday on my personal calendar.

Not that it was a pleasant thing to admit, but there comes a point when many of us stop being good sports and start wishing some ill-will on our more favored peers, no matter how talented they are. And Donald Margulies was a talented playwright, whose play *Sight Unseen* had recently won the Pulitzer Prize. Since then, he had been dubbed the official "Jewish-American Playwright" in some press-sanctioned ceremony to which (as usual) I had not been invited. My own Jewish play *Mickey's Home* had been beaten out several times by his plays, in one case actually getting knocked off a theater's roster when a new play of his suddenly became available. (That theater's artistic director, the very picture of WASP gentility, had actually said to me: "Well, you couldn't expect us to do *two* Jewish plays in one season, could you? We have subscribers.")

But now Margulies had crossed the line, he had climbed into my wheel-house and made it personal. Five years after my version of *God of Vengeance* had been produced at Playhouse 91 on New York's upper East Side—receiving seventeen rave reviews and selling out the last few weeks, despite losing our big-name star during rehearsal—I received a call from a literary associate at the Long Wharf Theater in New Haven, offering me thirty pieces of silver (alright, twenty) to be on a panel discussing a production of *The Donald Margulies version of* God of Vengeance.

I had put down the receiver and silently screamed at the playwrights' decibel (which not even dogs can hear) and then phoned a friend of mine who worked at Long Wharf. She had smuggled out a script, meeting me in the parking lot of a large shopping center, where I had to read the 200-plus page script on the spot, as if I was Julius Rosenberg memorizing state secrets. In the end, that production was cancelled (another twenty pieces of silver down the drain), but his version was out there, hanging over my head. So what if it had twenty-five characters and included a full klezmer concert? I mean, he was Donald Margulies, the darling of regional theater, the state-sanctioned "Jewish-American Playwright"—so what chance did my script have, right?

11

Except that Joe Chaikin liked my version better. Yeah. He loved my version, and he was going to direct it. *The* Joe Chaikin.

I looked across the table at Joe and his sister, who were lapping up the last of their spicy food, both of them bathed in midday sunshine. I smiled broadly, with what Herman Melville might have called "wordless enthusiasms."

Joe looked up, as if on cue, and smiled back. (Shami pursed her lips, looking suspicious.)

And then I did what I had promised myself I wouldn't do—launch into a fevered monologue on how much I loved Joe's work, and how deeply it had affected me.

The gist of it went something like, "Wow, Joe, I mean you are an artist, a real artist, I mean, I went to see the last season of the Open Theatre when I was like nineteen years old, and I was just so blown away by all the shows, I mean those images really stay with you, and it was all so dreamlike and freaky, except that it was very real and moving too, but then when you teamed up with Sam Shepard for that play about the dying man who had the voices of all those people speaking through him like he was channeling all the voices of the American landscape like he was some kind of Medium at the Mall of America—I mean, you're a real artist, Joe, almost alone among the people whose work I've followed all these years, you've stayed true to your vision, and I'm just so honored that—so honored to be—I mean, I read this quote from Stella Adler of all people: 'Joe Chaikin is all that's left of purity in this world,' and while it's a pretty silly thing to say, I also think there's some truth to it, and that's what I need in my life, Joe, I need some of that purity, I really do, I've been through some pretty bad times, some pretty fucking bad times, and I can't tell you how much I'm looking forward to . . ."

Joe sat there with the same smile on his face throughout. He seemed to be listening, but after awhile I had the sense that maybe he was just hearing his own inner music.

Shami, meanwhile, looked like she was going to lose her lunch. She had apparently heard many another nervous acolyte give their own version of this tribute to the master, and she was in no mood to hear another. It happens that Shami Chaikin has herself been something of a downtown theater icon, whom I had seen do wonderful work in a Jean-Claude Van Itallie play called *Bag Lady*.

I tried to shift gears and pour some of my free-flowing honey into her ears, but this only elicited a grumbled, "Got to get going," upon which she rousted Joe from his seat, and was soon walking down the street with him like an old country Mama with her twelve-year-old child.

Chapter Two

I Know What the "F." Stands for in F. Murray Abraham

WHEN I ASKED JOE what attracted him to *God of Vengeance*, why he wanted to direct it, he told me, "I was looking for a gay play. Even better, Jewish and gay. A dramaturg at Yale suggested this."

I found this kind of amusing. Not that there isn't some truth to it. The most notorious scene in *Vengeance*—and without doubt the scene most responsible for whatever revivals the play still gets—is a seduction / love scene downstage center in Act II between the "chaste" daughter of a Jewish whoremaster and his most sought-after prostitute. This was racy stuff when the play was written in 1905, and it still gets a rise out of an audience today if performed well. Whether the scene is about lesbian love or about a young girl's sexual awakening with the only partner she has access to is entirely up to the play's director—and will be a huge sticking point in Joe's production. But either way it entirely thrills and fulfills the imaginations (not to mention the libidinous fantasies) of Jewish hetero artistic directors with a rebellious streak (and most of them have it—otherwise they'd be rabbis).

As one prominent Jewish artistic director inelegantly put it, "Sholem Asch was a bad boy. I mean, writing a play about lesbian prostitutes at the turn of the century. You know he was trying to piss people off."

Something of this allure was certainly there for the Jewish Repertory Theater when they asked me to adapt the play for their 1992 revival. Ran Avni, the artistic director (who years later wouldn't help Mira Hirsch find me), explained that *Vengeance* was the first play produced by the JRT, in the basement of an old building. Eighteen years had elapsed since then—a mystical number in the Jewish religion, signifying a circle of life, a cycle of death and rebirth—and now they were preparing to present it again at Playhouse 91, their beautiful new 300 seat theater near the 92nd Street YMCA. But they needed a new adaptation, partly for the glamour aspect of creating a theatrical event, and partly to revamp an old play and give the actors language they could actually speak. And oh yes—"Make sure the play doesn't piss off the subscribers."

I didn't really know the play well at the time. (As far as Jewish classics went, I much preferred the folk mysticism of S. Ansky's *The Dybbuk*.) Also, I didn't read or speak Yiddish. And my main claim to fame at that point (if any) was as a theater features writer for the *Village Voice* and other publications, as well as a literary manager for the Off-Broadway company Primary Stages. So why choose me?

Apparently the JRT's associate director had read *Mickey's Home*, my play about an elderly Jewish couple who are haunted by memories and who may or may not have a son; they receive a surprise visit from a man who claims to be writing a history of their neighborhood. The managing director liked the play but felt its humor was too dark for their subscribers. However, if that same sensibility was applied to this dark Jewish classic, then maybe … "You know, Tom Stoppard and David Mamet have done it with Chekhov. You think they speak Russian? You could do the same thing," Ran told me.

Stoppard and Mamet were good. I liked that. Then Ran pulled an 800 pound rabbit out of his hat. "We haven't gone public with this yet, but the show will star F. Murray Abraham. We're going to sell out the run just with that."

Wow. A real Academy Award winner. And a really interesting actor, who could hit home runs from both sides of the plate. (I'm talking tragedy and comedy here. You got that, right?)

Not that I was totally starstruck, you understand. I mean, as an actor I had gotten to share the stage as fourth peon from the right with Piper Laurie and the young James Woods, among others. (Piper's sense of calm and well-being were of a sort I had only previously seen attained through a combination of drugs. Jimmy Woods was the most intensely funny and intensely serious actor I ever saw up-close; he could be kind of an asshole, it's true, but he was brilliant). I had spent time as an arts journalist with Lee Strasberg, Meryl Streep, Raul Julia, and scores of other terrific if lesser-known performers. As a playwright I had worked with many wonderful actors, including the young Stanley Tucci (the guy was just out of college and had no career yet, but he already had followers—fellow actors who strode behind him, imitating his walk). Then there was the sad case of Wayne Knight. A gifted comic actor, he threw away the chance of making $78 a week in the political satire revue I was producing and head-writing, bolting in the middle of rehearsals to take a supporting role in some nothing show (or show about nothing) called *Seinfeld.* What the hell was he thinking?

Anyway, I immersed myself in *God of Vengeance* and was thrilled to find it to be a fascinating if unwieldy play. Taking place in 1905 in a large town in Poland not far from Warsaw, the main action concerns Yankel, the Jewish proprietor of a ghetto brothel, and his hunger for salvation, for God. Yankel longs to attend synagogue with the rest of the community, to raise his voice with theirs—but his profession prohibits this. (He's a rich man now; but if he gave up his business, who would he be?) To appease his yearning, he has raised his daughter Rivkele as a chaste girl, a suitable match for a rabbi's son, even while he continues to ply his sex trade downstairs. And he has even taken the unusual step of ordering his own Torah Scroll—a very expensive proposition, which he hopes will protect his family from evil. This is the "instigating event" of the play, setting in motion a series of events which will climax with the fall of the "house" of Yankel, as he curses God from the ashes.

Written by Sholem Asch when he was twenty-one, the play cries out (even in bad translations) with a young man's anger and fervor and outrage. The great Yiddish writer I. L. Peretz, who was Asch's mentor, advised him to "burn it." The problem for many in the Jewish community went beyond even the so-called "lesbian" scene, and the sight of Jewish girls parading around as half-naked whores ("whores" is bad enough, but "half-naked" ones—much worse). No, it was one thing to point out the hypocrisy of the brothelkeeper, who exploited a stable of young women in his basement while raising a daughter of the same age as a snow-white virgin. But it was quite another to have a character like Reb Elye, a kind of rabbinical fixer (or in Yiddish a *macher*), who—for the right price—would finagle the purchase of a Torah Scroll, even though a man like Yankel was strictly forbidden to have one.

Reb Elye's hypocrisy hit right at the heart of middle-class values, at the way business was (and is) done, and it contributed as much as anything to the play's notoriety. This included the 1923 scandal surrounding the first English language production, when the play's Broadway run was shut down and the entire cast locked up (Rudolph Schildkraut, world-famous actor / director, among them) for lewd and immoral behavior.

And what force of American Puritanism was responsible for this raid? Was it some protector of moral values like Mr. J. Edgar Hoover? No. (Though by this time Hoover was already bedeviling the existence of that other Jewish firebrand, Emma Goldman.) It was Rabbi Joseph Silverman of Fifth Avenue's Temple Emmanu-El—sort of the Grand Poobah of snobby East Side Jews (like my maternal grandparents). Rabbi Silverman claimed, "This play libels the Jewish religion. Even the greatest of anti-Semites could not have written such a thing."

All of which whetted my appetite to no end for jumping into the fray. (As it would Donald Margulies, and probably David Mamet too, given my luck.) I mean, it's not just that sex sells, or controversy sells, or anything as obvious as that (though they didn't hurt). It's that this play exists alone in the Jewish canon. It may as well have been dropped down from Mars, or from some unsuppressible Jewish fever dream, by way of Russian novelist Fyodor Dostoevski (himself a big anti-Semite). No wonder the hetero artistic directors and the gay Jewish women were fighting over this play. It had the most important quality in the history of world drama: it made our parents squirm. It wasn't respectable. People couldn't ignore it.

For my part, I could already see the girls parading around in the lower depths while F. Murray prowled restlessly upstairs, chewing the scenery then spitting it out in God's face. Was this my idea of fun? You'd better believe it.

Ran had been very clear about some of the changes he wanted. In between the upstairs scenes in the family apartment and downstairs scenes in the brothel, there were a few street scenes where beggars and supplicants came into Yankel's house and, in effect, put on a circus / variety show to get contributions. These interludes gave the play some nice local color, but they made the same dramatic point over and over: Yankel is a rich man but isn't respected; he enjoys his power, but longs for people's respect. Eliminating these scenes would also get the number of characters down to ten. Ran would prefer eight (this is what artistic directors spend their time thinking about), but ten would do.

I had read and re-read the three English language versions of Asch's play that existed. I had also sub-commissioned a Yiddish scholar to do a literal translation, so I could get a better sense of Asch's linguistic intentions. Then I got another call from Ran Avni.

16

Ran was so afraid of offending his subscribers that he had already called twice to say the production was being cancelled. But it was too late for that now—F. Murray's star turn had been announced, the entire run was sold out. In fact, Ran was calling to tell me that F. Murray now wanted control over "every aspect" of the production. This extended to my adaptation. Ran demanded that I submit a sample scene for F. Murray's approval.

"What?" I said. "That's ridiculous."

I hadn't even formulated a strategy yet. Besides, it wasn't in my contract. (So far JRT had paid me only a small commissioning fee.) And what criteria was F. Murray going to use? Did he have his own gaggle of Yiddish scholars whispering in his ear?

"It's up to you. Take it or leave it," Ran said.

"Leave it," I told him.

"Then I'll find someone else. And I know plenty of writers with better credits than you who would do this for nothing."

Who can argue with such crystal-clear logic? I handed in my scene four days later. Three days after that I was summoned for a meeting with his Murray-ness.

For some reason, I'm a little vague on where this meeting took place, whether at a rehearsal room at the 92nd Street YMCA on Lexington Avenue, or a few blocks east at Playhouse 91, where the production was slated to run.

I guess I was pretty nervous that day. The truth was, I really wanted to do this adaptation. I had gotten very emotionally attached to the play. And I had nothing to gain and everything to lose at this meeting, where the commission could be so easily (and to my mind so unfairly) snatched away from me. But didn't stunts like that only happen in Hollywood, where writers had sold out their creative control for a barrel of money?

Apparently not. When Murray showed up—late, sweaty, wearing old gray sweats, drinking Poland Springs water ("Ha, ha," I thought. "*Poland Springs*")—he took out the four page scene, a simple dialogue near the start of the play between Yankel and his wife Sore. Murray looked down, shaking the pages somewhat sternly, as if they were unruly Yeshiva students. I was already thrown by the fact that he hadn't shaken my hand when he walked in. (Who in this business doesn't shake hands? The theater was like some Marx Brothers orgy of hand-shaking. It's what people gave you in lieu of money.)

I kept waiting for him to look up, to look at me long enough to make eye contact. I gave great eye contact, looking back deeply, unflinchingly. I knew

I could win him over with charm if I hadn't done so already with talent, if he only gave me the chance. But he didn't.

F. Murray turned to Ran Avni—the only other person in the room—and said, "Tell Mister Fife that this is a promising beginning."

"So he has the assignment?" Ran asked.

"Tell him he can proceed," F. Murray pronounced.

I took a deep breath. Internally, I shouted a victory cheer.

"Thanks," I said, smiling at F. Murray, waiting for him to drop the severity routine. I would laugh—even at my own expense—if this was supposed to be funny, but his manner was more that of a judge pronouncing a lengthy prison sentence. My "thanks" rattled around in the room then faded away like an embarrassment, some kind of faux pas.

"Tell him that the language is too literary," F. Murray told Ran. "I don't want to fall into the trap of doing a "classic.""

"Try to be less literary," Ran told me with a straight face, as if he was translating from a language I couldn't possibly understand.

"This is a seething, passionate play," F. Murray told Ran. "That's what made me want to do it in the first place."

"Of course," I interjected, speaking directly to F. Murray, trying to break through this logjam. I told him how I was having a literal translation made so I could get closer to Asch's language, his original intention. "Like stripping cheap paint from a beautiful antique," I said, plucking a phrase from a speech I'd concocted on the bus ride over.

F. Murray looked around perplexed, twitching his nose slightly, as if someone had passed some gas. After a few moments Ran told him, "He's going to work on it."

"Good, good," F. Murray said. "Just remember that I have final say on everything. If it all comes together in a unified way, it could be very powerful."

"It's already sold out," Ran said. "Producers are calling me about Broadway."

"First things first," F. Murray said, standing up.

Now that the meeting was over, I was hoping to get the handshake that F. Murray owed me, maybe even the nod or the smile. But no. He nodded at Ran, saying, "You'll keep me informed of everything?"

"Of course, Murray," Ran said, but the F-man had already bolted, probably late for his next Mission of Charm.

"Who's directing this play, Ran, you or F. Murray?" I asked.

"Just let me worry about that," he said. Ran is an Israeli expatriate with brusqueness to spare, but even Ran seemed a little put out by F. Murray's high-handed ways. "You just keep thinking about Broadway, and your name in lights," he said.

Broadway was good. My name in lights wasn't too shabby. But what size would F. Murray's ego have swelled to by then? It would be like a Macy's Thanksgiving Day balloon in a small room—Porky Pig blown to his full girth, crushing everyone inside with his porkiness. And how had this happened? Just because he won the Academy Award for *Amadeus?* I'd actually known F. Murray in passing some years before, when his main claim to fame was his role as a dancing grape in the Fruit of the Loom commercials. He'd been in scores of plays with friends of mine in obscure little theaters (to call some of these venues "toilets" would be a compliment), where he'd earned my allegiance by never shying away from an acting choice, no matter how outrageous.

(Come to think of it, though, I had heard a story that seemed more credible now. Right after he'd won his award, F. Murray was cast as Shakespeare's Scottish King opposite Estelle Parsons as Lady Mac on Broadway. He'd shown up at the first rehearsal, placed his Oscar downstage center, then assumed his seat with the others. The next day Estelle Parsons had placed *her* Oscar down center too. While this hadn't really settled anything, and the production had been a disaster, at least she'd had a way to retort. What did I have? Some letter of recommendation from a college instructor, saying, "It is my considered opinion that Stephen has a real flair for words . . ."?)

Still, I was convinced that the F-man could be tremendous as Yankel. He was physically unattractive, even repellent, in a way that entirely suited the hard-driving, self-loathing brothelkeeper. And he was sexy in an oily, somehow obscene way. Yet he could hit the high notes as well, you could really believe that he'd been driven half-mad by his suppressed yearning for God, and that he would not flinch from taking the Creator to task, matching Him rage for rage. (What did that "F." stand for anyway? "Frank?" "Fred?" Neither seemed Jewish enough to go with "Murray" and "Abraham.")

Yes, all in all, Ran was right: I was better off taking the abuse, the rewards were worth it. Now if we could just get a script.

That had been Ran's parting question, muttered through his dark scraggly beard, "When can you have a complete script?" I had told him not to worry, it was only May, he would have it long before Labor Day, which was when auditions began (the first preview was October 24). But in truth, there *were* reasons to worry.

The pressure of turning out the sample scene for F. Murray had completely exploded my relationship with the Yiddish scholar I'd been working with. He was a soft-edged young man with a shock of brown hair that hung in his eyes and a burning love of *Yiddishkeit* (the revival of Yiddish culture), matched only by his burning ambition. From the beginning there had been questions like, "Why can't the program say it's adapted by the two of us?" When I explained that I was the one who had gotten the commission, he had countered with, "How about if it says, adapted by you *with* me?" When I'd nixed this as being too confusing, he had laid low for a while. But when we were working up the sample scene, he made it clear that he was turning out his own version of Asch's play, whether I liked it or not. I didn't like it and fired him.

The subtext of this little power struggle was this scholar's belief that he was the more qualified of the two of us, even the more deserving, to create this adaptation. In fact, even more basically, he felt that he was the more *Jewish*. After all, not only did he speak Yiddish and live on the lower East Side, he also located his identity in the world of the *shtetl* (Eastern-European Jewish village / ghetto) that Asch was writing about. Whereas I was an upper-West-Side-private-school Jew, with much of the ambivalence toward my ethnic heritage typical of the breed. It was all part of that very familiar Immigrant Success Story, where assimilation (read: social-climbing) and financial freedom (read: acquisition of power) were the keys. Judaism was a fashion accessory to be worn on suitable occasions, then put in a closet and forgotten about.

There is no doubt that the scholar's sense of deserving was legitimate (which in a situation like this will get you fired ten out of ten times). But I felt it more keenly at this point because of experiences I'd gone through some years before, with regard to my own Jewish identity. That was around 1980, when I was just out of college and had received a federal writing grant through a Jewish organization. I was one of seven writers who received this particular grant, which required us to do a certain amount of work in the public sector. I started out by giving talks in the public school system on various topics of Jewish culture, such as Jewish Humor and Immigrant Literature. I also spoke about the Holocaust, going to far-flung places in Brooklyn, Queens, and the Bronx, where I tried to explain how six million Jews had been led to slaughter—as if such a thing could be explained. I had followed this up with a ten-month residency in a Jewish old-aged home on the lower East Side, where I collected oral histories, which I edited and published as a small magazine of the residents' writings. When the grant ran out, I hooked on as an art reviewer with a short-lived publication called *The New Jewish Times*.

I remember my Mom's description of going down to the newsstand to purchase the first issue of this weekly paper. "As soon as your father said the word 'Jewish,' the news vendor came out with three other papers with 'Jewish' in the title. One of these wasn't even in English." Ah yes, I could see the Ben Shahn drawing now: the dealer reaching over with thick grubby fingers as the two upscale liberals recoil in horror from the word "Jewish." I had to admit, that picture satisfied something basic in my rebellious nature.

But it would have been far more satisfactory for me (and probably for this book) if I had emerged from my experiences a deeply changed man, with a spiritual zeal and profound embrace of all things Jewish. The truth was, I did feel deeply changed on an emotional and—yes—spiritual level. And I did feel Jewish in a way that I hadn't before. But when Shabbat came, and the other bright young men at *The New Jewish Times* rose up and danced in a clomping frenzy of religious glee, I mostly hung back in a corner, reading my Kafka.

The intervening years had done little to clarify my position. I had married a Mexican-American woman, and I had worked for years on a series of plays about van Gogh, which focused on his battles with his Lutheran upbringing. Yet I also wrote plays with Jewish subject matter, such as *Mickey's Home*, whose taking off point was very clearly my experience collecting oral histories. I longed for a relationship with the Jewish theater community, which I was hoping *God of Vengeance* would give me.

Given this degree of cultural schizophrenia, it should come as no surprise that I ended up hiring a Yiddish scholar who was a perfect specimen of Aryan superiority: blonde, shapely, attractive, keenly intelligent. She was born in Germany, of full-German parents, with nary an errant Jewish gene in sight. Yet somehow these pure bloodlines had managed to produce a woman whose turn-ons were Sholom Aleichem, klezmer concerts, and neurotic New York Jews. More than that, she was a serious scholar getting her PhD in Jewish Literature from Columbia University (where, in fact, she was writing her dissertation on Sholom Aleichem).

She was also a no-nonsense collaborator, who gave me invaluable insights into Sholem Asch's language and purpose, pointing out how the physical dichotomy in the play of upstairs / downstairs was mirrored in Asch's recurrent use of the terms *kosher* (sanctioned, blessed) and *treyf* (vulgar, garbage).

Rather than go for a literal translation again, I asked this scholar to give me a textual comparison between Asch's original and the three English versions, and then to translate only one scene. The scene I chose was one in which two young prostitutes return from bathing in the rain to reminisce about their families and the path they have chosen. It is a sad, tender, funny, beautiful scene, suffused with nature poetry and biblical imagery. It was filled with compassion for these poor girls who were never given the chance to determine their own destinies (in fact, their only "choice" was between doing their father's bidding or being an outcast), and I was determined to do it right.

(When John Simon critiqued the production for *New York Magazine*—giving one of the two negative reviews it received—he singled out this scene as being the most egregious example of how I had "sensationalized" the play by unduly emphasizing sexual content. When of course I hadn't changed a word from Asch's original, treating the text here as holy writ.)

With my Yiddish scholar's help, I was able to hand Ran a completed version less than two months after receiving F. Murray's approval. Large sections of the original had been cut out, new sections had been written (either to provide necessary transitions or to go more deeply into character / motivation). There seemed little left for me to do than to kick back, play along with Ran's and F. Murray's games, and await the ascension to Broadway.

I had two more "story" meetings with F. Murray that I remember—but, memory being what it is, these two have compressed in my mind into one indelible meeting.

It was hot, sultry, muggy—midsummer in urban New York. Ran and I were there first, exchanging pleasant chitchat about designers who had joined the production, etc., moving on shortly to what we were looking for in the upcoming auditions. Then his F-ness entered (what did that "F." stand for anyway?) wearing his sweaty gray sweats and carrying a large brown paper bag. F. Murray opened the bag and took out a six-pack of beer. (I think it was Miller High Life.) He gave a can to Ran, ripped off a can for himself, popped the top, tilting it up, swigging.

("It's alright," I muttered. "I didn't want one anyway.")

There was some casual mention of the play, which would eventually prompt me to express an unbidden opinion. If F. Murray had any response to what I said, he would tell it to Ran, who would turn and tell me. These exchanges would inevitably end up with F. Murray re-stating that he "wanted control over every aspect," etc.

Then would come the real point of the meeting (as I soon came to realize)—discussing pornography. F. Murray or Ran would start describing a recent porno tape they had rented, and they would be off on a description of positions, escapades, body types, genitalia. There were serious discussions of titles like *Hot and Nasty* and *Wet XXX,* along with a debate on the best way to administer sexual pain. In fact, if I had to give their repartee a title, it would be "The Joys of Degradation (Yours Not Mine)," or "All Women Are Sluts (If You Can Only Get Them to Lie Down and Shut Up)."

I kept reminding myself how this related to themes of *God of Vengeance,* especially the *treyf* part. When that rationalization wore thin, I tried humming "Lullaby of Broadway." But eventually I couldn't help looking bored. That's when Ran turned and accused me of being "a yeshiva boy."

"What's the matter with you? You're so pure?" he asked.

Not at all, I said. This just wasn't my idea of fun.

"Oh? And what is?" he asked. "Going to poetry readings?"

I don't think F. Murray noticed the interruption, he popped the tab on his third or fourth beer (I lost count) and launched into another colorful tale of big boobs and body fluids, leaving me once again to ponder: What did that "F." stand for? Fleonce? Felton? Fester? Furman? Frittata? How about Frankenstein? (Hey, *that* sounded Jewish.)

All this frivolity came to a screeching halt toward summer's end, just before auditions were about to begin. I could tell something was wrong when Ran called me, his usual tone of glumness tinged with actual pain.

"Murray left to do a movie in Italy," he said.

"When is he coming back?" I asked.

"They offered him a million dollars," Ran said.

"But he's coming back in time to do the production. Right?" I asked.

Wrong. F. Murray was gone. Broadway was gone. The sold-out houses were gone. It was all we could do now to salvage the production.

Ran managed to do that, replacing the F-man ("Fleer?" "Flyaway?" "Faithless?") with veteran character actor Lee Wallace. Lee's wife, Marilyn Chris, took the role of Yankel's wife, Sore. Soon auditions arrived, and the rest of the cast fell into place.

The rehearsal period showed Ran to be an effective manipulator of actors with zero artistic vision. The actors were fine, especially Marilyn Chris, whose early career moxie as an experimental theater actress (with Robert Kalfin's Chelsea Theater) served her well in the role of a mother with the heart of a prostitute. Lee Wallace was fine too, except for one problem: he bore an uncanny resemblance to Ed Koch, only three years removed as Mayor of New York City. (Lee had in fact played a Koch-like mayor in the film *Pelham One Two Three*.) Lee grew a beard, wore a Polish cap, whatever: he just looked like Ed Koch with a beard and a cap. This tended to distract audiences from the issues at hand in the play. (To the very end, I would hear people leave the performances saying, "And that Ed Koch guy was good." "But he looked just exactly like Koch!")

Juggling the "hats" of artistic director and stage director, Ran Avni's attitude throughout was nothing if not consistent. Instead of paying a technical crew, he gave all the money for building the set of a house (spanning the forty-four foot width of the stage) to one homeless-looking guy, who camped out in the theater a week before the first preview, completing the job (sort of) just in time to give the actors one day to rehearse on it. On opening night, Ran threw a party for his best subscribers in the theater after the show, but only Lee and Marilyn from the cast of ten was invited. (Lee and Marilyn were so upset, they hosted a cast party in their apartment on second night, complete with personalized mugs for everyone.)

My Yiddish scholar came to opening night ready to be dazzled, but she left horrified by the shallowness of the show, begging me not to mention her in any interviews. I knew she was right, the production lacked any conviction or passion, any real reason for being. Most disappointing to me were the brothel scenes and the "love" scene. I thought the prostitutes had that same generalized air of "saucy" behavior so familiar from summer stock and even college productions. The actress playing Manke—the most charismatic and sexually-liberated of the whores, who seduces Yankel's daughter Rivkele— was astonishingly sensual and mysterious (almost feral) in her audition, but she never attained anything close to that intensity in the larger confines of Playhouse 91. True, the scene did cause the audience to break into an epidemic of coughing, and I observed many women fanning themselves with their programs; but it was a mere shadow of what it could have been.

(I only saw one audience member ever get up and leave. I stopped this man in the lobby and asked what had offended him. He told me point-blank that he would be glad to stay if there were any man-woman sex scenes upcoming.)

Yet from the beginning, audiences and the press liked the production (except for John Simon and Howard Kissel of the *Daily News*). *The New York Times* had run a feature story in the Sunday "Arts & Leisure" section prior to opening, and their daily reviewer later wrote: "Under Mr. Avni's direction this cast makes [the characters] vivid human beings whose hopes and schemes and delusions seem chillingly familiar." Clive Barnes in the *Post* titled his review "*Vengeance* Is Fine;" he praised Lee and Marilyn, along with my adaptation. *Variety* lauded the "taut production," asserting that the play "retains its uncompromising power." The Jewish papers and the gay papers gave the show a warm embrace. Even the *Village Voice,* which usually ignored my work or kicked dirt on it, chimed in with hosannas. The remainder of the run was soon sold out.

Talk, of course, immediately began about extending or moving the production. Such talk almost *always* begins just after opening, even if the show is the usual bland piece of cheese, because that is the hope, the wish, the small flame nurtured in the heart throughout rehearsals (just as I nurtured my "Lullaby of Broadway") and then stoked by one's friends during previews (mostly with big fat lies, but that's why they're one's friends). But in this case, with seventeen positive reviews—ranging from solid endorsements to outright raves—there were very good reasons to keep hope alive, keep those home fires burning. Fires that were being fed, in fact, by Ran Avni himself, who kept chucking on log after log.

"Keep your schedules open," he told everyone. "Try not to make any plans for the rest of the year." We had opened on November 1 (after a week of previews) and were slated to close at the end of the month. So there was only a two week window to make a decision and get the new advertising campaign in place.

There was something of a side drama here, that I (but no one else) was aware of. The production had a co-producer named Alexander Racolin. Mr. Racolin, a retired entertainment lawyer, had also been co-producer for many of the shows produced by the Primary Stages Company during my tenure as literary manager. On one of these occasions, the show had scored critical raves and attracted a group of investors who wanted to move it to a large Off-Broadway house for an open run. (Touchdown! Goal! Home run! You get the idea.) This was going to be a huge step forward for a very young theater—our first show to move—and everything was going fine, everyone was in agreement—except Mr. Racolin. He refused to give his consent to the venue that had been chosen, though he had nothing substantial to suggest in return. By the time he had finished dicking around, the venue was lost and the group of investors had gone elsewhere. In the end, Mr. Racolin had moved the show himself to an obscure little theater in the West Village that no longer exists. No one came. The show closed in two weeks.

I had never actually met Mr. Racolin (literary managers never get to meet anyone). I kept waiting for him to show up at Playhouse 91, so I could

25

pour on the charm and try steering him in a commercial direction (as if any producer ever really listened to the playwright, much less the adapter). Meanwhile, though, I was having a ball as Sholem Asch's surrogate self.

I was living at the time almost exactly due east of the theater, in a condo apartment on 90th Street between Columbus and Amsterdam. I had recently moved there in a misguided attempt to save my marriage. (It actually turned out to be a very guided attempt on my soon-to-be-ex-wife's part to acquire a better residence.) Every late afternoon during the show's run I would hop on a crosstown bus or walk around the jogging path in Central Park to Fifth Avenue, then stroll over to Second Avenue around 91st Street, where I would have something to eat (either alone or with friends) at one of the many excellent bars and restaurants. At around 7:40 I would saunter over to Playhouse 91, where I would hang out in the lobby, nodding to acquaintances and conversing with friends. Probably the most thrilling night was when Sholem Asch's only surviving son (John) flew in from London with his wife Evelyn to see the play. John was in his late eighties I believe, thin and frail, but still sharp; he shook my hand afterward and told me I had done his dad proud.

Of course, I knew that this was small potatoes compared to Broadway and high-end Off-Broadway productions. (Probably the most impressive event I'd attended, from a playwright's perspective, was the Broadway opening of Wendy Wasserstein's *Heidi Chronicles*. It seemed as if every playwright from Playwrights Horizons, along with a slew of other Broadway and Off-Broadway notables, was there. I roamed the aisles at intermission, looking for someone I would enjoy talking to. I finally came across the eccentric self-styled genius Harry Kondoleon, who had been a playwriting teacher of mine in the Columbia MFA program, and who would die of AIDS a few years later. He was seated with the playwright Paul Rudnick (who later wrote the films *Jeffrey* and *In and Out*) in a strangely isolated row of their own. The two sat there preening like Siamese cats, knowing that—by definition—any event they attended had to be fabulous.)

Still, this production was big-time stuff for me: a good cast, excellent acoustics, wonderful sightlines, a real refreshment stand in the lobby (as opposed to that folding card table I usually got), and sold-out houses every night at almost $30 a pop—from which I was slated to get a six percent cut. Not to mention all the blown-up critic's quotes on the walls, saying ecstatic things about the show.

It was on one such Thursday night, almost four weeks into the five week run, that Ran Avni took me aside in the lobby, saying that he had something

26

to talk over with me after the audience had gone to their seats. I was sure this had something to do with the extension or move, since time was running out to make an announcement. (Once a show closes, that's it, the parade has gone by; all that's left is to sweep up the confetti.) I speculated to myself that maybe this had something to do with Mr. Racolin, maybe he was again throwing a wrench in the works. If only I'd been able to meet him!

"Look," Ran said, when the lobby had emptied, "it's now or never for this extension. I have to take out an advertisement in tomorrow's *New York Times* if I'm going to do it. And I am prepared to do it—a two week extension. That's two more weeks for commercial producers to see the show. Two more weeks for agents to come see your work. And two more weeks of employment for the actors. But it can only happen on one condition."

I looked at him, completely puzzled. What could he be talking about?

"You would have to forgo your royalties," he said.

"What?" I asked. "You mean for the extension? Well, I don't think that's really fair, but if it means keeping the show open for another two weeks—"

"No. You'd have to forgo all your royalties."

"For the whole show?" I asked, stunned. Ran nodded.

For months now I'd been watching the actors collect their 300 or so dollars a week, while I'd gotten only a $1,000 commissioning fee—more than half of which I'd paid to my sub-contractors, the Yiddish scholars. Could he really be serious?

Ran actually put his arm on my shoulder, saying, "It's so sad when the theater has to be balanced on the back of its artists, but sometimes—"

I shook off his arm. "What about you? Why don't you take it out of your salary? Just don't pay the director."

"The thing is, my salary comes out of a separate budget," he said. "But your money comes directly from the funds needed for any extension—"

"No," I said.

"Then you're killing the production," he told me.

"Oh, so I'm killing the production?" I said.

"That's right, you are."

"Fuck you," I said, moving away from him. "Fuck you."

I didn't speak with Ran for the remaining week or so of the run. Ran, in turn, didn't speak with the actors, choosing to send the stage manager back with the news that there would be no extension. Ran didn't even go backstage closing night to thank the actors for their contribution—something I believe that even vermin do when they put on shows.

I saw Ran once more, two months or so after *God of Vengeance* had closed, when he finally had my check ready. "Oh look—it's yesterday's news," the associate director had sniped as I entered the office. I picked up the check and looked at it for a long moment—the total was around $5,000—then I turned on Ran and told him how ashamed I was to have been associated with him, how he had ruined a great experience.

"You'll be back," Ran said, shrugging. "The actors too. Where else will you go?"

I stormed out of the office, glad to be rid of him. But at the same time I knew that, despite his best efforts, he hadn't really succeeded in ruining everything. After all, this had given me the chance to work on a remarkable play, to work with remarkable actors, and—oh yes—to find out what the "F" stood for in F. Murray Abraham.

This had come out quite by accident during an interview with a red-haired reporter from National Public Radio, for an arts segment they were doing on the production (as I said, the press liked the show). The reporter told me how taken he was with Lee Wallace's delivery of the brothelkeeper's arguments with God. I agreed, saying I thought Lee's performance held its own with what F. Murray would have done. When we were off-air, the reporter casually remarked, "You know what F. Murray's first name is? Fahoud."

"Fahoud?" I said. "Fahoud? You've got to be kidding."

"Nope. I did a story on him a while ago."

"So he's passing for Jewish?" I asked.

"You got it, baby."

Fahoud Abraham. Wow. I didn't even have a clue.

Though the more I thought about it, the more I could see it really wasn't any different than all those Jews who had changed their names from Gar-finkle to Garfield, from Archie Leach to Cary Grant, from Fivelovsky to Fife. For a moment I felt a real kinship.

That's when I resolved to forget about "Fahoud" altogether and just substitute a four-letter word I felt close to, that was devoid of religious or ethnic associations, for Murray's "F."

Chapter Three

Jews Don't Pray with Clasped Hands

I N THE SUMMER OF 1980, I found out that someone I knew was assistant directing for Joe Chaikin's Winter Project, and I wrangled my way into a rehearsal. Joe was working with five actors and a few musicians on a still-untitled theater piece, which would later be performed at La Mama under the rubric *Tourists and Refugees*.

This was, as it turned out, the heyday of Joe. After the demise of the Open Theatre in 1974 (I caught this last gasp), he knocked about a bit before finding himself in the work of his two Sams, Beckett and Shepard. He directed Beckett's *Endgame* at Manhattan Theatre Club in early 1980 and would have a memorable meeting with The Great Stone Face himself in Paris when the production transferred there in late February. Joe's association with Shepard went all the way back to a dinner party in 1964. They had corresponded since then (with Shepard declaring, "I am an apprentice to Joe,"), and this had led to a wish to collaborate (Shepard had already contributed a few monologues to the Open Theatre). In 1978-79, they developed two separate pieces (*Tongues* and *Savage / Love*) for one actor (Joe) with onstage musicians. These were performed first at the Magic Theater in San Francisco, then at the Public in NYC, where I was among the lucky few to catch them (the theater space, as I remember, only held seventy or so people).

The evening was a poetic meditation on themes of love and death, a talking-score song cycle accompanied (often in a slyly-humorous, illusion-puncturing way) by musicians with homemade percussion instruments. Joe was an everyman character, a naked self thrust into a confusing, many-voiced world, wandering the ambiguous and uncertain terrain between birth and death. (Even death was ambiguous—by no means necessarily the end.) There was a shamanistic quality to his pitch-perfect performance, as he emerged from a coffin-like bed to raise the spirits of the dead and hidden parts of ourselves, the unseen aspects of our lives which we did our best to avoid in our waking hours, and which emerged (if at all) only in dreams. I remember a thread running underneath the words, which conveyed something like, "The world is an unknowable place of great joy and great grief, and I accept it." There was also a strong sense of mourning, of longing for life even as it slips away, slips through our fingers.

This quality was also present in the rehearsal I attended on that long ago summer day. Joe was having his small troupe of actors run through improvisations on the theme of "homelessness," and there was a general sense in the ensuing work of lostness, uncertainty, of being trapped somewhere between here and there. I remember improvs with a suitcase, mostly about American travelers in foreign places who did not know themselves, whose destination seemed to recede farther into the distance the closer they approached. Most of all, though, I remember Joe himself, who was looser, funnier, earthier than I would have imagined. A short man (around five foot four) with curly brown hair, his stage presence was spare (though not solemn) with a deep emotional resonance. But I noticed then how physically agile he was, at home in his body, as he joked and horsed around with the actors (who included two Open Theatre actors—Paul Zimet and Tina Shepard—and a dynamic young actor, Will Patton), making the occasional off-color remark.

I couldn't remember having seen this sexier, earthier, even coarser Joe Chaikin onstage (though all I could remember from the Open Theatre pieces was a general dream-like sense of anti-materialism). He certainly wasn't in evidence in *Texts*, the one-man Beckett play Joe co-adapted (from *Texts for Nothing* and *How It Is*) and performed in the large Martinson Theater at the Public. Joe held that 400-member audience spellbound by the force of his Chaplinesque grace, his ability to flesh out Beckett's sense of unbearable isolation. In the lingo of Peter Brook (a hero of Chaikin's), this evening exemplified the "Holy Theater" and the "Immediate Theater" (asserting itself in the present tense). But what about inserting a jolt of the "Rough Theater," with its joyous vulgarity?

I was just starting to write plays, and (of course) I kept thinking how cool it would be to write something in that vein for Joe. Maybe a sleazy gang kingpin or a late-night comic with a gambling problem. I kept mulling over these ideas, making false starts, trying to string together enough scenes that I could pique Joe's interest. Then, sometime in 1983, I heard that Joe was

30

going to Harvard to work on another play with Sam Shepard. "Damn!" I thought, in a fit of Shepard-envy. "When is it going to be my turn?"

Except that, shortly thereafter, I heard that Joe had had a stroke on the operating table, in the middle of his third open-heart surgery. He had almost died. And, even though he had survived, he now had aphasia, which rendered him speechless, unable to care for himself.

So much for Joe Chaikin. So much for the world's seeing any further sides of his talent. And so much for any chance of my working with him.

Except that Joe Chaikin did not fade away.

He completed his collaboration with Sam Shepard, titled *The War in Heaven*, about an angel who is caught between heaven and earth. More than that, he performed it himself, Off-Broadway and around the world. And he continued making theater—sometimes about his affliction, sometimes directing plays by Shepard, Ionesco, even Arthur Miller.

Of course, I had lost track of Joe a long time ago. True, I did go see him perform *War in Heaven* at the American Place, where super-titles were projected around the space to help jog his stroke-damaged memory. (They also created a deeply evocative physical environment, a sense of the word made flesh, as Joe's "angel" struggled to find salvation, in a performance that still defies medical explanation.) My wish to work with Joe, to have him perform or direct a play of mine, had long ago given up the ghost, replaced by other wishes, other dreams of collaboration with actors, directors, or theaters whose work I had admired, or whose rising star I simply wanted to attach myself to.

And then the phone rang out of nowhere, on a warm February day in Santa Monica, and the next thing I knew, I was here in Atlanta working with Joe Chaikin—on a piece of "Rough Theater," no less. My chance had indeed come along, eighteen years after the notion had first taken root in my thought.

Could someone be any luckier?

The flu that had percolated on my flight to Atlanta and had driven me from the first rehearsal subsided just as quickly as it came. Of course, I couldn't know that three days later it would return with a vengeance, bite me on the ass and knock me out for the weekend. On this Wednesday morning, I woke up feeling flu-free, stretched my extremities (still cramped from being squeezed into airplane seats) and gave myself permission to attend rehearsal and endanger the health and well-being of the company.

Truth was, I could hardly restrain myself. I had recently re-read Joe's book on making theater, called *The Presence of the Actor*. Published in 1972, it was still seething with that manifesto-making, draft-card-burning, fist-thrusting energy of the 1960s.

"I renounce the person that the System intended me to be ... Everything I do is to subvert the System." And: "All prepared systems fail ... The aesthetic remakes the system." And about the Open Theatre: "How can we support a revolutionary voice and avoid serving the capitalist machine ...?" And of course, that evergreen classic: "We have moved to a sense of full solidarity with our sisters and brothers in prison."

("Yeah!" I thought. "Yeah! Stick it to The Man! Whoever that was anymore ...")

But the more prevalent tone in Joe's book was a kind of practical mysticism, a celebration of the actor's "presence," with pronouncements like: "An actor must in some sense be in contact with his own sense of astonishment." And: "The joy in theater comes through discovery and the capacity to discover."

That's what I wanted, Goddamnit! A little joy of discovery, a little sense of astonishment from the actors. Yeah! Was that so much to ask?

God knows I'd seen little enough of it from Ran Avni's production, where the major concern was always not to offend the subscribers. Come to think of it, I hadn't seen much "astonishment" from any production of my plays (except perhaps the astonishment that the damn things had been done at all). But now I was working with the Master of Astonishment himself, Joseph Chaikin. I'd seen the joyful noise he had created with those actors in the Winter Project. "Gimme some of that," I thought, as I navigated the accident-strewn arteries of Interstate 285, through the clogged heart of Atlanta.

This time I managed to arrive at the rehearsal room before the day's work had commenced. Joe stood near the doorway, conversing with Faye Allen and Del Hamilton, the co-artistic directors of 7 Stages. (Del, a local theater legend, was also playing the key role of Reb Elye, the deal-making rabbi.) Joe saw me and nodded. I nodded back, smiling. My smile's subtext was, "Yeehaa! Let the magic begin!" I smiled even larger, trying to make this crystal clear. Joe looked perplexed.

Soon the company of ten actors was assembled. They smiled at me. Their smiles said different things. From some, there was an edge that conveyed, "We already told you we loved the play. What more do you want?" From others, there was a more open hostility, which I read as, "We were told the playwright was dead." All seemed to share the general sentiment towards me of, "Why are you here?" I just smiled back.

32

Joe started again with some physical warm-ups, then quickly moved on to a few improvisations. (Hot-diggety-dog! I thought.) The first one involved only the four actresses who played prostitutes in the downstairs scenes. Joe asked each to do an exercise in which she chose physical actions appropriate to her life in the whorehouse. (Yeah, very funny. Not sex.) So one girl started combing her hair, two others were putting on makeup, while the fourth was washing her clothes. After a little while, Joe told them to interact with each other. So the two girls putting on makeup turned and, giggling, started putting it on each other. The girl washing her clothes went over to the girl combing her hair and started braiding it. There was a little flicker of life, the beginnings of an ongoing reality. Joe stopped the exercise. Everyone clapped.

Next, Joe moved on to an improv between the actresses playing the wife and daughter of Yankel the brothelkeeper. After they had agreed on an activity (setting the table), they went ahead and put it in motion. Joe said, "Add words." They immediately started conversing in that sort-of-real-sounding-but-basically-fake way actors affect when they don't have a clue who their characters are, taking lines from the play and twisting them around to sound "personal."

"Can I wear makeup?" the daughter (Rivkele) asked.

"That's not a good idea," the mother (Sore) responded.

"Can I wear earrings?" Rivkele asked.

"You know your father wouldn't approve," Sore replied.

"But why does Manke get to dress up like this, and I can't?"

Manke was Dad's big moneymaker downstairs, the resident Whore of Babylon, who, for some time now, had been allowed to come upstairs and play "innocent" games with Rivkele to pass the time.

After Mom explained how Manke was a "bad girl" and shouldn't come upstairs anymore, she launched into the play's exposition about how "your father has bought a Torah Scroll, and we are going to spend every night praying to it for His blessings." Heidi, the actress playing the Mom, accompanied her words with a gesture of prayer.

"No. Jews don't pray with clasped hands," Faye Allen interjected.

"Right. And they don't go down on bended knee either," I put in, just in case she was thinking of going there.

Heidi looked out at us, stupefied. "How do they pray then?" she asked with a southern drawl.

"Not like Christians," Faye told her.

33

"Wow," Heidi said. "What else should I know?"

I wanted to say, "We don't use silverware, we wear hats to cover our horns, and our underwear has a special pouch for our tails." But Joe was already looking upset at the interruption, and besides, I was afraid she'd think I wasn't kidding.

It soon became clear that the vast majority of the cast wasn't Jewish (there were two, both playing older men). Not that there's anything wrong with that, you understand, an actor's an actor, blah blah blah, yadda yadda yadda. But the play takes place in a Jewish *shtetl* (town, sort of) in Poland in 1905, and there's a certain tribal aspect which is hard to simulate. (Have you ever tasted a *goyische* matzoh ball?) Since I'd been told there were 80,000 Jews in the Atlanta area, I had to conclude that very few of them longed to be actors, and that those who did were very bad. Unless, of course, it was the notoriety of *God of Vengeance* itself that scared them off.

Now it may just be my paranoia (something that I, like many of my Landsmen, had in abundance), but I'd seen this happen before. I've already mentioned how, in Ran Avni's production, the *shtetl* population got very Irish when it came to the whorehouse. A few years later, my adaptation was revived by a Jewish woman dramaturg at the University of Maryland's graduate center, where a cast of ten well-meaning white students made me want to crawl into a *kreplach* and die.

On the basis of this scant evidence, along with a lifetime's experience of Jewish shame, I was on the verge of formulating some kind of conspiracy theory. I was tentatively calling it "The *God of Vengeance* Jewish Girl Fear of Scandal Scandal." Or maybe it was the "Fear of Daddy" scandal. In any case, it fit into a more general pattern of behavior in which American Jews were still too uncertain about their place in the society (or their own core sexuality) to have the dicier aspects of their (human) character publicly examined.

(Come to think of it, though, I had had a not totally dissimilar experience a few years before, when my play *Mickey's Home*—yes, that again—had been the only play chosen for presentation at a North American Conference of Jewish Theaters in Rochester, New York. Well, one of the play's characters is an old Jewish man who hails from Poland and at times breaks into fits of Yiddish. When I went to rehearsal, I found that not only were all the characters played by non-Jewish actors (we're talking cocktail hour WASPs, folks), but the Yiddish passages were being spoken with a Swedish accent

34

that would have done Ingmar Bergman proud, followed each time by the director's stepping forward and speaking my translation of these passages in an oddly-clipped voice. Yikes!

Once the cast had pried me off the director's stiff upper lip, I really did crawl into a *kreplach* and die, only to be reborn into a whirlwind of bagel-tossing fury. I mean, this was a Jewish Theater conference without Jewish actors! What were they thinking?

So maybe I have to re-think this conspiracy theory. Maybe it's more than a "Fear of Scandal" or a "Fear of Daddy." Maybe it's a "Fear of Being Jewish" thing. Hmmm.)

One of the two Jewish actors in the production was the star, the show's brothelkeeper, Frank Wittow. Frank was apparently the Laurence Olivier of Atlanta, or something close to it, as I was to learn the next morning at a photo shoot for the local Jewish publication. A tall, vigorous, barrel-chested man, whose robust voice and manner belied his seventy years, Frank had a list of local performance credits as long as, well, Olivier. There was great anticipation about Frank's working onstage with Del Hamilton, or so the young Jewish woman reporter was eager to inform me.

"They're two living legends down here, and they've never acted together before," she said with a syrupy southern twang.

Whoopdee-do, I thought, in my caustic New York way. (All this southern dipsy-doodle was causing my inner yankee to break into a rash.) I mean, it was all fine with me if it put behinds in the seats. I'd had my fill of empty theaters, thank you. Just a year before this, *Mickey's Home* had finally been produced in New York at a downtown venue. The play had even received a good review in the Friday *New York Times* (the issue with optimum arts exposure), and still hardly anyone came. So if this was the local theater equivalent of

Frank Wittow, the Laurence Olivier of Atlanta

35

Waylon Jennings and Willie Nelson in concert, I'd be there with bells (or anything else) on.

My attention at that moment, though, was more focused on trying to get into the group photo that was about to be taken. The truth was, the playwright hardly ever gets in these photos, not unless he's David Mamet or Donald Margulies (even Margulies isn't a sure thing). It's a sad fact that nobody really cares what the playwright looks like. I mean, sure, most people know that folio picture of Shakespeare, and maybe Beckett too, and Tom Stoppard's shaggy-maned, big-jawed visage has made the rounds of glossy magazines and artsy talk shows (think Charlie Rose), but who else would you recognize in a police lineup? Okay, yeah, Sam Shepard, but he's also a movie star, so that's not fair. Trust me, there's only two: Neil Simon and Wendy Wasserstein. Two Jews who get into *every* picture. And really—I want you to answer this honestly now—do we really need to see them again? I mean, haven't their visages already been burned into our cerebellums for life? Isn't it time for a fresh face or two? (I smell a conspiracy here.)

In any case, I'd been told to show up at 10:00 AM at the 7 Stages Theater (where the show was going to run), and to me that meant one thing, "Say cheese!" *The Atlanta Jewish Times* may not have been *The New York Times* or even *The LA Weekly*, but it was a start. I'm talking twenty years of playwriting here, not one published photo. Zip. How was I supposed to have any public profile if nobody knew what I looked like?

So you'll excuse me if I hung close to Joe and Frank and Del, shadowing them like a stalker. I knew *they* were going to be in the photo. (The only other person there from the production was Mira Hirsch. Since she was artistic director of the local Jewish theater, I knew of course that she was going to be in the photo. But she was also an attractive woman who didn't know me very well, so stalking her was ruled out.)

Dina, the Jewish reporter, buzzed between Joe and Frank and Del and Mira, asking them bright-eyed questions, while the staff photographer went about setting up his shoot a few feet away. Every now and then Dina would buzz over my way, with a question like, "What attracted you to this script in the first place?" But each time she came over, I noticed Joe and Frank and Del and Mira hunching closer together in a tight bunch. Oh, I get it, I thought. I tried to mingle, to stay in their orbit, but after awhile I felt like one of those molecules spun out from the nucleus, unable to find its way back to the core. "Be Pro-Active!" I told myself, even though I hated that phrase. I plopped myself down next to Joe, like I had something urgent to tell him. Since I didn't, I just sat there like a boob, making very small talk. ("I really love the cast. Everyone's super.")

A few moments later, the photographer made a show of clearing his throat. I looked up. He avoided my eyes, looking over at Mira. "We're ready," Mira said, glancing at me.

"Yes?" I said, leaning back in my seat. I mean, I was here already, and I was hoping no one would want to offend me by asking me to get up.

"He needs to work with us now. To find the right pose," she said, as if explaining things to Forrest Gump.

Her "us" couldn't have excluded me more clearly, and yet I still felt constrained to say, "You mean, you don't want the adapter ...?"

I suppose I was daring her to nod her head at me, which she immediately started doing. Soon I noticed that everyone was nodding, even Joe, whom I had counted on for support. I slunk away to the back of the theater, hovering there like the spirit of playwrights past. Couldn't they hear my chains clanking? Wouldn't they have second thoughts and take me back?

But no, I couldn't have been more "out of mind" than if I had been hurtling through space in the shuttle. (Come to think of it, that would at least have gotten me into the photo).

As it happened, the shuttle was very much in my thoughts at that moment. The big news of the day was John Glenn's return engagement with the vastness. Liftoff was scheduled for the same day as our first preview. Everybody kept talking about how old he was, and it was bumming me out, making me feel old as well. Forty-five years old, to be exact. People were supposed to have lives by this point, to be set in their ways. What did I have? No money, no children, no agent. An ex-wife who wanted to skin me alive, and a life-partner who often seemed to share this worldview. And I couldn't even get in the photo.

Joe came up to me after the session and asked if I would drive him to lunch at the Ritz-Carlton. I thought for a moment that he felt badly for me, that he picked up on the unsung riffs of my playwright's blues. But it turned out that his assistant Scott was simply otherwise occupied. Joe didn't drive, so he asked me.

It felt odd not being in rehearsal by the middle of the day. But rehearsals were limited to three or four hours a day due to Joe's infirmity. (Today's started at two.) His medical condition also limited his diet, proscribing against any food made with oil or salt (which could kill him), but he still found lots to choose from at the Ritz-Carlton's lavish lunchtime buffet. We carried our heaping platefuls over to a table by a burbling indoor fountain and sat.

"How did the photo session go?" I asked, munching on broccoli quiche.

"Boring. Hate having my picture taken," Joe said, making a face.

"Right," I said, as if this was a constant problem for me too.

I loved the idea of sitting next to this gurgling fountain, which was kind of a stand-in for the babbling brook that ancient philosophers were always lying beside while they discoursed about the world and its sad little problems (that is, when they weren't buggering each other, à la Socrates and Plato). But in this instance, it was a big mistake.

Joe's aphasia had permanently impaired his speech, causing him to speak in soft staccato bursts of clipped language. Even in the best of circumstances, it wasn't all that easy to understand (not until one's ear had made an adjustment, anyway). So in rehearsal, he was limiting himself to comments like "Not clear" and "Gray area" and "Good. Try again." But now the splashing waters were completely overwhelming him, as if we were trying to converse while swimming laps in the hotel pool.

I could just make out that he was saying something about Allen Ginsberg the poet, that Ginsberg (who had recently died) had been a neighbor and good friend of his for years in the West Village. Then there was something else about Ginsberg's long poem *Kaddish*.

I think he was saying that he loved the poem but hated the 1970 stage adaptation (which, coincidentally enough, had been a breakthrough performance for Marilyn Chris, she of the Ran Avni *God of Vengeance*). There was something else about wanting to stage a new adaptation. Did he already have the new adaptation? Was he possibly asking me to adapt it? Did he have the rights?

I wanted to ask a bunch of questions, but I didn't for fear of embarrassing him, making him feel self-conscious. So I just sat there nodding and smiling, smiling and nodding, to the degree that I expected at any moment to hear myself say, "Life is like a box of chocolates," or some such Gumpism. So I just excused myself before this could happen and went back to the buffet for some of the highest cholesterol food this side of the Mason-Dixon line. (Hey, I'm a playwright. Someone else was paying. You do the math.)

When I came back, I launched—apropos of nothing—into a gushing tribute to Joe's performance as the title character in Georg Buechner's *Woyzeck,* in a production I'd seen at the Public Theater in the mid-1970s. For some reason, this was the only thing I could think of to say, by way of a segue out of my confusion. Joe nodded and smiled, smiled and nodded. Any moment I expected him to say, "Life is like a box of chocolates." (That is, if I could hear him above all that splashing.) Instead he said, "Buechner. Interesting writer. You like him?"

Like him? Do I like Georg Buechner? Whoa. Just kick back, I felt like telling Joe, "Cause I'm gonna crank it up now." Or as my forebear Al Jolson would have put it, "Watch me go into my dance . . ."

I mean, here's a guy who practically invents all of modern drama out of two plays (*Woyzeck* and *Danton's Death*) and the fragments of a third (*Leonce and Lena,* brilliantly funny and original and entirely *different* from the other two), who writes a short fragmentary novel (*Lenz*) that for my money is the best piece of German 19th Century fiction (okay, except perhaps for the stories of Heinrich von Kleist, E.T.A. Hoffman, and some of Goethe), and who ultimately *changes the way people think*—all before dying of the flu at age twenty-four. (And oh yeah, he still found time to become a doctor, get married, and be a source of political opposition to the ruling elite.) That's why, in my humble opinion, his death was the greatest tragedy in the history of Western Literature, greater even than the death of Keats. Now it's true that Keats gets all the press. And "Ode to a Nightingale" and "Ode on a Grecian Urn" *are* unparalleled poems. Add five or six others, mostly sonnets like "When I Have Fears That I May Cease To Be," and you have an indisputably first-class talent. But Keats' work was actually getting *weaker* when he kicked off at the ripe old age of twenty-six. (And he would never have gotten it up to marry Fanny Brawne, so stop your boo-hooing.) Whereas there is no telling how high Buechner's star could have risen.

(By "changing the way people think" I mean that he showed the world stripped of its moralizing veneer, he ripped off the overlay of a benign bourgeois God and displayed life unvarnished. And he was no untutored savant; this university graduate knew what he was doing, writing to his family a year before his death, "One would have to go blindfold through the streets not to see the indecencies, and must needs cry out against a God who created a world in which so much debauchery takes place." (Who writes a letter like that to their family? I mean, really.) Of course, nobody really cared that much at the time, but fifty years later this kind of stuff was making people riot in the streets when it turned up in the work of Ibsen and Strindberg. And, I'm not even touching on Georgie-Boy's tragic sense of language—what one commentator calls "man's inability to grasp the words that will save him." We're talking savage here, folks, even Gene "Droopy-Eyes" Ionesco has to take a back seat. But please, don't make me go into it, I'm already *verklempt*. Just talk amongst yourselves . . .)

I watched Joe's eyes for any telltales signs of glazing over. He wouldn't have been the first; this kind of stuff has its esoteric aspect for some people. (Not you, of course, gentle reader.) I myself start nodding out after a few minutes of string theory, though I could listen all night to wave particle theory. Go figure. But no, Joe seemed to be with me. He even asked to hear more.

Truth is, I had read all of Buechner's work by nineteen in both English and German (okay, I kind of skimmed the German), and I really thought his was a great idea for a life. I mean, you start writing at twenty, you're out by twenty-four, and you leave the world changed. Bing, bang, boom. I couldn't really see any downside. (Okay, you're dead, but even that has its pluses, because all these lit-crit types will be saying things like "We'll never know how high his star could have risen." Whereas if you hang around, you're just gonna screw it up. Right? I mean, just look at Giorgio de Chirico. He paints astonishing surrealist canvases in his twenties, then nothing for fifty years, when he starts *copying* his own youthful paintings, trying to pass them off as the real thing. What a yutz.) The only problem with the plan is you have to write *Woyzeck* when you're like twenty. Who can do that? You have to be like an alien. Or a genius.

Joe started talking about the production of *Woyzeck* I'd seen him in, lo those many years ago. *Woyzeck* is the first play ever written about a lower-class protagonist (in this case a soldier), a man exploited by his superiors and by science until he commits a violent act in a meaningless world. It shares with *God of Vengeance* a young man's sense of outrage at the world's hypocrisy (Asch authored his play at twenty-one), especially as regards religion, and the way this is used to keep the lower class in its place. Joe was saying how disappointed he'd been by the Public Theater production (which he didn't direct), how it hadn't reached the heights or depths of Buechner's text. I said something about trying to make sure that didn't happen with the chance we had here. Joe agreed.

Then I looked across at Joe, and it suddenly dawned on me: I am talking with Joseph Chaikin about Georg Buechner and other things that I love. I mean, I have the kind of opportunity here that I've longed for all my life, that I would have gladly paid for with an appendage when younger.

Now I was here, and all it had cost me was twenty-five years of struggle. Just twenty-five years . . .

Chapter Four

"Yo!" (or "Oy!")

TWENTY-FIVE YEARS? YEOW!!! How DID I get into this in the first place?

That's the kind of awkward question that reporters are always asking in interviews. "So how did you ever get interested (or *involved*) in the theater?" (I'd probably asked the question myself, of Joe Papp or Sandy Meisner or someone else I was in awe of, though under oath I would deny it.) As if "interest" had anything to do with it, or could sustain so much disappointment. And, God knows, my "involvement" in *The Theater* has so far been not nearly as great or as grand as I had hoped.

I mean, look at me. Oldest of four sons of a well-to-do Jewish family, raised on Central Park West on a diet of chocolate chip ice cream and shlag (okay, so it was Cool Whip), I had—as the obituary notices always say—"everything going" for me. A loving and attentive mother (a little overly shame-based perhaps, but aren't we all?), a father who—while an obsessive businessman—would always find the time to trounce me in a game of one-on-one. Brothers who withstood the blows that inevitably reigned down on them from someone bigger and stronger (me), then declined to take their revenge when they grew to mammoth proportions. (Okay, maybe not "mammoth," but they were big enough and could have hurt me, I'm sure.) I attended a wonderful grade school (Columbia Grammar), where I was elected President of everything except the Chess Club (I think some nascent Bobby Fischer beat me by one vote). I moved on to that renowned prep school, Horace Mann, where I was again elected class president, and from which I would graduate with Honors amid pronouncements from the school's writing guru that I would soon win the Pulitzer Prize. Then it was on to Columbia University, home to Trilling, Barzun, and other literary lions, where I soon ended up on the Dean's List ...

But already the Dorian Gray portrait is beginning to crack, that other blood-soaked one in the attic is seeping through.

I mean, so what if I was president of this or that in grade school? Only two memories from that time have any real staying power for me. One is my own version of an Afterschool Special, when a girl I had a crush on in fourth grade invited me to her family's empty apartment, where we kissed and stripped and rolled around naked on the cool sheets. The other took place the following year, when I played The Tin Man in a school production of *The Wizard of Oz*. I was okay with the acting part (having already essayed the challenging roles of Long John Silver and the Ugly Duckling, among others), but singing for an auditorium full of my peers—no. I was not blessed with my forebear's pipes (not to mention that whacky-legged Al Jolson rhythm), and in rehearsals my voice was rising with fear into uncharted registers. Mom eventually convinced me to "do a Rex Harrison," speaking the song in a vaguely melodic patter rather than trying to sing. This worked out okay, though I will never forget the shrieks of terror echoing through my brain as I looked out at the giggling faces of classmates while my mouth was chirping, "If I only had a heart ..."

(And speaking of Rex Harrison—one of my most thrilling early memories involved being taken to see him in *My Fair Lady* when I was seven or so. He was so *big* onstage, such an outsize personality, and his rendition of "I've Grown Accustomed To Her Face" opened up worlds of sadness and regret that I never knew until then existed ... Though, boy, I do now.)

And then all that Horace Mann stuff: president, honors, Pulitzer. Please! I gagged on all that at the time. That is, when puberty woke me up with a jolt from my ice-cream-and-shlag-induced slumber, and I looked around and saw I was in a fucking *all-boys school* run by a bunch of closet cases who longed for the good old days of British public school education when they could take the students out to the woodshed and give them what for. If I'd had any real balls, I would have done as Kerouac had some years before and lit up on campus (a cigarette or a joint, whatever) and blown smoke in some teacher's face, instead of having it blown up my butt for the better part of six years. But no, I had asthma so I couldn't smoke cigs. And when I smoked pot on school grounds, I did it furtively behind large trees like all the other disaffected youth. Because we were too sensitive for confrontations (read: scared shitless of losing out on more ice cream and shlag). We planned revolutions from our vantage point in the bushes, we were the greatest lovers the world had ever known, but when it came time for asking some thin pimply-faced girl to dance at one of those God-awful school mixers (how could Dante not have given them their own exclusive circle of hell?), then we quaked in our boots and jacked off in our Levis.

I do remember being shocked when I lost my cherry at fifteen. A girl's hole was so hot and so damp. I somehow hadn't expected that. In fact, I knew so little that I kept apologizing to the girl (a friend from camp) for the forty-five minutes we screwed, because I couldn't manage to come any sooner. (Little did I know that's how Jewish guys talk during sex, "Sorry, excuse me, I didn't mean that, are you alright, are you sure?") It was exciting and repulsive at the same time, with so many tastes and smells and sensations, so much mingling of flesh and fluids, not to mention the flume ride of emotions. It was so hot-breath-intimate, so here and now and goose-pimply real in a way that nothing else is or was or perhaps ever will be. It pretty much blows everything else out of the water, including the so-called "moral values" that the closet cases at Horace Mann were trying to drum into us.

Please remember this was the late 1960s, before "sex, drugs, and rock 'n roll" had calcified into a slogan, and when "sexually-transmitted diseases" were the stuff of comedy, easily treated. I was hanging out with the school literati, laughing at the pomp and circumstance of prep school life from the sanctuary of our "superior intellects," and railing against the unjust war in Southeast Asia and the general hypocrisy of our elders. It all sounds pretty much like a cliché now—"The Woodstock generation!" blah blah blah—and I suppose in a sense it was. It's true that left-wing rhetoric and a pipeful of hash almost insured that you would get laid. (Eventually all you needed was the hash.) But there really was a war going on, you could really be drafted when you turned eighteen, and it gave the already-disaffected youth something to be really disaffected about.

As far as risking anything real, I did get arrested a few times, including once on the Fort Knox army base in Louisville, Kentucky with a pal and two girls. We were all fifteen and had been recruited by an anti-war group from our nearby social work camp. (Hey, don't laugh. Where else can you learn how to save the world?) We handed out literature in the base's main square, until the MPs picked us up after a few minutes. They held us in a guardhouse at the main gate for twelve hours—alternately yelling that we were traitors and shaking their heads at how we'd ruined our lives (so that's when it happened!)—only releasing us after they'd gotten our parents' permission. This was supposed to make us squirm in our seats, but I wasn't too worried.

In fact the tall square-jawed MP meandered over with a bewildered look on his face, asking me, "What's wrong with your Mom? She was squealing with joy, like you'd *won* something." (Hey, it's a liberal Jewish thing, okay?)

But I'm getting off-track now, I'm sorry (excuse me, I didn't mean that, are you alright, are you sure?). Getting loads of free love at fifteen and sixteen undoubtedly has an influence on behavior (and I'd be glad to volunteer for a study, if I could try it again). But I can't say that flower-power pussy led me down the road to perdition (the theater), not right away anyway. The thing was, the world itself was just too damn exciting, there was too much going on.

A directing teacher of mine used to say that the task of theater is "to beat the street," but how could you beat Abby Hoffman (barring Richard Pryor, the most dynamic comic I've ever seen) working his charismatic ways in Washington Square or Central Park? How could you beat going down to the Electric Circus on New Year's day and ending up in an orgy? Or having a cheap date on the Staten Island ferry turn into a speed-snorting session with Gerry Ragni, co-writer of *Hair?* (Okay, I'm name-dropping now, I admit it. It's not an attractive thing, but neither is my sitting here in my underwear, watching "X-Files" reruns. I have to cling to something. So sue me.)

The whole world seemed jacked up on speed, and there was no way that Chekhov, Ibsen, or Shakespeare could compete. Not even Joe's Open Theatre, which was breaking new ground with ritual-based works like *America Hurrah* and *The Serpent*, would have been able to get my attention.

Then some girl I was involved with dragged me down to see Peter Brook's *Midsummer Night's Dream*, and I was hooked. Absolutely. (It's always a woman's fault, isn't it?) It wasn't just that the acting or directing was top-notch. It was the whole thing, the *experience*. I mean, the set was this iceberg-white box with a balcony jutting out over the stage, overlooking the action on three sides. This balcony was inhabited by characters in white garments—courtiers in the Athenian scenes, fairy spirits in the forest. Each was equipped with a hollow piece of tubing, like a corrugated white elephant's trunk, which gave off a deep whooshing sound (kind of like blowing into an empty beer bottle) when waved through the air—something they would do periodically to comment on the main action. This action took place on a stage entirely empty except for two open doorways, through which actors would enter or exit. The whole thing was infused with a spirit of tremendously boisterous fun, though with an underpinning of genuine sorrow for human folly. But it was the poetic nature of the production, the "bodying forth" of a world of the imagination, that really grabbed the audience by the gonads and said, "Pay attention!" And made one ask, "How could I be a part of something like this?"

The strange thing is, just a year later I was playing Laertes in a revamped version of *Hamlet* at La Mama ETC—hub of the East Village experimental theater scene—and I had met and conversed with Peter Brook himself at the Brooklyn Academy of Music. You see, I was sleeping with this girl from the Living Theater, who introduced me to her mentor Julian Beck, a skeletal dude with otherworldly eyes and a kid's excitement at making theater, who in turn introduced me to—

(Whoa. Hold on. I just remembered—it wasn't a girl who took me to *Midsummer*. No. It was a guy, a schoolmate from the last year of high school, his parents had given him tickets, he convinced me to come along. Man. The "girl" thing sounded a lot cooler, didn't it? And now I can't really blame the whole thing on women ...)

(Also, it's not exactly true that I didn't see any theater in the late 1960s. I saw the original *Hair*, and my Mom gave me a birthday present of second row tickets to *The Great White Hope* with James Earl Jones and Jane Alexander. This was before Jones became a bobblehead TV pitchman, and the sweaty heat he generated with Alexander, the sheer body-flinging thrust of their black-white sexuality, went way beyond anything the subsequent movie was able to convey. Though it was almost overshadowed at the time by what was happening in the row behind me, where an ancient Groucho Marx was cracking wise, surrounded by a bevy of thirty or so lovely blonde girls. I was with a lovely blonde girl myself, though none of that evening's events impressed her sufficiently to allow me to penetrate her shiksa reserve. The play did inspire me, however, to have my only black girlfriend. She was lovely and smart, a true flower of black womanhood, but the times we went to bed, it was like Martin Luther King himself was sitting in the room, intoning, "I have a dream ..." A great speech. One of the greatest. Not a great lubricant.)

I didn't want to go to college, didn't want to submit, to do what was expected of me ... but in the end I caved, filled out the forms, and got rejected by a slew of Ivy League reps who didn't take kindly to my smartass patter. Yet—after managing pretty effectively to dash all my hopes on the rocks of convention—I somehow washed up on the shores of Columbia University, a none-too-shabby safe harbor. How or why they took me in is beyond me.

The thing was, I went to Columbia as a poet. That's what I had been in high school, that's what I thought I was meant to be. Then something happened. Something even more unexpected than sex. My aunt died in a fire on New Year's Eve, along with her only son, the youngest of her four children. She was Mom's only sibling, a thirty-seven-year-old professor in the Psychology department at NYU. The fire started after midnight in the family's winter rental in the Hamptons. Most likely, a stray gust of wind had blown around some embers from the fireplace, a curtain had gone up in flames. The house had a bifurcated stairway leading to the second story. The side of the house with my aunt's two middle daughters was spared, and they were able to jump to safety. The side with my aunt and her eight year old son—whose screams had woken the house—was completely consumed. (My uncle and the eldest daughter were back in the city.)

My parents and brothers were out of town at the time, on vacation in remotest Mexico. I had elected not to go with them, even though the trip coincided with Columbia's winter break. Truth was, I was simply depressed—not making a smooth transition to college life, not happy to have chosen to stay in the city—and I didn't feel like being with family. (Certainly not in the colonial role with "natives" that such a trip entailed.) I was feeling so down that I'd skipped some final exams, not handed in some term papers; languishing instead in my room, writing sad poetry. I figured I'd get myself together during the break, make up the missed work. In the thirty-six or so hours it took my family to get back to the city—it really did feel like a much longer time—I slowly lapsed into shock. Everything went into slow motion, attaining a not-entirely-disagreeable sense of not being real.

I remember the funeral, my three beautiful brown-eyed girl-cousins sitting on a black leather couch at Frank E. Campbell's, crying, crying, crying, streams of water flowing, the tears forming small puddles on the highly-buffed floors. I remember writing a poem on the way to the grave-yard, a sonnet, that came out all at once, mocking (even as it emerged) the sad poems I'd been trying to work on:

> Touch us with noble anger
> To cry so the dead may hear
> The sorrow that stays with the living
> When the dead have no longer to fear
>
> The shriek of a child at midnight
> The waiting for her to appear
> Who has promised her love. Smite

Us with resolution

To fill the unhallowing air
With cries that resound like thunder
That roar beyond lengths of year
Of a life that is fierce with wonder

And a death that is without fear
Of what lies so far under.

And I remember the reception at the grand apartment where my aunt used to live on East 67th Street. The place had an enormous livingroom, of cathedral-like dimensions, with a ceiling two-stories high, worthy of a Tiepolo fresco. My uncle was a doctor with a thriving practice, and the room was filled to bursting with his medical associates and other people I didn't know, all laughing and talking and cramming themselves full of pastries and sweets.

I stood on a second floor balcony overlooking the scene. I kept imagining what it would be like to throw myself down, to land on some well-appointed doctor's wife guzzling champagne. Yes, I wanted to do it so badly, I could see the scene unfold as in a movie: my standing for a moment on the railing, the eyes of the wealthy strangers looking up at me, my launching myself into space, falling in slow-motion, the looks on the strangers' faces turning to horror as I landed with a thud on some overweight, big-bosomed matron who probably never even knew my aunt, never knew what a great person she was, what a truly great person, a paragon of sweetness and light, of beauty and truth, of everything graceful and good that I'd ever found in the world. She of all people should not have died, and now somebody had to pay for it, had to feel pain.

But no, I couldn't do that to my cousins. I just couldn't.

The thing was, I couldn't stop thinking about the last serious conversation I'd had with my aunt. I know it may sound grandiose, or somehow self-aggrandizing, since I was just a *pisher,* a teen. But the conversation was about death, the very fact of it, which had really begun to disturb me during my last year in high school. My aunt was incredibly busy, with four children to raise, a large house to run, and a more-than-full-time career, but she still somehow found time to see me. My Mom tended to react a tad defensively if I brought up such a topic ("You're worried about what? Try making five different breakfasts in the morning, why don't you?"), but my aunt gave me her full nonjudgmental attention.

The thing I had fixated on, which I could not stop thinking about, was the whole "deer in the headlights" thing. I mean, why does the deer freeze in the headlights? Why? All it does is insure that he becomes roadkill. Same with people. Why doesn't the proximity of great danger cause us to react with an urgency commensurate to the immediate threat, instead of—more often than not—paralyzing us, thus making sure that we stayed in harm's way. This seemed a complete contradiction of the survival mechanism, which dictated how things were supposed to work out (or so I had thought).

My aunt had calmly explained the psychological and physiological reasons for "freezing up," pointing out that it could also serve a useful function, as we used the "freeze" time to assess the nature and scale of the threat. I went away grateful for the explanation, though not completely convinced. (I understand now that we don't react well to anything out of the ordinary, which danger usually is; though I'm still stumped by the deer, who should equate headlights with "haul ass" by now.) More important was the way my aunt had treated me, with love, concern, and an utter lack of condescension.

But all I could think about at the reception was how my theoretical question had become way too real. Had my aunt "frozen up" when she'd awakened in a dark house, the smell of smoke in her nostrils? Had she been paralyzed by fear—even for a few moments—when she was desperately searching for a way to save herself and her son? Or was it already too late by then, had their fate been sealed by her sound sleep and the tinderbox of a charming old wooden house?

But no, it was too horrible. Much too horrible to think about. Still, I couldn't think about anything else. Why had I even asked her that question?

Day turned into night, night turned into day. I couldn't sleep, so it didn't make any difference. I remember spending an entire day in a movie theater viewing Peter Brook's film version of *King Lear*. (In those days they didn't give you the bum's rush after one show.) It may sound like a bad idea, or like the setup for a joke, but if I'd gone to see a fall-down farce like *It's A Mad Mad Mad Mad World*, then I really really really really would have slit my wrists. As it was, I felt comforted by the barren heath on which Lear's sad tale unfolded. The film was in black-and-white, with rich depthless grays, and I felt visually and viscerally soothed. After awhile, I just wanted to walk down the center aisle and enter the screen, to throw myself down on the blasted heath and pound the earth with my fists, to wail my lungs out until I couldn't wail anymore, or until the world ended, whichever came first. (Why had I asked her that question? Why? What had I been thinking?) There was nowhere to go and nothing to do. Why couldn't I stay in this gray place forever?

In the end, of course, I did have to go. (Even in those days, the ushers weren't too good with people hanging out overnight.) I tried to write poems, but nothing came. I tried to call friends, but most people were away for the holidays. (And those who weren't wished they had been after they heard what I had to say.) I didn't sleep for several days (seven days? eight days? After the first three, I lost count). I started having dreams behind my eyelids every time I would blink.

I finally got some help from a shrink who had known my aunt. (He was at the reception; I might have gotten to know him even sooner if I had jumped.) He talked with me and gave me Valium. I got some sleep. (Of course I also ended up getting hooked on the Valium, but that's another story.)

It took me over a year to make up all those incomplete credits. Columbia, ever the sensitive institution, had me on probation the entire time. In fact, they made my twentieth birthday the cutoff date by which I would be kicked out if I hadn't handed in all my term papers. True to form, I gave them in the day before. A month later I received a notice informing me that I was on the Dean's List. But by that time so many things had changed, I couldn't stay in school any longer.

(I suppose I should say, on Columbia's behalf, that this was when the antiwar riots were going on. In fact, the third major protest in six years took place during the first semester of my sophmore year. A group occupied Hamilton Hall, after chopping up wooden desks and lighting a bonfire on the quad in front of it. I hung around, attracted by the political message. But when they started jerking off on the desks and smearing shit on the swivel chairs I split, not seeing what this had to do with the bombing of Laos and Cambodia.)

The main thing was, I could no longer sit in a room writing poems. (Why had I asked her that question? Why?) There was nothing more to do and nowhere else to go, and the walls kept closing in on me, closer and closer. I understood now: I was just a mayfly poet, whose brief poetic life span had had its day. I could see the time coming very soon when

I would be squashed like a bug, when my tiny creative essence would run out of me in little rivulets. A part of me welcomed that day, almost prayed for it. But another part of me didn't, wasn't ready to give in. I ran from that room.

I had terrible stupid love affairs with a succession of women, moving in with a few of them (anything to get out of that room). I went out to movies, plays, restaurants, concerts, any time of the day or night (just keep me out of that room). Oddly enough, I didn't use heavy drugs—more because I was afraid of what they would show me, of hearing those questions again (Why? Why? Why?), than for any other reason. I've never been much of a drinker—Hey, how many middle-class Jewish drinkers do you know?— but during this period I gave it the old college try.

In the course of my travels, I saw lots of remarkable plays. Pinter's *The Homecoming* was a revelation for how nasty the theater could be, how nasty and funny, and what poetry could be made of sexually-charged emotional violence. The Wooster Group's production of Sam Shepard's *Tooth of Crime* created a dazzlingly fun and strange world in which a muscular Spalding Gray (I kid you not), clad only in a silver athletic cup, did battle with a rebel rock 'n roller for the prize of a bare-breasted Joan MacIntosh. Little theaters were springing up all over the place, flinging sand in the face of the military-industrial complex (yes, people really did talk like that). This was clearly where the energy was. (And you could meet girls. Lots of girls.)

I took a playwriting class at Columbia, where the teacher advised me to improve my dialogue by taking an acting class. The only acting class at Columbia was taught by an ageless white-haired man of unlimited energy named Aaron Frankel, who seemed to be on the faculty of every theater program in town. He had great enthusiasm and love for the art form, which is probably the most important trait a teacher can possess at this level. Under his guidance, students awoke from their Ivy League-induced lethargy, their intellectual torpor, and let the unreasoning demons out of their cages. For me, it was exhilarating. I felt like Houdini, that magical Jew, wriggling out of death's grip.

Sometime during the early part of my sophmore year a woman came into the acting class, seeking performers for a show she was staging at La Mama Experimental Theater Company. It was called *Ophelia*, a reworking of *Hamlet* around the prince's girl. I ended up playing Laertes and the Ghost of Hamlet's father. All I remember about the show was that the title character was played by a half-naked dancer in platform shoes.

Also that, coming back into rehearsal one day, I was waylaid by La Mama herself, Ellen Stewart, who pressed me against a wall, planting a big smooch on my lips, while groping my privates. Today it would be grounds for a lawsuit. Then it was just Off-Off-Broadway. It was 1972, and I had something to put on a resume.

Later that year, our acting class received a visit from Bernard Beckerman, head of the Theater Department. He informed us that the university was withdrawing the option of a Theater major. From then on, every theater class would only count one-third toward a Literature major.

This is one of those plot points essential to the development of any realistic story, to give it the semblance of life. In point of fact, if not for this I probably would have stayed at Columbia (once I had gotten off probation and on to the Dean's List). Instead, I resolved to leave school and seek my destiny elsewhere.

Back at the ranch, the folks were not down with this. "You're going to be a bum! Just a bum!" my Dad shouted, employing his untapped powers of prophecy. Mom had been bitten by the prophecy-bug too, she muttered tense thin-lipped warnings like a Delphic oracle. ("You will cut off the head of your future." "There will come a day when you will need us, and we won't be there." "You will find yourself alone in the dark, with nowhere to turn, and …" Well, you get the picture.) Ever since her sister's death, Mom saw disaster popping up everywhere. (Not that Jews have any trouble seeing this when it's blue skies and sunny.) Now here I was creating calamity where none had to happen.

This exchange of ideas was taking place in Mom and Dad's new apartment, a cavernous duplex with a celebrity lineage (the two prior occupants were diva Ethel Merman and Bill Cullen, long-time host of the TV game show *The Price Is Right*.). A steady stream of friends and acquaintances would soon pass through the elegant halls, marveling at the diningroom with its Arabian tent motif, ogling the spectacular views of Central Park. On one of my occasional visits (I was checking out the new digs myself), I struck up a conversation with a visitor, a painter and set designer named John Wulp. It turned out he was starting an ambitious new summer theater on Nantucket island. He was looking to form an apprentice acting company to play small parts and do grunt work. I danced an impromptu jig and convinced him to give me a shot (my jigs tend to have that effect, as people will do anything to get me to stop).

The Nantucket Stage Company was one of those blips on the radar screen of the American Theater that deserves to be looked at more closely. A one-season wonder, it produced the world premieres of the Edward Gorey production of *Dracula* (which eventually ran on Broadway for five seasons, toured endlessly, and was made into a movie) and John Guare's *Marco Polo Sings A Solo* (later produced at the Public Theater, revived by the Signature, and included in many anthologies of great plays of the 1970s). It also employed the talents of such once and future notables as James Woods, Kevin O'Connor, Piper Laurie, Joe Grifasi, John Shea, Jimmy Tolkin, Grayson Hall, Diana Davila, Larry Arrick, Barbara Damashek, Mel Shapiro, Dennis Rosa, Beeson Carroll, Roger Morgan, Jerome Dempsey, Paul Benedict, Apollo Dukakis, Anne Sachs, Lloyd Battista, and many more. The publicist was Buzzy Bissinger, who years later would win a journalism Pulitzer and write several best-selling books, such as *Friday Night Lights* (about high school football in Texas).

It was a wildly impractical and giddy enterprise that cost the producer his cherished home on Nantucket and me the next twenty-five years, trying to find something else this exciting. (I mean, where else could you find a world-class artist like Edward Gorey *painting* the scene curtain—and doing it on a converted high school auditorium stage?)

It was an eye-opener for me, in many ways. It was the first time I'd experienced the comraderie of the theater, getting to know absolute strangers so quickly in such oh-so-intimate ways. It was also the first time I'd heard one man address others as "ladies," the first time I'd seen one grown man bitch-slap another (for missing a cue, no less). And it was the first time I was able to observe that strangest of creatures—the professional playwright—foraging for grubs in his native habitat. John Guare was up in Nantucket almost the entire summer writing and rewriting (and re-rewriting) his play, the Stage Company's third and final production. (And I do mean *final.*) Just watching a world-class talent like John at work was an indoctrination into theater.

As it happened, I had been thrown right into the mix, chosen to understudy the role of Renfield in the inaugural production, *Dracula.* Renfield is Dracula's slave, subsisting on a diet of insects and spiders while waiting to be summoned. Why the director, Dennis Rosa, chose me is a mystery, as there were several apprentices who were more talented, more experienced, and just plain better-suited. (Maybe it was because I looked wild, with long kinky hair and a scraggly beard.) Whatever the reason, it gave me the chance to sit through an entire rehearsal period, watching how the pros did it. (Dangerous stuff. It was a campy production, the actors were having way too much fun.)

The second show was a vanity deal, written by producer John Wulp. Where *Dracula* was a huge critical and popular success (and could have sold out all summer), this wasn't. But it did give the apprentice company the chance to perform several small roles. There's nothing like getting stage time in front of a paying audience to make everything else look pretty drab.

Then came *Marco Polo Sings A Solo*. A more wrong-headed choice for summer stock on Nantucket would be hard to imagine. John's play included a filmed sequence in which Jimmy Woods and Piper Laurie jumped up and down on trampolines, reciting dialogue from Ibsen's *A Doll's House* in Norwegian. It also had a thirty-minute monologue (for which it has become somewhat notorious) in which a woman describes how she impregnated herself with her / his own sperm. And it concluded with that surefire summer stock knee-slapper, a man castrating himself. Oh yes, and the running time on opening night was a mere *three hours and forty-five minutes* (!!!). (This was actually down by a half-hour from final dress run-through.) The auditorium had one of those big brown institutional clocks on the side wall, but it had to be taken down after opening night, as more audience began watching that than the stage.

The real fascination for me, though, was observing John Guare. My biggest task in the production was hanging out in the stifling attic for most of the (endless) third act, until my cue finally came to toss a pink flamingo down to the stage. John, in my world, was that pink flamingo. A very hot playwright at the time, coming off the huge success of *House of Blue Leaves*, he was by turns uproariously jolly and bitingly (sometimes maliciously) sarcastic. He dispensed a seemingly endless stream of bon-mots, and ideas gushed out of him in geysers. My forebear notwithstanding, he was a UFO in the atmosphere of my solid middle-class values.

Of course, later on I saw some of the careful calculation behind this persona, the enjoyment John took in playing the genius playwright. But at the time I bought it completely, and I went to school on John, trying to decipher his utterances, the source of his wit, so that one day I could speak that language. John, for his part, encouraged me in a general way. That is, he never made me feel I had any particular talent, but he did give me a certain measure of friendship and respect, which meant a great deal at the time.

I went on to study playwriting with John the next spring at the National Theater Institute, the student wing of the Eugene O'Neill Theater Center in Waterford, Connecticut. By that time, I'd been a college dropout for five months, living my "bum's" existence in a fifth-floor walk-up on the upper West Side (which I shared with a black playwright so angry, I thought he was going to ax-murder me for not spit-shining the tub). I was trying to see if I could make a life as an actor. Toward that end, I went to auditions, took classes, sent out 8 × 10 glossies of my very unglossy mug. I did manage to land a few stage roles (such as the gay St. Peter I mentioned before—and probably shouldn't have), along with a slew of lead parts in small movies, mostly by Columbia or NYU grads. At one point I made six or eight films in a row, the directors handing me off from one to the other like a favorite whore. (It was pretty much the same plot each time: I lusted after a pretty girl, she wouldn't have me, so I jacked off in the men's room, or my bedroom, or *the girl's* bedroom (yikes). In other words, the classic story of a man and his dick.)

I had my doubts about how long I could sustain this (not to mention the lovely jobs I was trying to hold down in the wide world of telephone surveys). But the O'Neill Center was an oasis, a little theatrical hothouse where the flowers of imagination (and wishful thinking) could flourish. There were twenty-five or so students, fairly evenly split between guys and girls. We cohabited in two residences close by each other, with no particular adult supervision. (In retrospect, it's surprising we didn't give birth to many little O'Neills.) Instructors included Guare, Lloyd Richards (later the head of Yale Drama School and director of many August Wilson plays), Fred Voepel, David Hays (later a best-selling author), the modern dance master Danny Nagrin, the actor Kevin O'Connor (the original "Young Man" in early Sam Shepard plays, he deserves his own volume), video artist Kirk Nurock, and Larry Arrick, a noteworthy director who ran the school with his equally-talented mate, Barbara Damashek. Jerzy Grotowski, the Polish theater guru, had been a visiting artist the prior semester (we had a Kabuki master from Japan), but even without him it was a formidable crew.

Of course, the thing about all theater programs is that they're pretty much theoretical. Few of them can guarantee you a job, much less a career (except perhaps for Yale Drama, at least in the old days), and the chances are good that you'll never get much of a chance to hone the skills that you've spent so much time and hard work (not to mention money) in learning. So the most you can really ask of any program is the same thing you should ask of any production: to give you an indelible experience, a sense of what theater can be under the best of circumstances. That is, for the most part, what NTI gave me, concluding with a two week bus and truck tour of a fairly daring performance piece (a highly theatrical adaptation of Ovid's *Metamorphoses*). It filled me with hope and enthusiasm about making a new kind of theater, a new kind of life, much as seeing the last season of Joe Chaikin's Open Theatre had done the same year (1974).

Perhaps I should blame the National Theater Institute (and Joe Chaikin) for leading me down this road to perdition (or whatever it was), for filling me with expectations that are so seldom realized. But I can't do it. The only job of any school (or any artist) is to stoke the hidden fire of dreams. Most dreams aren't strong enough to survive the light of day, they fade away (as they should), disperse into the ether, leaving only a vague memory behind. But every now and then a dream survives, perhaps even thrives, spreading into the minds of others, creating a wildfire, where it (hopefully) generates enough heat and light to help audiences see this world more clearly, or perhaps even to imagine a new one.

Chapter Five

Franz Kafka and Neil Simon Walk into a Bar

ACCORDING TO CERTAIN WHITE supremacist groups, the Jews are an all-powerful people, able to plant subliminal thoughts in the minds of unwitting "purebreds," and God knows what else. These groups have evidently never done Passover Seder with a Jewish family—"Ooo, these bitter herbs are so *bitter*." "Hey, you're only supposed to take a sip of wine, not drink the whole glass!"—much less taken a gander at the flyer for the 7 Stages / Jewish Theatre of the South production of *God of Vengeance*.

This flyer truly must be seen to be believed. It was created by Andy Suggs, Art Director of Carroll / White Advertising—an acknowledgment I make out of prior agreement with that agency, not from any desire to demonize or even to blame. (Well, maybe a little bit to blame.) I'm sure Andy had only the highest motives when he took on this job, which he very likely worked on pro bono. But Andy, baby, did you even bother to read the play? And if so, then Andy what the hell were you thinking?

Let's start briefly with something Andy was not responsible for, in the upper left-hand corner, where not one—not two—not three—but *four* corporate logos are listed, including the town bank, the town newspaper, and a vodka distributor. You know you're in great shape when you have *all* those guys looking over your shoulder. (Actually, the vodka company was pretty cool, kicking in unlimited shots at the opening; I'm willing to bet dollars to donuts that the bank and the paper only came along for the free booze.)

We'll completely overlook the simulated brushstrokes or pieces of scotch tape or whatever the hell this "decorative motif" is supposed to be, and move on to the "production photo," which was taken weeks before rehearsals began. This purports to show Del Hamilton and Frank Wittow

in costume as Reb Elye and Yankel Chapchovich respectively, but the two men are holding things (a scroll and a tray with two candles?) in such a way that it looks like they're angry butlers. Then again, Frank's makeup is so dark, so chocolate-brown, and his expression is so "Master Thespian," that it brings to mind nothing so much as a hasidic production of *Othello*. ("Hey, that old black ram is, um, *shtupping* your white ewe. No, not me, you. I mean ewe. Your ewe. *Oy vey ist mir kineh hora*, just forget I ever said anything!") I mean, please! What's next, the Leni Riefenstahl production of *Fiddler?*

But no, the piece de résistance is in the lower right quadrant. This displays (and I do mean *displays*) a full frontal view of a naked woman hanging by her arms from the upper horizontal bar of a Jewish star. No problem there, right? I mean, serious Jewish play about the nature of God, naked lady hanging from a star—that sounds about right, don't you think? But here's where we run into issues. To my mind the woman doesn't look Jewish. No way.

I'm not saying this because she has a big rack, or even because she appears to be very buff. I'm sure there are many Jewish women who fit that description (please, ladies, send photos). No, it's the body language that gives me pause. The woman here has her legs curled slightly up toward her torso, in what can only be described as a highly-athletic—one might even say provocative—pose. Now, all the naked Jewish women I've ever seen swinging from a Star of David—and believe me, there have been several—have been somewhat self-conscious about it. I don't know if it's the nakedness as such, or the added presence of the most important symbol in all of Judaism, but I don't believe that a Jewish woman would be capable of the *casualness* of this attitude, much less the element of body-centered carelessness, even thoughtlessness, shown here. (Perhaps I'm stereotyping, I don't know; but there's simply an un-self-consciousness, and—yes, I admit it—a shamelessness, that I don't associate with Jewish women hanging from stars or from bars.)

No, the woman pictured here is a goy. More than that, I'm convinced that she's Aryan. I mean, look at her. No, look more closely. (Closer!) This woman isn't just in good shape, she's not just a body-builder. No. She's a *gymnast*. I mean, how many naked Jewish women gymnasts do you know? Okay, and how many of them have you ever seen do a dismount from a Jewish star? Right. Starting to get the picture now? This isn't just any naked Aryan woman (which I have nothing against, by the way). No, this one has been plucked right out of the opening frames of *The Triumph of the Will* by Leni Riefenstahl (yes, her again). You know what I'm referring to, right? Where the airplane swoops in and shows us the Hitler Youth workout, all those hot master-race bods sweating to Wagner, getting ready to people the world with little Adolfs? (Or else the woman could have been taken whole-hog from Riefenstahl's *Olympiad*, about the Nazi-hosted Olympics of 1936, which is almost as bad.) I mean, could anyone have come up with a more disturbing and frankly anti-Semitic image if they had tried?

(And excuse me, Andy, but what are those two circles surrounding the Jewish star, the red one inside the white? Is that some kind of code, like a Freemason handshake or something? Or is it more nefarious, some kind of Brotherhood symbol? I mean, Andy, really, were you trying to invoke the local chapter of the KKK?)

Come on, you see it too, don't you? Don't you? There's some kind of conspiracy here. What else could it be? I mean, what else could have provoked a nice, intelligent, *successful* guy like Andy Suggs of Carroll / White Advertising to create such an insult?

I don't claim to know the ultimate goal, though it could have had something to do with that ongoing global conspiracy (a matter of fact in some quarters) to make sure I don't have a career. Yeah, that's the ticket . . .

Anyway, these were the kind of flu-ridden thoughts that ran through my brain all that weekend, as I tried to sleep my way back to relative well-being in a stranger's house (more about that later). I would fall into a feverish torpor, roll around in bed for a few sweaty hours, then wake up in a strange room surrounded by computers (this couple was very into high-tech). First I would think about Georgie-Boy Buechner, who after all died of a strain of this same disease. Then I would turn on the light, look in disbelief at the production postcard (which I'd first seen on Friday), upon which I would let out one of those high-pitched Homer Simpson screams ("Aaaaaah!"). How could this be?

(I mean, really—how can you come up with an image that is, at one and the same time, anti-Semitic and still looks like an ad for the most boring and annoying Holocaust play ever written? I would almost be willing to call it a masterpiece of semiotic bad taste, if it wasn't *a flyer for a production of my own goddamned adaptation!!! My God, Andy Suggs, how much did my ex-wife pay you to try to kill me???* Aaaaaah! Aaaaaaaah!! Aaaaaaaaah!!!)

Okay. I'm calm now. It was touch and go there for a moment, but ... I'm okay.

Truth be told, though, it didn't necessarily take the influence of influenza to send most playwrights' thoughts rattling down a psychic back alley to Nightmareville. If Murphy's Law is the worst day in most people's lives, the day when everything that can go wrong does, then that pretty much represents life as usual in the playwriting world. This is not to say that wonderful, incredible things don't happen. They do. Actors can make your lines sound better than you ever deserved, directors can provide focus and meaning where there was little before, a group of strangers (to you anyway) can come together and create a world that is as full or fuller than the one you imagined. (Not to mention audience members who can be deeply amused or deeply affected.) But more often than not, this doesn't happen. More often than not nothing happens. And when it does, it usually gets messed up somewhere—wrong actor(s), wrong director, wrong designer, wrong music, wrong costumes, wrong publicist (if you have one at all), wrong producer, wrong venue, wrong time, wrong place, wrong audience, wrong millenium. Wrong, wrong, wrong. Wrong.

(A number of playwrights have recently tried to stack the odds in their favor by directing their own plays. Sam Shepard has done this for a while, with mixed results. Mamet does it compulsively—he's actually a terrific director of other people's work, but too much of a micro-manager of his own, which get very slow and drawn out. John Patrick Shanley completely *ruins* his plays, emphasizing all the weaknesses, obscuring the strengths. In general, I think that writers are too literal with their own words to make good directors, and they lose a great opportunity to blame things on somebody else.)

After awhile, this sense of "*wrong*-ness" becomes the default for many playwrights (at least the ones who hang out with me). You really do start looking for the cloud in every silver lining. (Is that enough of a cliché for you?) I was trying to suspend this in the case of Joe Chaikin, my youthful hero, to banish this mindset at least for the time being, but it wasn't easy.

For one, it appeared that "astonishment"—at least of the improvisational variety—was not going to be part of rehearsals. This was already the case by the second rehearsal (following that lavish lunch at the Ritz-Carlton). Joe immediately got people up on their feet and started staging the text, the actors stumbling around with scripts in hand like tourists in a foreign land consulting their guidebooks. This was disconcerting, to say the least. I had read so much about Joe's belief in "ensemble," which was practically a religious principle in the 1960s and 1970s.

(Joe had written in 1972, "The single most important concern of the Open Theatre is the continuity of our ensemble of actors and the collaboration of talented writers, directors," etc. But there was no continuity here, just a one-shot deal. Most of these actors had never worked with Joe before. And they had no particular passion for the subject matter beyond wanting to put on a good show and (hopefully) promote their careers.)

Then there was the Corky factor. Corky (only one name, like Cher) was the show's set designer. I had yet to meet him, since he had apparently not shown up for the last few production meetings. This was of some concern to both producing theaters, for obvious reasons, especially since Corky had never collaborated with Joe. It was of great concern to me because I knew how hard it was to devise a set for the schema of this play, which alternates upstairs and downstairs scenes. It had actually been easier before, when the script had those hokey "circus" crowd scenes in which to make the transitions. But since I had cut those out, it took some designer-inspiration to compensate.

In fact, Joe's major staging idea for this production was to incorporate an onstage violinist whose klezmer-influenced musings would make for smoother transitions, as well as establishing the hoped-for "old-world" atmosphere. Chip the violinist was my constant companion for the first few days, having little more to do than I did (sit and watch). During a break, he showed me a book of klezmer arrangements compiled by Henry Sapoznik. This completed a link for me, as Henry had been a good friend of mine while I was in residence at the Jewish old age home (eighteen years before—a Jewish cycle), when he was a bluegrass musician calling himself "Hank"

63

Sapoznik. But after hearing ten minutes of Sapoznik stories—"Did I tell you about the time he came over to my house for dinner and made me *buy* his latest album?—Chip looked like a caged animal, searching for any means of escape. He finally found one, and I didn't see him much after that.

I drifted over to Joe. I'd been snacking on a bag of sunflower seeds, and now I extended them to Joe, who took a handful. The gesture was so casual and off-hand, yet it filled me with joy. "Joe Chaikin is eating my sunflower seeds!" I thought. "Yes I would stay to watch rehearsal." So what if the actors were sending daggers my way, trying anything to drive me from the room. ("Were we there when you were adapting?" their looks seemed to say). And so what if there weren't any more "breakthrough" exercises to watch, no more fun and groovy improvs? This was my adaptation, goddamnit, I'd sure as hell sit there and watch the actors fumble over every freaking line, if it pleased me.

"Oh my God!"

A thought suddenly thwacked me between the eyes, stopping me in my tracks. These sunflower seeds are a mixture of salted and unsalted. *So I gave Joe Chaikin salted sunflower seeds! Deadly salt! I killed Joe Chaikin!*

(In an instant, the scenes raced through my head: Joe lying on the ground, the cast weeping, me standing there munching the murder weapon. Del and Frank see me looking as guilty as only a Jewish sunflower-killer can. They both get the same idea, they charge toward me, pin me against the wall. "You wanted more improvs, didn't you? Didn't you?" Del shouts. "But was that any reason to kill him?" Frank intones in his grief-stricken baritone. "It wasn't like that. You have to believe me. I loved him!" I plead, as the cops grab me and toss me in the hoosegow. *New York Magazine* runs a big investigative piece called "The Playwright's Revenge"—"He wanted more improvs!"—they interview my ex-wife, who is only too happy to spill her guts about our fourteen-year marriage. "It was horrible, horrible!" she'd cry (she did that well), citing chapter and verse. She'd tell them about the poetry teacher I had an affair with. (But what about the eleven years of monogamy that came before? Don't I get any credit for that?) And my photo would finally get in the paper! Some agent at ICM or William Morris would see it, they'd think, "Hmm. Playwright's Revenge. Sunflower Killer. Sounds like big bucks!" And the next thing you know—)

Wait a minute. What about Joe?

I turned around. He was standing there (Thank God!), talking with the actress playing Manke (Yankel's daughter's "special friend"). I watched for any evidence of Joe chewing. Nope. His right hand was cupped, the fatal seeds must still be there, lying in wait, getting ready to plant their roots in Joe's system, to sprout their sunflowers of evil. But not on my watch!

I bounded over. "There's salt on those seeds," I informed him. (What a sentence!)

Joe half-smiled at me, he went on talking with the actress. Moments later, I saw him dump the seeds in the garbage, brushing salt off his hands.

And then I was out of there. One attempt on Joe's life was enough for this playwright. I could almost hear the actors applauding as I slipped from the room.

Truth was, neither theater had really wanted me to come down here at all. They could see no particular upside (my adaptation was already completed), and plenty of downside. I did manage to convince them to spring for my airfare, but no amount of cajoling could get me a room. Since I wasn't about to rent one myself (it was a freelance writer thing, not a Jewish thing), I had gone looking for a friend with Atlanta connections. I found one in Amy S., a director, who had grown up in its suburbs. She was actually my girlfriend's friend, but she was about to inaugurate her new theater with a revival of my play *Mickey's Home*, so I felt okay dumping my problems on her. She made arrangements for me to stay with her recently-divorced cousin Ben, after I spent the first few days with her twin sister (half of the high-tech couple).

As it happened, this was my day for moving into Ben's house. I had already shoved all my things into the trunk of my rented Dodge Neon. Since Ben wasn't going to be home until later that afternoon, I decided to take a jaunt to the Jimmy Carter library, which I had passed many times on my way to rehearsal. My agenda here was not so much a patriotic thing as a chance to bask in the nostalgia of a simpler time (before AIDS and my failed marriage), when a healthy neurotic male could at least fool himself into believing that at any particular moment he might get laid.

Driving up, I found the symmetric stone buildings and surrounding Japanese gardens to be nearly as impressive as the brochure-speak. ("Located in a wooded, thirty-five-acre park ... [the] spectacular grounds include formal gardens, a wildflower meadow, a cherry orchard, and waterfalls tucked between two small lakes.") A plaque informed visitors that the library contained twenty-seven million pages of documents and 40,000 objects (didn't they throw anything away?). But what interested me couldn't be found among those endless reams of official papers, those political artifacts. I was looking for the comedy and sexiness of the Carter years, a little tour down memory lane of loves and lusts past.

Ah yes, I felt, looking around at the somewhat cheesy-looking exhibits in their high-school-hall-of-fame display cases. Here were Jimmy's hokey campaign commercials ("Why Not The Best?"), his inaugural walk down Pennsylvania Avenue (loved that), and Amy Carter at eight-years-old, looking (to my jaded eyes) reassuringly small and unmarked by experience. Here was Billy Beer, and Miss Lillian talking too much, and Jimma's cartoonish face (rubber cheeks, goober lips) painted on the side of a peanut.

It was all enough to make a body laugh and cry himself sick. Long dormant memories rose up and stood erect, aroused by the aphrodisiac of Carter's drone. I had finished up my college years at Sarah Lawrence (yes I went back to school, if only to prove to Dad that college graduates could be bums too). There were 80 men and 800 women on campus, and half the men were gay. There was also a well-organized contingent of women who were not pleased by the presence of youthful y-chromosomes on campus, heckling and berating the guys ("Get out! Boo! We don't want you here!" often screamed in your eardrum). Nevertheless, there was much to be said for the presence of so many smart, sexy, overly-sheltered young women. But the memory that kept coming back to me was of opening a door at someone's party and beholding a tall black girl in all her unclothed Nubian-princess beauty. Embarrassed, I excused myself, backing out; but she smiled, completely unfazed. I smiled back and started approaching, and then … hmmm (long sigh).

When I opened my eyes some minutes later, I found myself in front of a Leroy Nieman painting of Camp David that made me wish I had never been born. Seriously. You have to wonder at the fate of a people who could produce such a monstrosity, much less put it in a museum. Anwar Sadat looked like one of the Temptations, Menachem Begin like a Borscht-Belt comic, and the color scheme! Oh my. All I could do was let out a silent Homer Simpson scream ("Aaaaah!") and pray that this memory would not be passed on to my future children.

Moving along, I came upon a diorama of the Camp David accord that was almost as bad. It showed wax figures of Carter, Sadat, and Begin against a psychedelic background (hey, it wasn't my idea). Carter's smile was big and goofy, he looked like Howdy-Doody. Of course, Carter's smile *was* big and goofy, and he *did* look like Howdy-Doody. But it was depressing to be reminded.

There was a small section devoted to the Iranian hostage crisis, but (of course) nothing about the failed rescue mission which doomed his presidency. There was nothing as well about his other defining moment, the infamous *Playboy* interview (yeah, *that* they threw out). That's where Jimma confessed that he "lusted in my heart for other women." This seemed kind of touching right now (it was 1998, the country was in the forceful grip of Monica Lewinsky), but it also brought back other, more disturbing, memories. I remembered laughing about his faux pas with my ex before we were married. Yes. To my great horror, Jimma Carter's "lust" made me remember when I loved my ex-wife.

I hadn't expected this, not at all. I'd gone in for a quickie peep show of my Carter administration self, a sexual highlight reel of a beloved era when it was still "anything goes" (though condoms were stored under the counter and porno was still a source of some shame), and I'd come up against this ... this ... obscenity!

I staggered out of the visitor center, almost falling into the meditation pool (where I would probably have been devoured by the piranha of my unconscious). I hopped into my trusty Neon and hit the road, zipping in and out of traffic until I found what I was looking for: a Stuckey's. I ran inside, bought ten pecan logs and stuffed them into my mouth, one after the other. I sat in my car and chewed and chewed and chewed, waiting for the sugar-high to take effect, to obliterate this unwanted memory. (It was quicker than booze, and much less of a hazard for driving.) After awhile I did go into the first stages of sugar shock, but it was still not enough to get rid of the nasty aftertaste, the image of my ex-wife as a sexy and sensitive woman, which still lingered underneath. I turned on the radio and jiggled the dial until I found what passed for a rock 'n roll station here in Atlanta, hoping that really loud music would help do the trick.

Of course, I had to turn the radio down when I pulled up to Ben's house, a small split-level on a leafy suburban street not far from the rehearsal space and theater. I sat in the car for a few moments, trying to compose myself, to rid my mind of this snapshot of the ex and I looking at each other with such affection ... Out of the corner of my eye, I saw a curtain in the house pulled aside, somebody was looking at me. I took a deep breath, smiled for the camera, and got out of the car.

Ben turned out to be a large, prematurely-balding man in his mid-thir-ties, who looked like a high school football player gone slightly to seed, soft around the middle. He had been involved with local theaters as an actor and director, but his big thing now (he was eager to tell me) was directing films. "You got any scripts I might want to option?" he asked. "I've got the financing all lined up, no problem."

If he had asked me this even five years before, I would probably have been only too happy to hand over my hard-earned scripts and treatments and fragments of concepts, in the belief that this could be "it," that something really great was going to happen. But my limited experience in Hollywood, along with a brief interlude developing scripts for Dustin Hoffman, had changed all that. "I don't really have anything I'm giving out right now," I said. Of course, this could change on a dime later on if we became buddy-buddy (or if he really had that "financing," which people almost never do, especially people without a track record who toss out the line in the first two minutes of meeting you).

I tried to be as friendly as possible in my demurral, but Ben's mood immediately turned prickly, surly, even resentful. (Come to think of it, he hadn't seemed that happy to see me.) Ben's cousin Amy had told me that he had recently gone through a painful divorce (is there any other kind?). I brought it up now, figuring it would help us "bond."

"My divorce just came through a few months ago," I told him. "It took me four years of struggle to get it."

"Uh-huh," he responded, his surliness only deepening. "I'm not sure how long this arrangement is going to work out for," he added.

"But Amy said you could put me up for three weeks," I said.

"I'll have to see," he tossed out. "I may need my own space."

This announcement sent shock waves through me, as I had nowhere else to go and my credit cards were almost maxed out. (Also, no man had ever told me that he "needed his own space." Just hearing those words coming from a man's lips was frightening. I mean, why would I want to be in "his space"? Just leave me a little, you can have all the rest. In fact take all of it, just don't come too close to me, Ben.)

"Okay. Whatever," I said, feigning indifference. "I'm thankful that you're putting me up at all. Sorry for imposing," I added. Ben nodded, his mood lightening up a bit. I asked him where I was going to sleep.

We were standing in his livingroom, a medium-sized room in the middle of the small house, with a washer and dryer to my far left, and an open kitchen behind me, with only a long counter separating it from this room. There was a large-screen TV and VCR to my far right (with several boxes of videotapes piled up alongside), and a small sofa in the middle. "Right here," Ben said, pointing to the sofa.

I looked at the sofa more closely: it was actually more of a bench with springs and thin orange cushions, barely six feet long, so rickety I was amazed it hadn't buckled under Ben's weight before now. "Please tell me you're kidding," I said. Ben shook his head.

I was aware of a strong scent of bug disinfectant in the house. I had smelled this when I first walked in, but it had gradually receded into the perceptual background. Now it rose up again, I could already taste it in the back of my palate as something chemical, bitter. I was also aware of an electronic hum in the room, from some appliance or other, that came to seem louder and louder, until it was almost deafening.

"But you have a house," I said. "It must have a spare bedroom?"

"I'm using it as a workout and storage room," Ben told me. He escorted me a few steps back to a small interior room with a large gleaming bench press, surrounded by several half-opened boxes of books and papers and a blizzard of shoes, socks, shirts, pants, and underwear. A yellowed jockstrap was hanging from one of the bench press handles. There were no windows, no sources of ventilation. Still, I could see where there was room enough to clear a small space on the floor.

"Do you have an extra mattress?" I asked. Ben shook his head. I asked if there was anyplace nearby where I could buy an inflatable mattress.

"Hey, if you want to sleep on the floor, go right ahead," he said, shrugging.

It was crazy, it's true, but so was the idea of sleeping on that sofa. It wasn't just that the sofa was small and bench-like (though these were not good things), it wasn't even that it got direct sunlight from half-curtained windows. No. This sofa was right in the middle of the room. I can't sleep like that, I need a wall. This may seem overly precious, I guess. But sleep was not a casual thing for me. After my aunt had died, it took more and more valium to make it happen, until even that wouldn't work. Then it took years to be able to fall asleep without it. Insomnia is a great joke if you don't have it, but I'd spent too many nights staring up at the ceiling to risk doing so when there were any alternatives.

Of course there was another alternative: pay for a motel room. I'd practically hissed this at myself when I bought the red rubber mattress ($80, or two nights in a Motel 6). And if I'd been looking at a stay of a week or less, I would have done it. But the Playwright's Economic Survival Code dictated that I could not spend more on this trip than my royalties would cover. Since my rental car was already eating up half the total, how could I justify spending that much again for something that would surely have been pretty seedy and depressing itself?

This argument had plenty of holes in it, but I overlooked them in my quest for free sleep. Ben had cleared a space on the floor at the base of the bench press, between the two metal legs on the left side. He had also removed his yellow jockstrap (for which I was grateful). He came in while I was blowing into the supposedly self-inflating mattress and asked me if I had dinner plans. When I told him I didn't, he invited me to come with him to visit his parents. "Sure," I said, embarrassed by my heavy breathing.

His family was interestingly different from the mostly-yankee Jews I had known. His father was tall and relatively lean with the hard-bitten manner and ambling shuffle of an Arizona ranch-hand. When I came back to say hello, he was barbecuing a mess of ribs slathered with his own homemade sauce. "So you really don't eat meat?" he asked, as if suspecting that someone was pulling his leg. I nodded. He pointed to a bowl of chicken parts off to the side. "We won't let you go hungry, don't worry."

(I hadn't eaten pork since 1980, and I'd given up all meat and fish when I left my ex-wife, an inveterate meateater. But my resolve had gradually weakened, and now fish and fowl were once again no longer safe from me.)

Ben was in a surly mood when we got back to his place, but at least this time I felt like I understood why. During dinner his family had asked me lots of questions about the production. At a certain point it came out that Ben had worked at the Jewish theater himself on a few occasions, though not for quite a while. He had also submitted plays to them, which had been rejected. Meanwhile I had waltzed into town from the Hollywood area and taken his spotlight. Oh yeah, this arrangement was gonna work out just fine.

I told Ben that I'd be happy to look at his plays; he just gave me a withering look and slammed the door to his room. I washed up and went to the workout room, where I spread a sleeping bag Ben had lent me on top of my narrow mattress. I noticed two framed pieces of paper on the wall, which turned out to be Ben's correspondence with Neil "Doc" Simon. Ben asked, "What advice will you give a young writer in today's market?" The Good Doctor replied, "Just forget about the market and write." Good advice, no doubt. Still, I couldn't help wondering if this was before or after his movie *The Slugger's Wife?* How about *Odd Couple 2?* Or the windbag epic *Jake's Women?*

But hey, I had to admit feeling a bit like one of those Neil Simon losers myself (maybe a little less lovable), lying on the floor of that windowless room. The bug-spray smell was stronger down here, but it was almost drowned out by the dried-sweat smell coming off Ben's piles of unwashed clothes. Then again there was another smell too, less definable but still very present. It was a musty sourish smell, like something had fallen behind the refrigerator and died and was now decomposing. I had smelled it before, many times, in the apartments of various women I'd gone home with after leaving my wife. Often very vivacious women, but then they'd open the door to their place, and this sad sour smell would come wafting over you, and . . . well, it didn't bode well for the immediate future.

Christ, I really was a Neil Simon character, wasn't I? A would-be Lothario whom women were attracted to because they saw right away that I was the marrying type. They saw right through me, no matter how hard I tried to pass myself off as some kind of artist-stud. I remember this one two-day span, after a week of snowstorms in New York City, when three different Jewish women stopped me on the street, gave me their cards and told me to call them. Just like that. I'd love to say I saw lust in their eyes, but no, only wedding bells. And another time, this language teacher, right in the middle of our making love, she looked in my eyes and told me, "You're gonna get married again very soon. I just know it." "Well, not to you," I'd said, highly offended. (In general, I think coitus is a bad time to share mind-blowing insights.) Still, I knew deep-down that she was probably right. How else to explain the many years I'd spent with my ex-wife?

Of course, even with her, things had started off promisingly enough. She was a beautiful and talented actress from a Mexican-American family, where an acting career was not an option (not that there were many options then for Latinas). I was a would-be playwright from an upper-middle-class Jewish family, where a playwriting career was highly discouraged. We lived and loved in the dream of someday working together. Then we finally did—and it was a disaster. She spent the entire rehearsal period refusing to follow direction, telling everyone she was the playwright's wife and would do as she pleased. I was on the phone constantly with the director and other actors, reassuring them that everything would be all right. Still, she was able to convince me (read: withhold sexual favors) into casting her in two more productions, where it was pretty much the same story. Finally even she got the message. She announced that she was quitting acting to become a Mom.

However, this involved overcoming two big obstacles. First, by this time I didn't really *want* to have a child with her. And second, she was unable to conceive without the help of fertility doctors, whom we could not afford. Being a resourceful person, she solved both problems in one fell swoop by withholding more sex and running a big fat guilt trip on me, lying around the house crying, "Don't mind me, my life's over." Soon, Mother Fife had forked over thousands of dollars to sweet-talking men in nice suits, and Jughead Dufus McIdiot (me) was jerking off into a cup. Except all this still didn't add up to a baby, so we did it over and over and over. Finally, in desperation, she enlisted the help of her youngest sister, who came to New York and donated her eggs. At last she got pregnant. ("Why didn't that make me feel happier?" I'd asked myself. Duh.) But only seven weeks later she had a cataclysmic miscarriage, losing half the blood in her body. This was a blow, and I felt badly for her. My parents felt so badly, they helped us finance the purchase of a two-bedroom apartment on the upper West Side. The idea was to move somewhere new and start over.

But there was no starting over. My wife was still fixated on having a child, but even a Dufus McIdiot could refuse to go along now. (We were barely on speaking terms anymore. Enter the high school poetry teacher ...) Then the commission for *God of Vengeance* came, and my playwriting career started heating up. I got one agent, then another; had my gig working with Dustin Hoffman, had readings of my scripts at the Public Theater and other venues.

(One note about my brief stint with Dustin: I never experienced the crazed control freak that other collaborators of his have described. The Dustin I saw was a sharp, funny guy whose mind never stopped throwing off sparks. But he had just endured three flops in a row, and I was shocked by how anxious he was about the future. "Hey, you're Dustin Hoffman!" I wanted to cry out. "I mean *Midnight Cowboy! Tootsie! Rain Man! The Graduate!* You think people are gonna forget that?" Then a few years later, Dustin tumbled from the ranks of headlining stars. So, wow, I guess the guy knew what he was talking about after all. And the moral of the story is—altogether now, class—"*Never doubt the star.*" (Unless, of course, you should. See F. Murray Abraham story.)

Around this time I wrote a play called *Savage World* about blacks, Jews, and the search for justice. It was first alternate for the National Playwrights Conference (a big-deal in the fishbowl world of the theater). I had meetings all over town, with the likes of HBO, New Line, yadda, yadda, yadda. I was approached by the Broadway producer Anita Waxman, who swore that *Savage World* was the best script she had read in years. The Shubert Organization also expressed interest, and I was summoned by the head Shubert, the King of Broadway himself, Gerald Schoenfeld.

Stepping into the Shubert offices, off Shubert Alley (in Shubert World), it indeed felt like I was entering some inner sanctum, some secular temple of Show Biz. The thick Persian carpets set off a hush that made me feel like falling to my knees and intoning new versions of the songs of my forebear, Al Jolson—"Shuberts! How I love ya, how I love ya, my dear old Shuberts!" There was a Palazzo-like capaciousness to the waiting room, which had a double-high skylighted ceiling and was surrounded from above by an elegantly hand-tooled wooden balcony (affording ample opportunities for offing truculent directors and playwrights, no doubt). Oh boy, it was all happening, baby. Oh yeah.

Except somehow it didn't. Mr. Schoenfeld—a modern-day Pasha holding the promise of riches for any Scheherezade able to keep his attention— showed me a reader's report calling my play "a bandwagon that we need to get on;" but then he handed me a list of changes that had to be made (the play's style, characters, and dialogue) before he'd consider hitching his star to that wagon. (What was it exactly he'd liked?) Meanwhile, Anita Waxman offered me a contract for the stage and film rights ("We're going to get Larry Fishburne!" she vowed), but this fell apart at the last minute when she partnered-up with an even bigger producer who wasn't partial to my script (or the size of the ten-actor cast). All the film companies rolled up their red carpets and rolled away. Then Alexander Racolin (remember him?) announced that he was going to open my *God of Vengeance* in London, only to find that his contract with Jewish Rep didn't give him the rights. He offered me $75 for them. ($75!!!! Wow, now I could almost afford to go to the theater!) My agent, feeling this was not a good sign, turned him down.

By this time I had told my wife that I wanted a divorce. She reacted by saying, "In your dreams," then going rollerblading, where she fell and broke the humerus bone in her shoulder. She would go on to re-break this four more times—five operations in four years. (Yes, I've heard the jokes. "Very humerus." Ha ha.) I pleaded with her to work out a settlement with me without resorting to lawyers. I suggested we sell the condo, split the proceeds, and go our separate ways. She would have none of it, screeching, "What about the last fifteen years? Am I supposed to just let it all go down the drain?"

And so here I was now, broke, lying on the floor beneath a bench press, groveling towards sleep, praying for some respite from thoughts that wouldn't leave me alone. All these bug-killer fumes were going to my head, putting a Kafkaesque spin on my Neil Simon knee-slapper.

Oh yes, I've got it now, the title of my little chronicle. Let's call it "The Cockroach Kid." (Of course "The Marrying Bug" isn't bad either.)

Chapter Six

"The World's Greatest Humus" and Other Conspiracies

WHAT CAN YOU SAY about a city where every other street is named Peachtree, where the main freeway (Interstate 285) suddenly changes its mind for no discernible reason and shifts from an east-west axis to a north-south one, and where the most elite, upscale neighborhood rhymes with the word "fuckhead?" Don't get me wrong, Atlanta is a nice enough place to visit, but you could also get pretty much the same effect by kicking back in a lazy-boy drinking a coke while watching CNN, reading *Gone With The Wind*, and listening to a CD of Dr. Martin Luther King's speeches. (Sticklers for historical detail might get one of those gas station maps of the city, place it in a metal wastebasket, and torch it.)

Then again, Elton John loves it, so what do I know? Sir Elton even has a house in Buckhead (hey, that's the real name, folks), and he claims to love puttering around the city like the queen in her own private garden (I mean Elizabeth, of course). In an interview for the local newspaper, he painted a charming picture of himself queuing up every Tuesday at the local Tower Records for new releases from 'N Sync or the Backstreet Boys or whomever. He claimed not to be hassled for autographs while he was in line, but I'm sure that was only because he blended in so well with the twelve-year-old girls.

As it happened, Sir Elton's musical *Aida* was receiving its world premiere just then at the local institutional theater (the Alliance), where I was able to catch the final preview. Now I know that the show went through a huge overhaul before it opened on Broadway, and Heather Headley was smashingly good as the titular slave girl, but what I saw here was major caca. I mean, yes, some of the songs were tuneful enough (even if they all sounded the same), and the lighting and costumes were spectacular, but we're talking big-time pop-culture *kitsch* here, of a dangerous variety. By which I mean that this love story of a black slave girl and her white oppressor was completely divorced from any sense of context or reality, appropriating the symbols and signposts of another culture with no interest whatsoever in examining them, in exploring the "other-ness" (from our viewpoint) of Those People in That Time and That Place.

Now I know it sounds silly to get all hot and bothered about a Disney-produced pop-musical spectacle, to call something "dangerous" that has no thought in its head beyond selling top-price tickets to tourists. And I'm by no means oblivious to the charms that pop-kitsch can have in the right hands (say those of Charles Busch or Charles Ludlam). But does the name Karl May ring any bells? He was Hitler's favorite author, a very effective pulpmeister who specialized in enormous soap opera sagas of the American West without (of course) ever having been there. That is, to him Americans were "the others," and he was able to project his obsessions with blood-purity and the noble savage onto that past in a way that made little Adolf dance with delight. But Karl May was a master of verisimilitude next to this *Aida*, which cast the Egyptians with California surfer dudes and ended with the doomed lovers being transported to heaven without first bothering to die. (Seriously—the lovers were encased in the pyramid for two seconds, and then poof! their souls were flying up to The Big Guy's lap faster than you can say, "Mickey Mouse.")

Now, all apologies to the lovely Sir Elton, but this is Nazi art pure and simple. That is, a mass entertainment designed to justify the audience's own sense of a-historical cultural superiority, a feel-good spectacle intended to affirm a lust for world domination. Denial of Death was only one aspect, but it typified the airbrushing of all unpleasant and inconvenient aspects of *reality* from this picture, until there was only the emotionally-pleasing masturbatory fantasy. ("And after all wasn't that really what matters?" our egos coo to us in a fit of self-gratification.) Certainly the Nazi-like eagle and other symbols of domination on the set did nothing to dispel such thoughts from coming to mind. And the fact that the evening was not unpleasant to watch, that it succeeded in lulling the audience into a receptive stupor, made it seem all the more dangerous to me.

Of course, all of this could be easily dismissed as the demented rantings of a paranoid left-wing liberal who saw conspiracies everywhere, even in the "failure" of the world to recognize and adequately reward his talents. Maybe so. But I took some comfort a day or two later when a local scene designer

I was speaking to (about my fears of Corky having gone AWOL) happened to let slip that she had been on the *Aida* tech crew.

According to her, the original set for the show included Egyptian hiero-glyphics all over the stage that closely resembled swastikas. She said it made her and many other members of the building crew very uncomfortable. "Everyone noticed it, but no one seemed particularly concerned," she told me. Then two weeks before the first preview, the Lion King himself, Michael Eisner, came to rehearsal, and he was very concerned. "Get rid of those things," he said, and they too were airbrushed away. What could not be removed, however, was why they were there in the first place, and the shadow they cast over an enterprise that purported to be about the eternal power of love, while actually celebrating cultural self-love and the eternal power of the almighty Buck(head).

(Then again, all this pre-dated the show's reworking by the estimable David Henry Hwang, author of *M. Butterfly* and master of cross-cultural identity issues. Perhaps he was able to find a pulse in this mummy, to unwrap the layers of gauze and expose some signs of dramatic life. I'll let you know when I sell a screenplay and am able to afford the price of a Disney ticket.)

I'm afraid I gave the impression before that I found all of Atlanta equally unappealing. That isn't true. It had the ills of many modern cities: an impersonally-corporate downtown area, an uneasy mixing of new and old architectural styles, a suburbia of endless malls and strip-malls and gated communities, and roads that couldn't bear the hyper-increased volume of traffic. Even Sir Elton agreed with me on that last one, complaining, "The drivers here ... are really the worst ... I'm sitting behind the wheel yelling, 'Come on!' They're a nightmare."

But I loved the area called Little Five Points, where the rehearsal space and 7 Stages Theater were located. This was in the northern section of the city, shading east, around Moreland Avenue between DeKalb and Ponce de Leon. It was described to me as this city's East Village. It was indeed the flower-child section of town, with candle shops, bookshops, a juice bar, small boutiques, antique clothes shops, a very good Carribean restaurant, a small Mid-East café ("The Olive"), a wrap café, a large health food co-op, and a variety of small shops, bars, and restaurants. These included a combo head shop / general store, which displayed used hippie duds and a sign for "The World's Greatest Humus." This was an invitation I couldn't resist, and

I slipped in and took a seat at one of the three or four small tables. A tall, rather burly man of Pakistani descent approached and took my order. When I asked if the humus was indeed the world's best, he beamed from ear to ear, assuring me that I would never taste better.

I started out feeling charitably disposed, charmed by the man's handwritten sign and personable manner. But after twenty minutes of waiting (there was no one else in the store), I found myself muttering, "It had better be the world's best fucking humus …"

The man finally came back carrying a tray, and with that ear-to-ear smile still beaming. He placed the tray in front of me with all the pride of a parent displaying his first born. There were several triangles of pita bread on the tray, surrounding a good-sized white bowl containing "the world's greatest humus." This humus was made up of what looked like mashed falafel balls in a sea of olive oil with huge chunks of garlic cloves on them. I was partial to the whipped humus myself, the kind where all the ingredients were mixed together in a nice reassuring solid mass. "If it's not the world's greatest, then it's certainly the world's oiliest," I thought. But hey, I guess this was how they made humus in Pakistan. Wasn't I always up for trying something different?

The man stood over me impatiently, his smile rapidly turning into a scowl. I picked up a pita triangle, dipped it in the unappetizing-looking concoction, and popped it into my mouth.

"It's good, right?" he asked.

Oh yeah, definitely the world's oiliest. And the garlic scent was so strong, I could barely sit at my own table. I mean, wow! did I reek. "Yes, it's quite different," I said.

"Different?" he asked, his scowl growing deeper.

"Well, different than I've had before. But very good," I added. (I was prepared to go very far in my lying, but "the world's greatest?"—only if he pulled out a sharp object.)

"This is how humus is supposed to be made!" he boasted. "Not like some others do it." He waved in the direction of the Olive Café across the street, his eyes blazing. Now I'd been in the Olive Café and eaten their humus and loved it. It might even have been the world's greatest. But I could see that from now on, I was going to have to sneak around and duck inside there like some kind of man on the lam.

The proprietor continued to stand over me, awaiting the pleasure of watching me eat more of his pride and joy. I forced myself to consume half the triangles, praying so hard that someone would come in the store that I was afraid my chant was going to become audible. ("Somebody please come in. *Please* come in. *Please!*") Finally a girl did walk in and browse around the used jeans, but the man did not move a muscle, he did not waver, his eyes remained fixed on their target.

(Was I the only one who'd ever ordered the humus? Was I the only sucker who'd ever fallen for that handwritten sign? Was there a word on the street that I hadn't gotten? I mean, where the fuck was I when everyone else got the warning? Or, maybe, just possibly, had I been set up? Was it—dare I say the words?—*A conspiracy?* "Don't tell the Jew, he's certain to fall for that sign?")

The worst part was, this portion was huge, it was enough to feed a table of hungry Semites. (Was I being punished for often complaining about how small the portions were at most restaurants? Was that how the world worked?) At last I had to toss up my hands and say I was finished, I couldn't eat another bite. The man's face did indeed fall, it looked like he was going to cry.

"It was great, just—great," I said, tossing down dollar bills.

"The World's Greatest?" he asked, not cracking a smile.

"Absolutely. You bet," I said, hightailing it out of there.

My intention had been to stop by rehearsal after getting a bite, but how could I do that now? I literally reeked from every pore, I could almost *see* the fumes coming off me. I could barely stand to be in the car with myself, much less in a small room with people. I went into the health food co-op and bought a few bottles of water and some gum, then I got back in my car and decided to take a short tour of the surrounding area.

Looking further south on Euclid Avenue, the view was all leafy green trees and weather-beaten white two-story dwellings, a lush southern landscape. I turned away from this (west, I believe), tooling around with no purpose. Around fifteen blocks away, the city-scape suddenly changed. Leafy streets gave way to cement lots, paint-peeling shacks. It looked more like darkest Mississippi than anything connected to Ted Turner's Atlanta.

I stopped in a small shopping center (or what passed for one anyway). There was a liquor store and a grocery store, both with bulletproof plastic shields over the windows. I went into the grocery. There was nothing on the shelves. Well, okay, there was something, but only two boxes of Cheerios, a box of Frosted Flakes, some Bisquick and powdered milk (probably dating from the Vietnam War era), a few boxes of Tide. The cashier was a middle-aged black man in a small booth, surrounded by plastic shields. I tried to make small talk with him, but he couldn't seem to understand a word I was saying. (Forget Mississippi, this was a Johannesburg township.)

A hundred or so yards away was a music store called Spin City. Now I'm a big fan of down-and-dirty blues, the authentic stuff, and I thought I might find an obscure Muddy Waters or Son House CD here. But when I opened the glass door, I was almost blown back by a grenade blast of "hate-whitey" hip-hop. Still, as angry and violent as the music was, it was nothing compared to the glares of the two young black store clerks. I had been expecting a cozy little setup with bins of CDs for customers to peruse; instead, all the product was behind the three-sided glass counter facing the door, as were the clerks, both tall and thin, who made me understand a little better how James Meredith must have felt walking into that lily-white school in Alabama. (Okay I'm exaggerating, but I hadn't felt that hated since I stumbled into a roomful of ex-girlfriends at a Mabou Mines benefit.)

For a moment I felt a tinge of actual fear, a tingle running up my spine to the back of my brain. Could I really be in any actual danger? This had been a problem for me when I was a kid, I had a bad habit of shooting hoops in the wrong playgrounds and having to fight for my ball; then, when I went to Columbia, I had been robbed at knifepoint, gun-point, and several other points; but I tended not to think about such things anymore. However, I was suddenly very aware that I was in hostile territory, and these guys were looking at me like I was lunch. My only real weapon (it occurred to me) was my bad breath. Then again, my breath was *very* bad, and I doubted that these guys were prepared for anything like it. (It occurred to me also that maybe that cashier *had* understood me; I had an image of my breath filling up his tiny booth like a deadly gas.)

I did that "white guy smiling" thing (one of the main things I'd learned at Horace Mann), my lips crinkling and spreading out over my teeth. (It was about as effective in masking fear as the "white guy dancing" thing was in displaying rhythm.) I added a little nod, as if I was some kind of Irish leprechaun about to come out with a "Top of the marnin' to you," or perhaps a rendition of "Danny Boy." Then I backed away, letting the rageful rap music blow me right out the door.

I hopped in my oh-so-cool (not) Neon and drove to rehearsal, chewing stick after stick of gum. (I kept thinking about my forebear, Al Jolson, singing "Swanee" in blackface from the bottom of his Lithuanian heart; what a strange confluence of cultural cross-currents were at work to make this a highpoint of that era's idea of entertainment!) Even after going through the

80

whole pack, I could still sense myself emitting a cloud. Oh hell, I thought, "Just another reason for everyone to wish that I wasn't there."

The actors were in that awkward stage where they had acquired a certain familiarity with the lines but still had no idea who their characters were or why they were saying these things. Some of the relationships were starting to form—upstairs between Yankel and his wife and daughter, and between Yankel and Reb Elye (Del) and the Jewish scribe; downstairs between the whores and the pimp Schloyme (a swing character, who works for Yankel but wants to set up shop as his rival). But everyone was behaving way too nicely for the rough, lower-depths world of this play. Only Chip, the free-floating violinist, seemed convincingly to belong.

Frank, as the brothelkeeper, was coming along, though it was hard to get past his strange attire that day of formal blazer and cheap Bermuda shorts. (He looked like an absent-minded banker who had wandered away from his tailor in the middle of a fitting).

Yankel refers to himself in the play as owning "a house," but Frank kept calling it a "whorehouse," making it seem as if he might break into a chorus of "The Best Little Whorehouse in Poland." He also confided to me that he was going to "play against the melodrama" and get down to the raw fear and shame, which I said sounded peachy.

For reasons I couldn't fathom, Del was wearing a funky brown hat. Perhaps he believed that it gave him the distinctive look of a hasidic Jew, but in reality it made Reb Elye look like a pusher. ("Hey Mamele, I can take you higher.") The truth was, you could dress up Del in a black suit, yarmulke, and tallis (prayer shawl), slap some pais on either side of his face, and he would still look and sound like he should be roping steers in Wyoming.

Joe, for his part, was taking everything in stride. He seemed more concerned with the place-ment of the actors onstage than

The brothelkeeper's family, at home in their "house"

81

with motivation. ("Stand at an angle, not facing front," he said. "Everything at an angle.") He was making minor adjustments, telling the actress playing Rivkele, "Stop. Take a beat. Continue." Then telling Heidi (as the mother), "Too fast with your daughter. Take more time." He was advising Jim Roof, playing the pimp, not to kiss Heidi because she was sniffling a bit. But meanwhile, the show was lying there like a lox. There was not the sense of burgeoning excitement (much less sexual heat) that should be somewhat apparent, even at this early stage. This was especially true of the Manke-Rivkele seduction scene, in which the two girls confided in each other like classmates at Miss Porter's School.

Of course it *was* early, so I held my tongue, not wanting to be seen as a negative presence. On the bright side, there had been a Corky sighting (or so I had heard).

Mira Hirsch told me that the set design was coming along just fine, everyone was very excited, and construction would begin by week's end. When I asked her if I could see some plans, she told me not to worry, I would see the finished version soon enough.

What, me worry? Hadn't I already seen what they'd been able to do with *their flyer?* What could I possibly have to worry about?

Several comments rose to my lips, but once again I didn't say them. I knew that I'd only be branded a smartass (if I hadn't been already), and I knew only too well where that could lead. Between my stints at the National Theater Institute and Sarah Lawrence, I was enrolled for a year as an actor at Carnegie-Melon University in Pittsburgh. A week after arriving I was placed on probation for telling a Scene Study teacher what I thought of his instruction. This teacher was then able to connive his way into becoming my faculty advisor, a position he used to give me the benefit of his great stores of wisdom. "If you were Laurence Olivier," he snarled at year's end, "I would still make sure you got booted." (Ah yes, *The Theater*. Ain't it grand?) This little piece of personal history was something I'd rather not be doomed to repeat.

In any case, I had enough to worry about with the roads in Atlanta. Just the day before, a small plane had made an emergency crash landing on the freeway at rush hour, so now I was keeping my eyes peeled in all directions. (Unlike John Irving's Garp, I believed these things came in bunches.) This wasn't helping my already-lousy ability to follow the map and the road signs (when there were any signs, which wasn't often). On this particular evening, I was trying to find my way to someplace called Stone Mountain, where

Heidi and her hubby were giving a party for the company. I got lost several times, driving around like a cartoon character, my head spinning around in frantic circles.

Finally I found an open bookstore, the man in charge looked like Mark Twain, with a silver mane of hair and a large salt-and-pepper moustache. He patiently drew me a map, and with this by my side I was able to reach my destination. (Though not before passing a three-car pileup, a four-car pileup, and a ten-car pileup—what kind of unholy place was this?)

The actors were in the process of bonding when I arrived, and I threw myself into their midst, hoping some of it would rub off on me. On top of everything else, a long distance e-mail argument had suddenly and quite unexpectedly broken out with my girlfriend Holly (more about this later), so I was greatly in need of some fresh, hot-from-the-oven actor-love. For my own part, I was a veritable whirlwind of positive vibes, clapping everyone on the back, giving group hugs. "I'll tell you anything wonderful you want to hear, just say something nice to me." (That was my subtext).

Frank Wittow was at the party with his "other half," Barbara LeBow. Barbara, a university professor, had written the Jewish play *A Shayna Maidel*, which had been a considerable critical and commercial Off-Broadway success in New York, and was currently being produced at venues around the country, and probably around the world. (As, of course, my *God of Vengeance* and *Mickey's Home* weren't.) This momentarily tested my "group-hug" frame of mind, but I was able to overcome the impulse to engage in an intellectual pissing contest and, instead, throw a fairy dusting of praise all over her, in an all-too-naked fervor of bonding.

Joe was at the party, of course. I drifted over, posing a question that had been on my mind for some days. "Tell me again about *Kaddish?* What's the story with that?"

Joe made it clear that he was hoping to stage a new version of Allen Ginsberg's poem, if he could find an adaptation he liked. Since he thought so highly of my Asch adaptation, he was encouraging me to try my hand with the poem. But it was unclear whether he had the rights. While I was trying to figure this out from his somewhat cryptic remarks, Joe asked if I would drive him back to his hotel.

I was a little taken aback, as I hadn't really finished my bonding. There were several members of the cast I had barely said hello to. The kind of mood I was in, I felt like I could bond all night, it was almost like a frenzy that ran through my veins. On the other hand, here was a chance to spend some quality time with Joe (with only sixteen days before the first performance). I tamped out my wildfires of bonding and said, "Okay."

As I navigated the way back on I-285 (and prayed that I wouldn't drag Joe along on another adventure to the "lost" world), I asked Joe if he'd ever driven. "Yes. When younger," he said. Why had he stopped? "I was distracted by the scenery," Joe told me. He added that he'd had three separate accidents, each time driving his car off the road into a ditch because he was transfixed by the sunlight filtering through the trees, by the rows of dandelions swaying in the breeze, by the sheer beauty of the landscape he was driving through. Finally his three sisters (he is the youngest of five children) had persuaded him not to drive anymore.

The funny thing was, that was the same reason why it had taken me until twenty to get my license. I was a young nature poet, easily fascinated by purple hills rising up in the distance, easily wounded by the spectacle of a flock of birds ascending towards the sun. After my aunt had died, when I was nineteen, my tendency toward introspective dreaminess took over most of my waking hours. But then I went into the theater, into acting, and my focus on the outside world returned. I was once again able to accomplish practical tasks like keeping my mind on the road. (Had I lost my purer self in the process, my chance at being a truly "pure artist" like Joe?)

We chatted a little about the production—Joe wasn't particularly sold on Corky the set designer either—until I was suddenly aware that Joe was pouring out his heart about a close friend who had recently died of ovarian cancer. She was a dramaturg who had worked with Joe since his Open Theatre days, traveling with Joe to Israel in the early 1980s to help him create a performance piece about Arabs and Jews called *The Other*. She was a confidante, a constant companion, who knew him as well as anyone on earth, and the loss of her had left him feeling lonely and bereft.

Joe then moved from this into a fragmentary monologue about his own illnesses, his three heart attacks. "Each time I thought I was dying, each time they took me to the hospital, a voice in my head was saying, "This is it. All over. Everything you love is ending."" Joe's voice and face were impassive, he looked straight ahead at the dark road as if seeing this scene.

I knew something about these events from Joe's book, *The Presence of the Actor*, from various interviews with him, and from his published correspondence with his friend and sometime-collaborator Sam Shepard. I knew that Joe had had rheumatic fever as a child, that he'd been sent to a sanitarium in Florida, where he was one of the few children to survive. I knew that Joe had grown up Jewish, gay, poor, and sickly in Des Moines, Iowa, that he'd moved to New York after college (Drake) in 1955, where he'd been making theater for twenty years before having his first open heart surgery in 1974. I knew that Joe had written to Shepard in 1979 that he was going to stay in a geriatric hotel while in San Francisco, "since I may never be old." Yet here he was, sixty-three years of age, if not old then certainly taking some definite steps in that direction.

Joe kept going on and on at a breathless breakneck pace, sentences running on, running into each other. "I did die once, you know. On the operating table. I saw the white light. But then I came back again," he told me.

"Did you get any glimpse of the other side?" I asked.

"No. Just the white light," he said.

Joe didn't mention when this had happened, though I assumed it was in 1984, when he suffered a stroke during his third open heart operation, leading to his aphasia. Looking at him now, small and spare and child-like, I saw nothing of the sexier, earthier, coarser Joe Chaikin whom I had observed in that 1981 rehearsal. All that was burned away, leaving just this pared-down poetic essence. But when the proprietor of the Olive Café referred to Joe as "the old man," I didn't know whom he meant. While his hair may have been graying and thinning, Joe didn't seem "old" to me, he had a Chaplinesque quality of movement, of inner grace, that made him seem ageless.

"All I kept thinking," Joe told me again, "was that everything I loved was ending. I would never do the things I loved, never see anybody ever again."

Joe's words came back to me at three AM when I woke up with a start. Or rather was woken up with a "thok!", which I soon realized was the sound of my nose smacking against the front left leg of the bench press. (Yes, my nose; not a big "Jewish" shnozz, just a regulation size honker with lots of moxie. I'm convinced that the bench press made a remark, and my proboscis was not amused.)

"Of course I had loved my ex-wife" was the ghostly thought that soon came floating through the pea-soup fog in my head. But that love preceded our court battle, and her attempt to extract a pile of money from my parents. Then there was the matter of my writing notebooks and personal papers, which she had taken hostage. The notebooks were the core of my work, and she had forced me to ransom them for a few thousand dollars (and made me pay further to have them messengered from her lawyer's office to mine). My personal papers—including twenty-five years of letters from friends and lovers, as well as all my professional correspondence—were never returned. I still couldn't believe that the woman I'd loved was capable of such a thing, and at moments like this it stung deeply.

(Among the "disappeared" papers were the love letters we'd written to each other so long ago. I couldn't fill in any blanks now, couldn't remember a single word of the love we had sworn to each other.)

So no, I didn't miss my ex-wife. I didn't even miss being married. What I missed was the general sense of goodwill, the feeling that, basically, life made sense, that *my* life made sense, that the future stretched ahead as an endless source of opportunity for good things to happen (and they *were* going to happen, goddamnit, I'd felt so sure of that). It was much harder to believe such things anymore, to get myself to swallow such dubious sentiments.

But of course I had to give it a shot. How else was I supposed to get back to sleep in the shadow of a sarcastic bench press at three o'clock in the morning?

Chapter Seven

LOL (Laugh Out Loud), Part 1

Subj: Happy Happy Happy
Date: 10/12/98
To: HollyG

Dear Birthday Woman (doesn't sound quite right):

So glad to hear about your great progress on your writing! That's really wonderful, and it has to make you feel good. I don't know what to say about your feeling more inspired when I'm gone; I guess I'll just have to go away more often. I'm just glad to hear you're getting work done, and I hope it continues.

I've been compiling lots of notes about Joe. I definitely want to do a book, and Joe will be a part of it, though not necessarily the central focus.

I feel badly that more people didn't show up for your birthday gathering. You certainly deserve better, because you're a great person, and such a good friend to others. So here's my best wishes for your next year, I hope it is a great one for you—with or without me.

All my love. Steve

Subj: Happy Happy Happy
Date: 10/12/98
From: HollyG
To: StevF

Thank you for being so kind and loving toward me. Thanks for the sentiments about it being a good year for me "with or without" you! I love you, you know, however the life-decision thing shakes down.

It was, after all, a fine birthday. Low key and not flashy in any sense, but satisfying and fine. I guess I'm finally adult enough not to need the "perfect" birthday. And when you let go of the need for perfection, you open up to the joy of imperfect but wonderful real experience. (Blah blah blah—my Alanon training may be slowly sinking in and paying off!)

Back at you (all *my* love).   Holly

Subj: Happy Unbirthday
Date: 10/13/98
To: HollyG

I had a terrific lunch this afternoon with Joe C., after having had a terrible time sleeping last night. (The room I'm in is so musty, I'm having trouble breathing, and there's this sweaty smell in the air from Ben's laundry; also, I was "sleeping" on the floor, which is harder than I'd remembered. Never let me take springs for granted again. I went out today and bought an inflatable mattress for $80—expensive, it's true, but useful for camping, and absolutely necessary if I'm going to get any sleep here.) I had convinced myself in my sleepless torpor last night that Joe wanted to ask me not to come to rehearsal for the next week or so, that I was distracting the actors. Instead, he kept going on about how much he loved my adaptation, and certainly left the door open to working together again. He mentioned something about being interested in working on a new production of *Kaddish*, the Alan Ginsberg poem, with a new adaptation. I'm of course going to question him further. All in all, it really was sort of a fantasy come true.

And oh yeah—the artistic director of Jewish Theatre of the South (love that name!) took a bunch of us to Simcha Torah services tonight at a conservative synagogue. It was very whacky. I got to carry the Torah, as did several other people. (There were at least seven Torahs in circulation at any one time.) We were dancing around and kept bumping into each other. It was kind of like Jewish bumper cars. Who knew that a night at the synagogue would be so much fun? (Isn't that a Marx Brothers movie—"A Night at the Temple?")   Steve

Subj: Happy Unbirthday
Date: 10/13/98
From: HollyG
To: StevF

You had me smiling from ear to ear with your description of the experience with Joe C., and then laughing out loud (which I understand from savvy e-mail friends is represented online by "lol") with your description of the "Simcha Torah free for all" and the Jewish bumper cars!

I'm just so happy and proud and excited for you that this experience with Joe has worked out so well. Wouldn't it be something to work on the *Kaddish* project with him!

I'm sorry that Ben is a jerk. Although, as you know because you can read my thoughts, I am worrying that you are not being a good or grateful guest . . . but I'll just have to live with my anxiety about that and keep it to myself—oh, whoops, I guess I just let it out . . . oh well. (And while we're at it, you will, of course, buy a "bread 'n butter" thank you gift for both Alison and Ben before you leave, yes?!) Enough of my fears and mothering.

I think the inflatable mattress is a great idea. I've been wanting one for a while, for numerous reasons. Is it a double, or only a single? (If it's a double, we could make love in front of the fire and sleep there one night, which I've always wanted to do . . .)

I'm really hit hard with this fucking cold. I woke up at noon today and only had enough energy to pick up Cheryl at the airport. Cheryl and Andy had an incredible time in Hawaii. Like everyone has told me, it is apparently truly Paradise. We have to go. (Maybe even a better honeymoon than Italy? Oh, I didn't just say that, did I? Whoops . . .)

Okay, talk later.   H.

Subj: Hi
Date: 10/14/98
To: HollyG

The air mattress is a large single (the double was $160!). It's okay to sleep on, though it doesn't replace a bed. (I'll buy a companion one for in front of the fireplace, okay?) It'll have to do for the time being, as there's no place else for me to stay here. Ben is not a bad guy really, it's just that there's no ventilation in his house, and he just had it sprayed with insecticide, so it stinks of spray and sweat. But hey, what can I do about it?

The 7 Stages producer told me today that the actors are worried because Joe is only able to rehearse for a few hours a day, and we have our first preview in only two weeks. She asked me if I would work with the actors overtime to help coordinate the lines and blocking, etc. I said sure, as long as Joe was okay with it.

Glad to hear you're feeling better. Take care.   Steve

Subj: Hi
Date: 10/13/98
From: HollyG
To: StevF

Wow, honey, it sounds as if the fact that you're there to possibly run lines and blocking with the actors will turn out to be a godsend, so you're not "superfluous" or anything like that after all. I knew this would be a good thing.   Love H.

Subj: Hi
Date: 10/15/98
To: HollyG

Still getting along great with Joe, but it's clear there are problems with the production—some resulting from Joe's lack of stamina, others resulting from his disinterest in character and psychological issues. The basic thing is, the show is not sexy. It's not dangerous. And it's not very believable. I mentioned these things to Faye (the producer) after Joe had left the rehearsal, and she absolutely agreed. She wanted me to get the company together to discuss this, but I declined, feeling that it would be unfair to Joe. Instead, I said I would speak to the actors individually and try to go over ways they could better locate some connection to this down-and-dirty environment (the women especially just look like actresses on a vacation). But the truth is, there's a limited amount I can do. It's not my place to be the director or run improvs with them. The cast is fine though limited. I'm always aware of how vulnerable and nervous they are, and I certainly don't want to make anyone feel lousy about themselves. But art isn't pretty, right?

Simply put, theater is hard work for little or no money. It's enjoyable when it works, but even then there's usually not much of a payoff. My payoff here has been working with Joe and getting to know someone who is really a transcendent spirit. There's no amount of money that can buy that.   Steve

Subj: Hi
Date: 10/16/98
From: HollyG
To: StevF

Yeah, theater is a lot of work for no money and very little payoff unless things go really well. We must all be nuts. It's just that every now and then

90

you see something that really does work, and it's transcendent. (You know, I don't have to tell you.) But I have to admit that I was secretly a little bit happy to hear you say that because, as a rapidly aging woman, I fantasize that this means you'll choose (of your own free will, of course) to concentrate on some other more lucrative career choice and do theater "on the side" so that we can have some financial security and a baby and all that. But no pressure. We all have to do what we all have to do.

Anyway, tonight I'm feeling very sad and lost and unrooted and … yes, I admit it … needy / lonely for you. But I find that I'm also focusing on some of the negatives between us—I don't intend to, but they rear their heads without my inviting them in. So that makes me feel guilty and horrible, like I'm betraying you and so on. I guess I just don't feel terrific right now, emotionally-speaking. Oh well.

It occurred to me today that you never told me if you had given your hosts bread 'n butter thank you gifts, or if you were even planning to. Remember, they're southern. (And it's the right thing to do anyway. But I'm sure you won't see this concern as my human and social grace and instead interpret it as middle-class bullshit.)   H.

Chapter Eight

The Asswipe or The Day Beckett Got Lost at the Mall

"You're on earth. There's no cure for that."
—Samuel Beckett, quoted by Joe Chaikin in
The Presence of the Actor

IT ALL SEEMED TO change in a flash.

One minute Del Hamilton was standing on the sidewalk in front of the theater, regaling me with stories like, "Two years ago Joe was directing Arthur Miller's *All My Sons* here. At the end of the first week of rehearsals, he had severe heart pains and had to be flown to New York City, where he was put on a respirator and then given a pacemaker. I mean, the man has had three heart attacks, two strokes, he's lived through rheumatic fever ... There's no explaining why he's not six feet under. And there's no way he should still be able to make theater."

The next minute (it seemed) Del was seated, jaw clenched, in the blonde-wood confines of his 7 Stages office. "There's too damn much reverence going on here," he steamed. "This show is flat. We wanted to do it because the characters had some spice to them, they weren't afraid to be ugly ... We thought if we could put that onstage, we would have something. But what we have now is just bland. The hero worship for Joe can only go so far, we have to be prepared to do whatever it takes to bring these characters alive."

But what could be done? Joe was directing the show, he was not a well man, he only had a limited amount of energy. Unless someone helped him. Someone unthreatening, with only the show's best interests at heart. Someone like me.

This was the suggestion of Del and Faye, that I make some arrangement with Joe and the actors to supplement Joe's direction. I wasn't comfortable

The Adapter with Faye Allen, and Del Hamilton, co-Artistic Directors of 7 Stages.
(Sorry, Mira, no room for you.)

with it, and I told them so. But I also had to agree that the production was in trouble. It had no urgency, there were several transitions that just didn't work, and there was that seduction scene that zigged when it should have zagged (to be honest, it hardly zigged). Joe had blocked it so that Rivkele and Manke (the prostitute) were sitting next to each other on a couch, earnestly saying lines to each other like:

Manke
... I uncovered your breasts and washed them with the rain water that ran into my hands. Your breasts are so white and firm, the blood in them cools under my hand like white snow. They smell like fresh grass in the meadows. And I loosened your hair, like this—

(*She* runs her fingers through *Rivkele's* hair) and I held it so in the rain and washed it. Its scent is the scent of May rain.

(*She* buries her face in *Rivkele's* hair)
Cool me with your hair, cool me so, let it wash over me ...

In Joe's staging, Manke touched and caressed the brothelkeeper's daughter at the appropriate moments, she stared deeply into her eyes, and none of it mattered, none of it *played*. The problem was that the strength of the scene lay in the rhythm of the lines, in their hypnotic sensual nature, rather than in any information they conveyed. Rivkele knew perfectly well what Manke had done to her in the rain, she didn't need to be reminded. But there was an erotic quality to talking about it, to reveling in what they had shared, had done with each other. There were any number of ways to stage this effectively, but simply illustrating the lines wasn't one of them.

94

I approached Joe after rehearsal to talk this over. It was a little under two weeks before the first preview, and he was besieged with questions from designers and tech people (no, not Corky, though his set was in the process of being built). By the time I got to him, Joe had the frazzled look of an eighth grade substitute teacher after his first day of classes. I was telling him my problems with the scene as gently as possible when I looked up and saw his eyes darting around, as if I was a new student whom he suspected of having a weapon.

"Anything wrong, Joe?" I asked.

He shook his head, but started backing up, moving away from me, a look of naked panic on his face.

"Look, Joe, it's no big deal," I said. "All it needs is a little adjustment."

I smiled and nodded and behaved as reassuringly as I could. (Okay, all I really did was smile and nod, but what other gesture would do the trick? Groveling on the floor or dancing like a pixie tend to produce other reactions.) But Joe continued backing away, muttering something under his breath that sounded like, "I can't now . . . I can't . . . can't."

"Hey, c'mon Joe," I said, a little put out.

I was going to ask him if he wanted to schedule a better time to discuss this, but he was already in full flight, scooting out of the theater as fast as his legs could carry him.

As I stood there watching his heels kick up little dust clouds, I was filled with conflicting emotions. On the one hand, Joe was my youthful idol, a man whose work and character I greatly admired. He was also someone, by this point, whom I regarded as a friend and felt very protective toward. But, goddamnit, he was also the goddamn director of my goddamn adaptation, and I would be goddamned if I was just going to stand around and let him make a goddamn hash of it. (Sorry, that last sentence was hijacked by the spirit of Holden Caulfield.) Also, his running away really bugged me. No director had ever done that before. Was I really that scary?

While I was pondering what to do, the actress playing Rivkele (Andrea) came up and asked if I had any notes for her. "Anything you can give me would be a big help," she said. "I'm really lost, and Joe doesn't have any time to go over it with me."

I told her (with some reluctance) that the key to her character was that she really loved her mama and papa, she really wanted to please them, but she couldn't understand or accept why it was wrong now to be friends with Manke. Manke—the only prostitute who was allowed upstairs—had been her friend since childhood, she loved Manke, loved playing games with her. Why was it suddenly forbidden for them to play together?

"So it's not a rebellious thing?" Andrea asked. "I'm not trying to get back at them? I'm not angry because they're such hypocrites?"

Not at all, I told her. It's all very innocent. Manke is her only friend, she loves her like a sister, so what could be wrong with anything Manke asks her to do?

Andrea thanked me, smiling, saying that I had really helped her. Which was a good thing, right? So why did I feel like such a schmuck?

Truth was, while there were several different ways to play Rivkele, the interpretation I'd given her was the only one that to my mind provided the proper payoff for the seduction scene later on. If Rivkele was too knowing or angry or rebellious then the scene turned into a coy excuse for two girls to get it on. While this would have undoubtedly pleased a certain segment of the audience (like that fellow who walked out of the Ran Avni production), and might have opened the play up to the raincoat crowd (probably not an inconsiderable number, judging from all the strip clubs and porno houses in town), it would also have robbed the scene of any dramatic impact. This comes from our seeing Rivkele lose her innocence *right in front of our eyes*, even as she and Manke revel in it, playing what seem like variations on childhood games. After these games have ended, however, we feel the terrible inevitability of what will surely follow.

This was the mastery of Asch's scene, as I understood it. (And to think he was only twenty-one years old when he wrote it in 1901!) But the key here is that this was *my* understanding, *my* interpretation, while it was *Joe's* production. However good my intentions may have been, on some basic level I was undercutting his directorial authority. So I felt guilty.

As I was leaving the theater, I heard my name being called, and I looked around. Joe's assistant Scott ran up to me, asking if I could meet Joe for dinner that evening. "Anything special he wants to talk about?" I asked. Scott started to say something, then stopped in mid-sentence, saying, "It's better if he tells you himself."

There was nothing unusual about eating dinner with Joe. We had eaten together several times, usually accompanied by Mira Hirsch or some other friend of Joe's. It was almost always in Indian or Thai restaurants, since they didn't use oil or salt in preparing their dishes. I can't say that these evenings had resulted in any memorable meals, but it was always a pleasure to be in

Joe's company, as we went over that day's rehearsal. In this case, however, my uneasiness grew throughout the afternoon, as I dreaded the confrontation that seemed to loom.

When I showed up at the mall Thai restaurant called The King and I (you can't make this stuff up), Joe was already seated at a table with a young woman named Emily whom I had met around 7 Stages. Much of the evening was taken up with Emily recounting anecdotes of growing up among the *PTL* (Praise the Lord), Jim Bakker's group of evangelical Christians who built their own religious theme park, and whose efforts would eventually drown in an outpouring of Tammy Faye's tears. Normally, nothing would have stimulated my appetite more than fun-filled true stories of Jim and Tammy Faye Bakker and Jessica Hahn (the church secretary with whom Jim was having an affair, and who went on to exhibit her virtues in the pages of *Playboy*.) But my stomach was so tied up in knots of anticipation that I could only shovel in half my Pad Thai, and hardly even touched the main courses. Finally I just turned to Joe and asked him, "Is there something you want to tell me?"

"Oh yes," he said, nodding. "Almost forgot." He motioned to Emily to hold on for a moment while he asked me something.

I braced for Joe's anger, whatever form this might take.

"Tomorrow afternoon. Emory University, Beckett Studies. Can you drive?"

"Me? Sure," I said, taken aback.

Joe told me what time to pick him up, then he nodded at Emily, who launched into another story of what it was like to grow up in an amusement park world dedicated to God that fell apart in less time than it took for the mascara to run down a drama queen's cheeks.

Even for an easily-confused driver like me, it was impossible *not* to find the Beckett Studies building at Emory University. All I had to do was keep driving around the campus of sloping hills, fir trees, and concrete buildings until I came to the wooden shack that looked like it might have been dropped here by some tornado, à la *The Wizard of Oz*. Seriously, this structure looked more like a hillbilly's still or perhaps a very spacious outhouse than anything you'd expect to find on a modern campus. ("Perfect," I imagined Beckett saying with a mordant smile. On second thought, scratch the smile.)

We were greeted inside by Lois Overbeck, a professor at Emory who was editing a huge chunk of Beckett's voluminous correspondence that had been donated to the university. (I'm sure I'm not alone in being amused that a man who wrote so sparely and (later in life) so sparingly would have left the world so many missives.) Among the 15,000 or so letters under Lois's domain were a few that older Sam (as opposed to Shepard, who was Joe's younger Sam) had written to Joe. Lois walked up to Joe, kissed him, and thanked him for "engaging with this incredible mind in such interesting ways."

Joe then introduced me to Lois, a middle-aged woman with short black hair and pale skin, who was wearing a black-and-white dress embroidered with flowers and leaves. She turned her smile on me, saying how much she was looking forward to seeing Joe's production of *God of Vengeance*. ("And what about *your* correspondence?" I queried myself. Oh yeah, that's right: I didn't have any. My ex chucked it all!)

On the inside, the Beckett shack lost some of its oddness and took on more of the trappings of Academia. There were the bookshelves stuffed with works by the Great Stone Face and his friends and associates (lots of James Joyce of course—the young Beckett was Joyce's secretary in Dublin), along with the biographies and monographs that had piled up in staggering numbers. There were the mail slots for staff and student interns, the copy machines and fax machines and computer terminals. And of course there were framed posters from famous productions of *Waiting For Godot, Endgame, Krapp's Last Tape*, and other Beckett plays. But the main room was dominated by a travel poster for Ireland, showing a lone farmhouse amid rolling green hills and winding stone fences. This sad, soothing image was tacked to the wall in a slapdash manner that I think Beckett would have appreciated.

I started reading some copies of his letters and poems that were stuck on a bulletin board. "Did you know that Beckett referred to his poems as 'turds' and 'asswipes?'" Lois asked me.

"Yes, well, many people have used those same words to describe my plays," I started to say, but then decided not to. I wasn't quite sure if she'd know it was a joke.

"I think that Beckett writes from a place where he is absolutely alone. There is no consolation. There is nobody around to hold your hand; only a few jokes."

Joe had written this in his 1972 book *The Presence of the Actor*, but it wasn't until eight years later that he'd actually met older Sam face to face. This took place in Paris, where Joe's production of *Endgame* had transferred from Manhattan Theatre Club to the American Center for a month-long run. Joe had an idea to create a one-man show by combining material from a Beckett play (*Texts For Nothing*) and work of fiction (*How It Is*). He met with Beckett at the latter's favorite sidewalk café to get his permission (often a prickly matter) and to discuss how best to construct the adaptation.

"We talked and talked and talked," Joe told me on the ride to Emory. "Beckett had so much in his head, so many more thoughts than I did. But then after awhile, he stopped, telling me, 'Enough. I can't go on.' And we didn't meet again after that."

Joe carried with him an enormous biography of Beckett, recently published, called *Damned To Fame* by James Knowlson. The book describes Joe as "the brilliant American actor-director and founder of the Open Theatre." It recounts Joe's café conversation with Beckett, going on to say that older Sam never saw the resulting one-man show, though he did hear a tape recording and offered reactions and advice based on that. It also tells how Beckett, just before his death, had dedicated the English version of his short play *What Is the Word* to Joe, assuring a certain kind of literary immortality.

(If only I could have something like that happen to me, I found myself thinking. Then the question of "Who the hell is Stephen Fife?"—so prominent in my lifetime—could resound down through the ages.)

I hadn't known Beckett, had not even met him, but I did have a Beckett anecdote (courtesy of the director Alan Schneider) which I liked to tell. It was a beautifully sunny day in London when Beckett met a few friends for a drink. Afterward they walked over to Hyde Park, where they walked through a perfectly manicured field of shining green grass. Lovers strolled by, hand-in-hand, alongside young mothers pushing baby carriages. One of Beckett's friends stopped and looked around, overwhelmed by the scene. "Beautiful," the friend said. "A day like this makes you glad to be alive." "Well," Beckett countered, "I wouldn't go that far."

Lois Overbeck told us some memorable Beckett stories of her own. One involved a man whose letter she had happened upon while going through the correspondence. "Sick and probably dying," the man had written, "I wanted to leave behind a legacy of some kind. Would you please write me a letter, preferably in ink?" Beckett, it seems, had written back to the man, who hailed from a small town in Maine. Lois called the morgue section of the town newspaper to find out when this man had died. The man at the newspaper told her, "Sure, I know who he is. Saw him yesterday at the store. He's healthy as a horse." Lois finally tracked down the man himself (henceforth to be known as "The Faker"), who was *very* evasive, refusing even to admit that he had written to Beckett. Lois subsequently went on the internet and found out that The Faker had written the same letter to at least twelve other world-famous authors.

Eventually, Joe went over the galleys of his Beckett correspondence with Lois, then we made our way back to the car. Joe still clutched the older Sam's biography to his side like a talisman, a Book of Life to which he had made a contribution, however small.

Back at rehearsal, Joe actually devised another improv. (Oh happy day!) He had the four actresses portraying the prostitutes "display" themselves for prospective customers, twirling around, thrusting out their hips, smiling suggestively. It was a blatant attempt to address the sadly lacking "lust quotient" in the show, as well as to inject a needed jolt of lower-depths sleaze.

Was it successful? As the Jewish scribe tells Yankel, when asked if God will forgive him, "Who can tell?" One thing I was sure about, though. If these middle-class southern girls of 1998, with their toned minds and bodies, and their sexually-liberated ways, had shown up in a working-class ghetto brothel in turn-of-the-century Poland, the line of Jewish men waiting their turn would have reached to the New World.

But what could be done? You couldn't exactly ask actors to change their body type for every role, could you (Robert De Niro in *Raging Bull* notwithstanding)? Well, in a sense, you could. Because in the end it had less to do with how much one weighed than in how one carried oneself, in the *attitude* one projected. I mean, how else could Eva La Gallienne score a huge triumph as Juliet at seventy opposite a twenty-year-old Romeo? It's true that audiences in the early 20th century were less literal than we are now, after so many years of TV-size reality. But those people weren't stupid or naive, they were simply overcome by the force of Ms. La Gallienne's charisma and imagination, her superior ability to create an illusion.

Which was exactly what was lacking here: not lust, but *conviction*. The kind of conviction necessary to transport a comfortable middle-class (largely Jewish) audience in late 20th century Atlanta to a radically different time and place. It was the sort of problem that pre-aphasia Joe would surely have been all over, working up endless exercises to stimulate the actors' imaginations and help them make that perilous but necessary leap. But the Joe of 1998 was a man dealing with a terrible disease that consumed much of his energy and left him with a limited ability to express his ideas. He simply was not in any position to push the ten-actor cast (if indeed anyone could have) to the lengths required to make magic happen.

All of which still didn't help me answer the question of what to do. I didn't want to step on Joe's toes, but if I had to sit there any longer and watch that seduction scene lay there like a bored housewife with a perpetual headache, I was going to scream. In fact, one day when I was already hearing unvoiced Homer Simpson shrieks echoing in my head ("Aaah! Aaaah!"). Joe's assistant passed me a note, written in Joe's unsteady hand on a yellow post-it, "Like your black jeans. Can you take me to buy a pair?"

"Aaaaaaaah!"

After rehearsal I drove Joe to a nearby mall complex, where there was a Gap. Walking with him amid the praline vendors, burger franchises, and electronics knock-off stores ("We beat any price!" surrounded by flashing red lights), I was never more keenly aware of Joe's otherworldliness, of the silence he carried around with him (like a curse? Like a blessing?). With his watery blue eyes and ambling, child-like gait, he really did seem to have sprung from a Beckett play ... perhaps one about a Lazarus-like man who has come back from the dead to look for a well-fitting pair of black jeans. In the real-life version of this event, Joe tried on pair after pair after pair, but they were all too big. Finally he found a suitable pair in the "Boy's" section.

I had resolved not to say anything critical about Joe's direction during our jaunt. As it happened, neither Joe nor I could remember anything about where I had parked in the mall's five-story concrete garage, and we ended up searching for almost an hour. (White Neons were far more popular here than I would ever have imagined.) We had pretty much given up hope when we rounded a bend and stumbled upon it. "Yeah!" Joe said, pumping his fist, and I was elated as well. But once we got in the car, my accumulated sense of frustration just bubbled over.

"Joe, that seduction scene just isn't working," I told him. "Faye and Del both agree with me, and ... I mean, I know you're dealing with a lot right now, and I don't mean to upset you or get in your way, but—"

"Fine. Why not ... you ... direct?" Joe said.

"Me? But you're the director, Joe."

"No. Please. Big help," he said.

"Really? You're sure?"

Joe nodded. I assured him that I'd only agree to do it if he was standing nearby, looking over my shoulder, overseeing the work. Joe smiled at me—a big generous smile, without a hint of darkness—as if I'd just offered to buy him dinner.

Chapter Nine

The Adapter Directs

- I wrote this play when I was twenty-one years of age. I was not concerned whether I wrote a moral or immoral play. What I wanted to write was an artistic play and a true one. In the seventeen years it has been before the public, this is the first time I have had to defend it ...

- As to the comment that the play is a reflection on the Jewish race, I resent the statement that *God of Vengeance* is a play against the Jews. No Jew until now has considered it harmful to the Jews. It is included in the repertoire of every Jewish stage in the world and has been presented more than any other play. *God of Vengeance* is not a typically "Jewish" play. A "Jewish play" is a play where the Jews are specially characterized for the benefit of Gentiles. I am not such a "Jewish" writer. I write, and *incidentally* my types are Jewish, for of all peoples, they are the ones I know best ...

- Jews do not need to clear themselves before anyone. They are as good and bad as any race. I see no reason why a Jewish writer should not bring out the good or bad traits ... I have written so many Jewish characters who are good and noble, that I cannot now, when writing of a "bad" one, make an exception and say that he is a Gentile.

  From an "Open Letter" by Sholem Asch, 1923, responding to the obscenity trial for the Broadway production of *God of Vengeance*.

HERE IS THE SETUP FOR THE "seduction scene" (or "love scene," depending on one's interpretation):

It is late one rainy night. Upstairs, the family—Yankel, Sore, and Rivkele—are asleep. Downstairs, in the basement, the lights are still burning, the brothel is still open for business. Manke is in her cubicle "entertaining" a gentleman from Lithuania. The other girls are bored, passing the time in conversation, since the rain has kept away the usual customers. They decide to go outside and play in the rain. Meanwhile, Hindl, the oldest "girl" (and something of a supervisor), is plotting to steal away Rivkele and start her own house with her pimp / husband-to-be Shloyme. To this end, Hindl encourages Manke to rouse Rivkele without waking Yankel. Manke taps a broom-head on the ceiling, and Rivkele soon appears. Manke invites her to come play outside in the rain, but Rivkele is afraid of Yankel hearing them. Finally Manke goes out herself, and Rivkele follows.

Hindl, watching this, sees her big chance. "Here's bread and butter," she says. "Now rent a place. Get married. You can be somebody. As good as anyone else." She prays for divine assistance, crying, "Give me good luck for once! Let me get what I want!"

When Manke and Rivkele return they are drenched in spring rain. Rivkele's teeth are chattering in the cold night air. Manke offers to warm her, saying, "Snuggle up close." Manke soon tells her, "Let me comb your hair like a bride's, parted in the middle, with two long braids. Would you like that?" Rivkele, mesmerized, is so scared and excited that she can barely bring herself to murmur, "Yes, Manke."

Manke then turns this into a game of a bride and groom on their wedding night, with Rivkele as the bride. "Your father and mother have gone to bed. Bride and Groom are alone at the table. We're shy and embarrassed ... Then we overcome our shyness and draw close to each other ... We're pressed together so closely, your flesh and mine, then we kiss each other so shyly, like virgins ... Then we go to sleep in the same bed. Our two bodies lying there, side by side ... Like two children who are without sin. But we're not children, are we?"

Then Manke asks the key question, "Would you like to sleep the whole night with me, Rivkele, in the same bed?"

When Rivkele murmurs her assent, Manke starts taking the young girl to her cubicle. Rivkele, however, is afraid of her father finding out. Manke then proposes, "What if I took you away from here? We could be together all day and night ... We'll dress up like officers and ride around on our horses. Wouldn't you like that?"

In a moment, Hindl is by her side. Rivkele is still terrified of her father's wrath, but Manke reassures her, and the three of them are soon walking to the door, making up a lame excuse when they bump into the other two (surprised) girls on the way out.

(Quick Note: Asch committed one *major* dramaturgical screw-up in the scene. When Manke emerges from her cubicle, she tells the other girls that her Lithuanian client has fallen asleep inside. But a short time later she tries to get Rivkele to come to her cubicle with her. Has she simply forgotten about the "*meshuggeneh* Litwak?" What if Rivkele had overcome her fear of Papa and taken up the offer? I guess the guy would have been a lucky Litwak, huh? But, in any case, the cubicle curtain is never opened, and the audience—in the heat of the moment—seems to have forgotten all about him as well. So I suppose any director can too. As they say in the sports world: No harm, no foul.)

My problem with Joe's direction of the scene—as I've said before—lay in its being too warm and cuddly. Sholem Asch was many things, but warm and cuddly he wasn't. His books are hugely ambitious, with biblical / Tolstoyan titles like *Salvation, The Apostle, The Nazarene, What I Believe.* He is given to making portentous (if provocative) statements: "It is my profound belief that only the Jewish-Christian idea contains in itself the possibility of salvation for our tortured world." (He was excoriated in his lifetime by many in the Jewish world for his perceived apostasy in embracing Christian ideals.) And, finally, *God of Vengeance* is not a warm and cuddly play. While it is astonishingly "modern" (whatever that means anymore) in portraying the brothel girls as three-dimensional people, it only does a disservice to sentimentalize them.

This is what Asch himself wrote about the scene. "This love between girls is not only an erotic one. It is the unconscious mother love of which they are deprived . . . I also wanted to bring out the innocent longing for sin, and the sinful, dreaming of purity. Manke loves the clean soul of Rivkele, and Rivkele longs to stay near the door of such a woman as Manke and listen within."

Then again, maybe we shouldn't listen too closely to what the playwright had to say. I mean, "unconscious mother love?" Puh-leeze. That may have sociological and psychological value, and might be useful to lit-crit types and the like, but how does it help an actor or director? That is, how can it be actively *played*? (Answer: It can't. It's a cerebral quicksand.) Worse, it pushes all involved toward exactly the kind of sentimental trap that Joe had fallen into. (Note to Reader: Playwrights often don't know dick about what they've written. That's why, for the most part, they make lousy self-directors.)

As for Asch's other idea, about "the innocent longing for sin" and "the sinful dreaming of purity"—well, that was more intriguing. It was something of a darker version of William Blake's *Songs of Innocence and Experience,* where the soul is transformed by the act of sex, i.e., partaking of the fruit from the Tree of Knowledge of Good and Evil. This mutual attraction of the virgin and the prostitute—though a little overly literary, not to mention a little too pat—still had some zing to it, it was something that the actresses and director could actively use.

Still, the main question to be answered was very straightforward: was this a seduction scene or a love scene? That is, was Manke seducing Rivkele in order to take her away to Hindl's house and thereby cause her to become a prostitute? Or was Manke simply so in love with Rivkele, so filled with passion for her, that she was looking for any way they could be together?

Joe had chosen the latter, which was by no means the wrong choice. Certainly the text supported the notion that Manke was completely taken with the younger girl (whether for Asch's reason of "innocence" or something else). Asch deliberately uses language in the scene that is culled from Solomon's *Song of Songs*, possibly the most passionate love poem ever written. His purpose is clear: this is not a mere infatuation on Manke's part, not the sort of seduction that Manke attempts twice a week. These two girls have known each other for some time, they are in a sense soulmates, brought together by an unreasoning and inescapable attraction. They will do whatever it takes to be together, no matter the dangers. (Personally I give their union two weeks before it burns out; but maybe I've just eaten too many apples from that same tree.)

No, where Joe went really wrong (in my humble opinion) was in keeping both girls seated on the couch. This is difficult even in a contemporary play, because it's so static; all the energy in the room tends to sag and go limp, and the audience's attention can't help but wander. But in a period melodrama like Asch's play, with such super-charged stakes, it's a disaster. The poetic dance of love and seduction between the two girls becomes merely a make-out scene, as we're transported to sitcom-land, where Manke and Rivkele have just come back from the lesbian prom. ("Golly gee, Manke, how could this be wrong when it feels so right?") Such an approach also ignores the very real life-and-death dangers that lurk all around them. Yankel could come down at any moment ... who knows what he might do in his rage? Who knows what he will do if he finds out from one of the other girls? At the very least, Manke and Rivkele would be separated forever.

The other big problem with Joe's direction was that Rivkele merely came off as a passive object of Manke's manipulations, rather than a willing participant. That is, she had nothing really to *do* except sit there and look mesmerized. Since most of her lines were, "Yes, Manke" (five straight responses) or, "I'm afraid of my father," she tended to disappear from the scene. Yet it was *her fate*, not Manke's, that was being decided. And as Asch himself had written, the attraction in the scene should be equally strong on both sides. Otherwise Rivkele was just a victim, which was not dramatically very interesting.

(To be fair, this is a built-in problem for any actress playing Rivkele. The character is really the second-most important in the play, yet Asch under-wrote the part, not giving her the lines to voice her internal crisis. (Yankel, after all, was written to be played by a big star.) This requires the young actress to bring a lot of ingenuity to the role, in order to find inventive ways to make her dilemma vivid and keep from being simply Yankel's daughter and Manke's girl toy. Otherwise, the audience won't identify with her on an emotional level. And without this, there is no tragedy, there is no play.)

I had my own ideas, of course, on how to fix the scene. But would they work? And, more to the point, would the actors really listen to what I had to say?

I tossed and turned in my little bugspray-smelling cocoon the night before the designated rehearsal. Yes, I was nervous about dealing with the actors in this unfamiliar way. But more, I was nervous about directing in front of Joe. No matter how genial he was in letting me try my hand at his job, it was in the end *his* job. Wasn't I simply making him look bad? I didn't feel happy about it, but I couldn't just let it go either.

I had been staying with good old Ben for something like a week by this point, though time had lost all meaning here. Seriously, I think the fumes had seeped into my brain stem, disabling some rudimentary but useful func-tions like counting. (And tasting. All breakfasts had come to taste like Ben's gym socks.) For the most part, though, I had adapted to my circumstances. Ben and I grunted when we saw each other but otherwise rarely spoke. I had reached a truce with the bench press, which no longer *thokked* me in the nose (but still made the occasional crack). And I had earned my moniker of "The Cockroach Kid," finally mastering how to fall asleep on the floor. Except not tonight.

I uncoiled from my bedding and scuttled into the livingroom, flipping on the TV. (Ben was snoring loudly in a different part of the house.) I searched the late-night offerings of Atlanta's basic cable, only to find the airwaves taken over by John Glenn, whose launch was coming up sometime soon.

Here was the young John Glenn, shooting off into orbit. Here was John Glenn the senator, striking out in his bid for the White House. Here was old John Glenn, getting ready to shoot into orbit again. And here was

Ed Harris playing the young John Glenn, getting ready to shoot into orbit. Enough already!

I flipped around the dial, finally settling for the nastiness of the Jerry Springer show. (More noise! Give me more noise!) This episode of "America's Scummiest" featured a heavy blonde woman with a big ass stuffed into toreador pants and a burly motorcycle dude with a punk hairdo riffing on the ever-popular theme I Cheated on My Partner on the Sly. The cuckolded husband sat on the side rocking slightly back and forth, a lanky man with slicked-back dark hair. Jerry asked him why he kept taking back his cheating spouse. "It's the sex, Jerry. I just have to have it," the man sputtered, spittle gathering at the corners of his mouth. (He promised to treat his wife better, but you just knew he would beat her silly when they got home.) The motorcycle dude then started bragging about his sexual prowess. When Jerry called his bluff, saying he was a big windbag in a leather jacket, the dude whipped out his equipment to show off his dick ring. The crowd (of course) went wild.

Yeah, it was stupid (and more than a little bit depressing), but "this is what the show needs more of," I thought to myself. That kind of energy. Less dicking around and more dick rings.

"Joe directed the scene to make it more like a love story, which I really liked. I mean, I thought it was really wonderful. But I can see that a lot of people aren't happy with it, which is making me very confused. I know that it's supposed to be this really hot, sexy scene, but I also know that it needs to have love too. I just feel so confused."

That's what Jenn, the actress playing Manke, had to say after I'd laid out my master plan for reworking the scene. A "wow, that's really interesting" would have been preferable, much less a "cool, let's give it a try." (A "hey, I never noticed what a really cool guy you are!" would have been nice too, though it had nothing to do with anything.)

But on second thought maybe her reaction was a good thing. Jenn was well-cast for the role, she was small and fetching with a slightly feral quality which she seemed somewhat ashamed of. She preferred to be nice, to do small gestures, to sentimentalize her sexiness and maintain control. Maybe the best thing I could hope for was to make her uncomfortable and confused, even at the risk of her turning against me.

Accordingly, I instructed her to move centerstage, away from the brothel couch, not long after entering. The couch, remember, was a black hole in the scene, sucking up all the dramatic tension. It worked fine at first, after Manke and Rivkele run back inside from the rain, and Manke coos to her, "Come, let's sit on the sofa." The two girls are sharing the physical delight of the rain, the cool delicious physical sensation, throughout Manke's first series of dialogue cues (which are accompanied by stage directions that have Manke playing with Rivkele's wet hair, including "washing her body" in it). But everything changes when Manke starts developing the game of bride and bridegroom. It was at this point that I had her move a distance away and continue the "game" from there.

The point, of course, was to highlight the manipulation that is going on in the scene. Manke may only be a few years older than Rivkele, but she is already a practiced and successful whore. We never see her express any internal conflict and / or bitterness with her lot, as the other girls in the house do. To her it all seems to be one big game (one might even say "child's play"), and she never appears to give a moment's thought to the possible consequences of her actions. So, as genuinely thrilled as she might be by the touch of Rivkele's wet naked skin, she is also very aware of where she wants this to go. She wants to end up in the sack with her virginal friend, spending the night in undisturbed lovemaking. Period. She doesn't seem to care if this takes place in her brothel cubicle or in the house Hindl has told her that she and Shloyme are renting, just so it happens.

So what's the obstacle? Rivkele is already mesmerized, already in love with Manke. She doesn't appear to have any problem with Manke touching her, with physically expressing the love "that dare not speak its name." Then what's the dramatic problem?

The problem is Yankel. Or, more accurately, Rivkele's fear of her father. Manke is never going to get what she desires as long as Rivkele flinches and starts to run away every time she hears a noise. She needs Rivkele to trust her completely, or at least to want her so badly that everything else ceases to matter. Which is why it's so important to have Manke move away from Rivkele at that early juncture—a move that will force Rivkele to overcome her resistance and come to her. In other words, the first part of the scene is all about giving the younger girl a taste of how wonderful it feels to touch each other freely, to share these exquisite sensations (that much more exquisite because they're taboo). Then Manke creates a distance between them, deprives Rivkele of her physical touch, even while spinning a tale of how they could be together like two shy "virgins . . . Two children who are without sin. But we're not children, are we?"

What this power play by Manke also does is set up the difficult transition at the end of the scene, where Rivkele is going to agree to run off with Manke. While Manke may indeed have no other thought in her head besides spending the night with her "beloved," Rivkele is only too aware of the terrible consequences that will accompany her flight. While she may push these away and desperately try not to think about them, she has known her father's wrath all too well to imagine that nothing disastrous will result. In any case, we need to see her make that decision for herself, something that can't really be physicalized unless we see Manke force her hand by moving away.

(It could be persuasively argued that Rivkele *wants* something terrible to happen, that she wants to destroy her impending arranged marriage to a rabbi's son. Certainly Manke's use of wedding imagery to seduce Rivkele makes an ironic comment on that situation, though Rivkele's own feelings are more to be inferred from the subtext of what she does than they are expressed in the text.)

The two actresses rehearsed the new staging with me while the rest of the company took a break. Jenn told me that she thought Manke's machinations were "mean," and her level of discomfort was still very high. On the other hand, Andrea (playing Rivkele) was delighted. "I didn't have anything to do before except sit there and let her paw me," she said. "Now I feel like I can breathe in the scene, like there's finally some room to work with, something for me to *do*."

All in all, it went very well, except for one problem: my own flapping lips. Ever "the writer," I couldn't seem to give a simple piece of direction without providing a paragraph's worth of description. At one point I caught myself talking about Sholem Asch's background, how half his family were yeshiva scholars while the other half were roughnecks and criminals. What the hell was I doing? I'd been an actor myself, I knew that the last things actors wanted to hear was information that had nothing to do with their parts, that they probably couldn't use. And at such a crucial moment too, when reblocking a scene! More proof (as if more was needed) of why playwrights (at least this one) shouldn't direct. The problem is, you spend all your time cooped up in a room or explaining to your family what it is you actually do; so whenever you have a captive audience, of course you start running off at the mouth.

In any case, the two actresses were finally ready to perform the scene for the company. I stood off to the side, house left, with Faye Allen, my eyes squarely on Joe. He sat in the very center of the house, around twelve rows back from the stage, a drafting table in front of him containing sketches from the various designers (like the enigmatic Corky). He watched the scene intently, his head cocked slightly to the left. When Jenn rose from the couch and moved centerstage, I felt as anxious as a proud parent watching his little one take her first steps. "Isn't she beautiful?" I felt like asking everyone. "Don't you think she's really smart?"

"It's better. Better," Joe said pensively, nodding. He flashed a brief smile at me.

He then modified my blocking, moving the actresses more Upstage Left (not so dead-center), so they didn't end up in such a nowhere zone before exiting with Hindl. He also modified the movements themselves, so that they seemed less imposed from without, and would hopefully read to the audience as more fluid, more human, more character-based. But the basic idea itself, of Manke's cross away from the couch and Rivkele's making a dramatic choice—that he kept. And it made me feel pretty great.

Later on we broke for lunch, and Faye came up to me, saying, "Jenn is really upset, she feels like she doesn't understand what she's doing anymore, or why she's doing it."

"Faye, I just have one question for you," I said. "Was the scene sexier?"

Faye thought for a moment, then nodded.

I smiled and walked away, feeling very much like a director.

Chapter Ten

LOL, Part 2

Subj: Hi
Date: 10/17/98
To: HollyG

You really have to let me have my own style. I will try to get gifts or whatever, but just keep your opinions to yourself sometimes. They are not really
asked for.

Anyway, it's not something I want to make an issue about (unless you
insist on it). I have a hell of a lot of things to try to get done here, and it's
difficult to organize one's day as a houseguest. Ben has become a lot easier
to talk to, and we're getting along fine now. But I'm still sleeping on a mat
on the floor, and it isn't comfortable in the least.

I know those feelings of loneliness you talk about. There's not much to
do with them I guess except sleep them off.   S.

Subj: Hi
Date: 10/17/98
From: HollyG
To: StevF

I'm sorry you see it that way. As far as I'm concerned, it's not a question of
"having your own style," it's a question of being a "good citizen," an adult
member of society instead of a self-centered and constantly "rebelling" little
boy. These people are my friends. I do a lot to nurture and maintain my
friendships and you, it seems, feel comfortable taking advantage of that but
not investing even a modicum of effort in the general (and, whether you
think it's middle-class or not, *civilized*) social contracts that are implicit
in smoothly running relationships. If you've noticed, you don't have that
many good friends. I know that's not important to you (so you say), but I

don't see you refusing the help or companionship of *my* good friends whom I've brought into your life. If you want to be a recluse, be a recluse. Don't live with me, don't live with others, and don't engage in the relationships that are lubricated by social proprieties. But it's hypocritical to enjoy the fruits of these relationships, on the back of your girlfriend, and then claim you're maintaining your own "style" and / or being some kind of personal radical.

For one thing, no one sees it as a statement. And as a style, they perceive your style as self-centered and immature (at best) when you enjoy their hospitality or other gestures of friendship and social interaction but don't go out of your way—yes, out of your way, nothing else is appropriate—to show appreciation. And again, they don't complain to you. I'm the one who hears about it. So you can suggest that I "keep my opinions to myself" because they are "not asked for," but I can only feel ashamed in silence, scramble to make excuses for you, or disassociate myself from you (i.e. break up).

I'm sorry that the play isn't going as well as you'd hoped. I've been supportive (up until now) and I still hope that you get what you want out of it. I was going to fly down and see it as a surprise, but it seems you'd rather not see me.

But anyway, I don't really care what you do—do what you want. It's your life. We all do what we want in the long run anyway. And now I'll keep my opinions to myself.   H.

Subj: Hi
Date: 10/18/98
To: HollyG

Thanks so much for your caring, deeply-felt letter.

Please tell me how to be as popular and beloved as you are. I can see now that that's all that matters. I will study to be more like you in everything.

Your greatest admirer

Subj: Hi
Date: 10/18/98
From: HollyG
To: StevF

Fuck you. It has nothing to do with being popular and beloved. It has to do with being sensitive to other people, not just sensitive. It has to do with being considerate. It has to do with being sociable. It has to do with being civilized and civil. It has to do with nurturing relationships instead of alienating them. It has to do with wanting to protect my contacts and friendships as part of your loving and protecting me.

Your sarcasm made me lol. If you think that I think "being popular" is all that matters, then I pity us both. But I know you know better.

Your greatest detractor

Chapter Eleven

Bread 'n Butter, Is That Your Mutter?

THE GREAT STAGE DESIGNER Robert Edmond Jones wrote in his landmark book, *The Dramatic Imagination*, that the designing of stage scenery demands above all the talents of a poet. "I want my imagination to be stimulated by what I see on stage," Edmond Jones wrote. "Everything that is actual must go through a strange metamorphosis, a kind of sea-change, before it can become truth in the theater."

Judging from his set for this production, Corky must have slept through this particular class (or else, more likely, he never showed up). The now-completed set was a two-tiered wooden structure, with the top part given over to the diningroom and parlor of the brothelkeeper's family, while the bottom shows the public room and curtained cubicles of the brothel. On the extreme Stage Left wing was a street level window that Rivkele peers through in Act II to see if Manke is in the brothel. The window was concealed by a complex lattice that had a tangled and spooky appearance, and made the structure look haunted, like something out of Edgar Allen Poe. Others described it less charitably as something left over from a college production of *Tobacco Road.*

"It doesn't even look good enough for a college production. It looks more like high school!" Faye Allen wailed.

To be fair, the set did provide a functional environment in which the play could unfold (and I'm sure we've all seen our share of snazzy sets that tripped up the actors). It also succeeded in physicalizing the essential hypocrisy of the play, where Yankel was able to raise his virginal daughter in wealth and splendor upstairs by exploiting Jewish girls of the same age in the basement. But this was also its problem. It committed what Edmond Jones called "the sin of Literalism," making the point with such thudding, thought-deadening obviousness. Edmond Jones described how a stage setting needs to have a certain "suspense, this indefinable tension." In contrast, this set told the entire story, giving the play nowhere to go. This was an especially big problem for a melodrama like *God of Vengeance*, whose weakest aspect was its creaky plot devices. These had diminished considerably in shock value over the years, already presenting a challenge for any production to maintain dramatic tension.

No, the really shocking thing was to have this be the set for a *Joe Chaikin production*. In *The Presence of the Actor*, Joe had characterized his purpose. "My intention is to make images into theater events, beginning simply with those which have meaning for myself and my collaborators." Richard Gilman, one of the premiere commentators on the modern American theater, had put it this way: "Chaikin's purpose is to free the actor from the tyranny of verisimilitude and make his living energy and presence the center of the theater event in a timeless, mythic present." But there was no way to attain this kind of freedom on such a set, which was in fact a model of "verisimilitude." And how could any "images" be created, when the imagination itself was so hemmed in on all sides?

"Maybe the lighting designer will be able to light it in such a way that she can isolate areas," a visitor to our rehearsal remarked. This visitor was a fellow Atlanta-based set designer who had worked with Joe before, but had been unavailable for our production. She kept trying to put the best face on the situation, which (as is often the case) just made everything seem more depressing. When pressed, even she had to admit that the set was large, cumbersome, hard to light, and quite uninspiring. "The energy is just all over the place," she remarked, cringing.

Joe, however, didn't seem overly concerned. He just looked at the hulking structure and shrugged, as if to say, "The set is what it is. Let's make the best of it, and move on." Taking my cue from this, I resolved to move on as well. God knows I had enough other things to worry about.

Tops on the list was, surprisingly (to me at least), buying a "bread 'n butter" gift for the two people who had put me up, Alison (Amy's sister) and Ben. Right beneath that was finding someone else who would put me up.

Yes, it's true, it had finally happened, the fateful words had been spoken: "I need my space." That's what Ben had said to me when I walked through the door of his house one afternoon after rehearsal, my head stuffed with lists of possible gifts I could buy him. (Barbells? The latest book on how to write a screenplay that looks and reads exactly like everyone else's? Two tickets to *Aida?*) (Sorry, Ben.)

Ben was standing in the kitchen, washing dishes, a pissed-off look on his face. "I want you out of here by tomorrow," he said.

"What? What did I do?" I asked.

I racked my brain, but couldn't come up with any capitol offenses like leaving crumbs around or not washing my dishes. Had I somehow misplaced his soiled gym socks, or otherwise disturbed the sanctity of his laundry?

"I just need you out of here," Ben said grimly.

"But Ben, there's only two more weeks until opening. I'm hardly here most of the time. Can't we work out a system?"

"Sorry," he said. "I need my space."

Yeow. Those words sent a shudder right through me. With Ben glaring at me like an attack dog, it felt as though we were doing a scene from *The Odd Couple* as adapted by *Murder, Inc.* What else was there to do except hand in my Kafka costume and move on to the next psychodrama?

Accordingly, I called Mira Hirsch and Faye Allen to let them know I was homeless and needed a referral ASAP. Then I sucked up my gut and strode into "my room" to deflate my mattress and break the sad news to the bench press.

The next morning, as I tossed the last of my belongings into the already-full trunk, I found myself wondering: why had I argued with Ben at all? Why hadn't I welcomed this change? (Ben, by the way, was already gone when I woke up the next morning, so I was denied a goodbye kiss, something that will certainly haunt me the rest of my days.)

It's true that I had nowhere else to stay for the moment. It's true also that my pointed inquiries on the subject to friends and total strangers had not met with any success before now. But surely some actor or actress or other member of the company would be only too glad to give me succor. I mean, I was a professional "contact," for God's sake. And I knew that people in the company really cared about me. Just two days before, a group of them had presented me with a canvas tote bag, on the promise that I would stop carrying my things around in a plastic bag.

By the time I arrived at rehearsal, I had convinced myself that there was indeed nothing to worry about. I sauntered up to Faye Allen, who was deep in conversation with Joe.

"Don't worry, I've spoken to Del, he's okay now with your staying on our sofa," she said. (He'd had misgivings before.) "You don't have any problem with cats, right?"

Actually I did. Highly highly allergic. (I have a veritable trove of "girl-friends with cats" stories—please notice I said "cats" and not "pussies," because I'm a highly-evolved male and would only make that kind of joke if I knew I could get away with it.)

Faye shrugged and told me, "We'll find something." She then went up onstage and announced my plight to the assembled company. "Anyone with a spare room or couch—and no cats—should go up to Steve during a break and tell him about it."

"I come with my own inflatable mattress," I said. It was meant as a laugh line, but somehow it came out sounding sleazy, like a strange kind of come-on. That's at least how I interpreted the nervous titters that greeted it. There was also a noticeable absence of people approaching me with offers of help before the rehearsal got into full swing.

Today's work focused on three major problems that Joe could turn his attention to, now that the blocking for the "seduction" scene was out of the way.

Two of these were difficult transitions. One came at the close of Act I, when the celebratory parade bringing the Torah scroll from the temple to Yankel's house was followed immediately by a highly-charged erotic kiss between Rivkele and Manke (which happened while Sore was offstage, telling Rivkele how wonderful her marriage to the rabbi's son will be). The second occurred after Yankel found out that his daughter had run off with Manke. The stage directions have him throwing a fit upstairs and wrecking the place; when the lights rise on the next scene (the start of Act III), he is supposed to be surrounded by disorder. But we didn't have that many objects to wreck, certainly not on a nightly basis. How was it best, dramatically-speaking, to show this?

The third (and biggest) problem was the offstage rain in Act II. This is the May rain that Rivkele and Manke and the brothel girls bathe in. The obvious solution was to play the sound-effect recording of rain during the scene, then have the girls come in soaked. But Joe didn't believe in using electronic sound effects. (He didn't believe in characters "freezing in posi-tion" onstage either, saying that such a device was imposed from outside and violated the organic nature of the stage reality.) So at present he simply had the girls going offstage dry and coming back wet. "Audience will understand how they get wet," he contended.

"But Joe," I interjected, unable to contain my impatience, "we have a basically realistic set. Sore brings Yankel real bread to eat, she serves her company real food. You can't then ask the audience to "imagine" the sound of rain."

But Joe shook his head, refusing to use "electronic" effects.

"But we're using electric lights, Joe," I argued. "We're not asking the audience to "imagine" the light … Can't we just hear what it's like with the offstage effect?"

"No," Joe said, absolutely unyielding. (Apparently my brief tenure as a co-director was over.)

The rehearsal broke for ten minutes soon after this exchange, and I parked myself in a conspicuous place in the rear of the theater. A few actors stopped by to say they agreed with me about the rain, while a few others wished me luck in finding new lodgings. But nobody made me an offer. Nobody. Not a dewy-lipped actress, not a hardboiled elder statesman. I saw Scott, Joe's assistant, and waved him over.

"What's going on here?" I asked. "Does everyone in Atlanta have cats?"

Scott hemmed and hawed, but he soon broke down under my grilling. "It's because of something you said last week," he told me.

"What?" I asked, disbelieving.

Apparently I had made a casual (and to my mind, very innocent) remark about how staying with people gave one such an interesting glimpse into their lives, how everything about them could be gleaned from the objects in their homes. (It was the other reason—besides saving money—that I preferred being put up in someone's place to staying in a sterile motel room.)

"Nobody wants you poking around in their stuff," Scott told me.

I tried to make it clear that I don't "poke around" in anyone's stuff. (I mean, everyone checks medicine cabinets, right? And if a list of "Ten Reasons I Hate My Parents" is left out on the kitchen counter, then …)

"I was just talking about it on a "character" level," I said. "About the interesting ways that people reveal themselves in their décor."

"Yeah, exactly," Scott said. "Nobody here wants to be looked at that closely. They're afraid of what you might see."

"You make me sound like some kind of psychological peeping tom," I complained. "So nobody's going to offer me a place to stay?"

Scott nodded.

"Come on, Scott. What about you?" I pleaded.

"Sorry, dude. I would if I could, you know that. But it wouldn't be cool with my girlfriend …" Then he made believe that Joe was signaling him, and he took off.

My serenity shattered, I made a bee-line for the pay phone and called Mira Hirsch at the Jewish Theatre of the South. She told me to call her back in two hours. "I'm not promising anything," she said, "but there's a good chance I might have a place you can stay starting this evening."

"Just tell them I have no interest in finding out anything about them," I said.

"What?" Mira asked.

"Nothing. Thanks a lot. I'll speak to you later," I said, hanging up.

By this time everyone else had gone back into rehearsal for a run-through. Since this was going to be of the stop-and-start variety (the show was still very rough), I opted for pursuing my other priority, buying those thank-you gifts. It was a dirty job, goddamnit, but somebody had to do it, especially after the war of words between Holly and me that had been exchanged on the subject. I would show her who was "uncivil," who was a violator of "the social contract." And I would show Ben too, now that he had his precious "space" back. No *God of Vengeance* for me, oh no! I was a New Age LA type of guy; all that time in La-La land may not have made me rich, but it had gotten me into this wonderfully mellow head with respect to people's foibles. I mean, so what if Ben had kicked me out on the street without any notice? He never had to put me up at all (on the floor or anywhere else), did he? But he had, and I was thankful, and I would buy him a memorable gift. (As long as it was under $20. I mean, otherwise I might as well have stayed in a motel, right?)

I walked outside, browsing the *tchotchke* shops that lined the streets of Little Five Points. At a certain point, I had the unpleasant sensation of being watched. Looking around, I locked eyes with the "Best Humus in the World" guy. He nodded with great animation, motioning me inside. I nodded back, smiling (that "white guy smiling" thing again), then walked down the street, moving swiftly, checking covertly behind me.

I browsed around for what seemed like a very long time (oh my God! How boring it is to shop for people you don't really care about much!), until I finally hit pay-dirt for Alison and her husband. They had struck me as very practical workaday people with an affection for cute pretty things. (Yes, okay, so I took a good look at their stuff. So what? It's like a doctor looking at naked women. It's all just part of the job. But do you think doctors have trouble finding people to put them up?) So, anyway, I bought them a soap-dish. "Boring," you say, right? But this wasn't the kind of soap-dish that Mom would have bought. This was a Balinese-style soap-dish of a gold-speckled green frog nibbling on a white lily pad. Pretty terrific, huh? (Oh, alright, maybe it was ugly as sin, but they really did need a soap-dish, and it only cost $15.)

Ben's gift was proving more difficult to find. I kept stopping in front of novelty items, like a plaque that read, "Being Fat Just Means There's More Of Me To Love!" or a small gold Buddah with the inscription "Buddah was Fat too." Moving away from the "fat" section, I wandered over to a display of children's toys. I had this sudden inspiration (well, it seemed like an inspiration at the time) of buying an easy-to-assemble model of a space shuttle. "Hey, I got your 'space' right here!" I could write on the card. On second thought, no, too hostile. I walked over to a used bookstore, where I found a mint-condition copy of a hardcover collection of Neil Simon's screenplays. "Wow, Ben would really love this," I thought, remembering that framed letter from the Bard of Broadway on his wall. I bought it, knowing in my heart (in that kind of "Zen" way one hears Hollywood people talking about all the time) that I had done the right thing.

I looked down at my watch (actually an Edgar Allen Poe swatch that looked back at me with an extremely malevolent—yet oddly comforting—eye) and saw that more than two hours had passed. I raced over to a pay phone and called Mira Hirsch.

"Good news," she told me. "You have a bed to sleep in tonight."

"Yeah!" I said, pumping my fist as if I'd won the Pulitzer.

I hopped in my Neon and drove toward the address Mira had given me. On the way I pulled into a supermarket, feeling something else tug at my heart: Fuck Zen. No way Ben was getting that screenplay collection. In its place, I would be giving him a super-size package of paper towels. (Remember me always, Ben.)

The new residence I was staying in was only a few miles from Ben's house, but it might as well have been on a different planet. In a different galaxy. Somewhere far far away, where people moved around in a quiet, orderly manner, and where the very notion of some middle-aged divorced scribbler camping out on the floor of an insecticide-laced, gym-sock-smelling exercise room could not even be imagined, much less actually happen. (Not even as a dark fable, a cautionary tale of life's little humiliations.)

The house itself, though larger than Ben's, was not what made the big difference. No, it was the people, the family, inside this comfortable dwelling, this home of observant Jews who kept a kosher household. (Which meant they followed dietary practices touched on in the Books of Leviticus and Deuteronomy, and elaborated upon in the Talmud, about using only certain specified plates and cutlery, eating only certain specified foods that were prepared in certain specified ways. Pork and shellfish, for instance, were big no-nos—which didn't stop Jews of most stripes from consuming many boatloads of the world's lobsters, not to mention a whole lot of bacon. And God help you if you mixed meat and dairy on the same plate, much less in the same dish. You would go straight to hell. If the Jews had a hell. Which we don't.)

In addition to the mother and father, there was a five year old boy and a girl who was almost three. They were all sitting around a table eating dinner when I arrived. The mother and father invited me to sit down and join them, but I begged off, saying I had a dinner engagement. (I didn't.) The father then showed me where I would be staying, a huge basement room with wall-to-wall carpeting, computer equipment, video games, and a fold-out couch that was already made up with blankets and pillows.

The gleaming white sheets beckoned my aching, sleep-deprived body, but I resisted for now. The father repeated his invitation to dinner, but I resisted again, even though the smells wafting my way were very tempting. Soon I was scooting out the front door and zipping away in my Neon, whose revving engine roar seemed momentarily to shatter the soothing cricket-less quiet of the suburban night.

I drove around and around and around, looking for somewhere to eat, finding nothing. I didn't want to go Indian or Thai, as I'd had my fill of that with Joe. Some really good Italian would be nice, but all the places I came across here were either too cheesy-looking or too expensive or both. Oh, for the gastronomical delights of New York's East Village! Where the only dilemma was in deciding which incredibly cheap eatery with incredibly fresh and distinctive food one would partake of that evening! Here it was all a wasteland of franchises, of Applebee's and Chili's and TGI Friday's and Domino's and Little Caesar's and Papa John's and Havaburger and Eataburger and Suckmyburger—aaaaah! (Big big Homer Simpson scream.) Why not just stick some smack in my veins and have done with it? At least I wouldn't be hungry. (On second thought, no thank you. The only needles I like are connected to yarn.)

Finally I couldn't take it anymore and ducked into one of the franchises, ordering a barbecued chicken and beer. Big mistake. As if to spite me, the booths were filled with chattering families and kissing couples. Some kind of easy listening crap was playing on the sound system. Suddenly waiters were singing "Happy Birthday" all around me, all the couples and families were singing along and eating dessert, stuffing their faces with mounds and mounds and mounds of unrefined sugar, the whole place was drowning in ice cream and *shlag*. Aaaaaah! Aaaaaah! Aaaaaah!

Hungry as I was, I bolted, nearly knocking over the clean-cut guy at the door, who still insisted on saying, "Hope you enjoyed it! Please come back again!"

No, what I really wanted was a lap dance. Yeah, that sounded like loads of fun. Problem was, I'd already gone through my lap dance period after leaving my ex-wife. All it did was leave me hornier and broker than before. (And pretty soon all I could see in the women's eyes was the child at home watching too much TV or the dental bill she was trying to pay off. No manner of shifting gears in my head could make that sexy.)

Light-headed with hunger and sick of my own company, I finally ducked into a dark bar and had a beer and something terrible fried. For some reason, I kept thinking about this story that someone had told me long ago about Sam Shepard. It was when Shepard was married to his first wife, O-Lan Jones, while having a thing with Patti Smith. Apparently the two women knew about each other and went along with the arrangement. At a certain point, though, *Sam* couldn't take it, he bugged out and hit the road, disappearing for a week or so. The two women were frantic, distraught, they huddled together, waiting day after day after day for the phone to ring. Finally it did. And what did the women say when Sam called? "Oh Sam, we love you, how are you, please come home, we miss you so much."

What planet did that take place on, and how can I get there? I mean, really. It was as unbelievable to me as a legend, something from King Arthur's roundtable, with Sir Lancelot and Lady Guinevere and some Lady Portnoy. I mean, maybe Thomas Mallory's stories are true, maybe there really were these great Arthurian Romances, but Patti Smith? Oh my God. Patti Smith is a great artist. And I've met O-Lan Jones, playwright and visual artist, she's not too shabby either. And she'd had a young child with Sam already! I mean, here he up and leaves his young wife and baby to go off and knock boots with a hipster poetess, then it all gets too much for him (poor guy!) so he takes off for the open road, where he probably picks up an all-girl band or the Swedish women's volleyball team, has crazy Kerouac sex with them for a week, then calls up the women he left behind, the mother of his child and the world-famous songstress, who do not yell recriminations at him, no, do not call him a bastard or lousy bum, do not tell him to get his fucking act together or don't bother coming back. *"Sam, we love you, we miss you, please come back and fuck us and leave us again!"* It was like science fiction, more incredible to me than an alien landing at Roswell.

(This may be a good time to admit that for years one of my abiding obsessions was to ask Shepard himself about the truth of this story. I thought this was going to happen years ago, when I was drinking buddies with Kevin O'Connor at the Nantucket Stage Company. Kevin was friends with Shepard and told me that Shepard was going to stop by any day. He invited me to tag along. By the time Shepard showed up, though, I was involved in some messy goings-on with my girlfriend at the time, and I didn't see Kevin again until I ran into him on a cobblestone street by a chowder house called Cap'n Tobey's, where he was just coming back from seeing Shepard off on the ferry. This started a remarkable string of near-misses for me, where for years it seemed like every time I walked into La Mama or Phoebe's bar or any number of other places, someone would tell me, "Oh yeah, Sam was just here. You missed him by, like, a minute."

(Cut to many years later, and I'm walking down West 55th Street in Manhattan, and there's Shepard loping up the street towards me, looking like he'd taken a wrong turn in Paris, Texas. Seriously, the man looked as out of place as a wild stallion at the Plaza Hotel, so it was beyond me to break into his reverie and ask him a question about something that probably seemed as long ago and far away to him as an Arthurian legend.)

I guess the closest thing in my experience to "The Shepard's Tale" (as I came to call it) was the affair I'd had with the Jewish poetry teacher (and poet) while living with my Mexican-American actress wife. In my version of the story, though, there were no children (just my wife's many unsuccessful fertility cycles), I worried about and tried to safeguard the fragile emotional states of both women (my reason for not telling my wife), and both women ended up hating me. Otherwise, the two stories were almost identical.

"And where was I now?" I asked myself, downing my second beer (I practically said the words out loud). I was intensely involved with Holly, a beautiful and talented Jewish woman, just a few years younger than I was. At first there was a great enthusiasm, a great meeting of hearts and minds, it seemed like we were soulmates; but now I just wasn't sure. I mean, the nightmarish twists and turns of my (seemingly endless) divorce had certainly taken a toll. But if a little thing like buying "bread 'n butter" gifts could escalate into the attack on Pearl Harbor, if this could cause the big guns to be hauled out, booming out words like "I hate you, let's break up, you asshole," then what did we really have? How could I build on this for the future?

All of which reminded me that Holly was no longer going to come and see the show and be there for emotional support (and, even more importantly, make mad passionate love with me). Instead—as I'd just found out—Mom was flying down from New York City. Perfectionist, politically-prominent Mom—former Deputy Mayor of New York City, and sophisticated connoisseur of sophisticated entertainments—was going to see this production, which was currently in such a state. So *unimpressive*.

I suddenly felt like the guy in the comedy who lets his friend house-sit his apartment, only to come back and find it's been used as a bordello—and his fiancee is coming over in half an hour with his stodgy parents-to-be! (Or something like that.) Oh my God, the place reeks! How will I ever get rid of the strong smell of *failure!*

Chapter Twelve

LOL, Part 3

Subj: Hi
Date: 10/19/98
To: HollyG

As you may remember, a few days ago you were writing me about how "needy" you felt, how much in need of affection. How did you get from that to the Queen of Criticism?

And yes, I do have my faults, and there are certainly people who get offended by what I do, possibly for very good reason. But the last thing I need in my life is somebody who feels obliged to point out every mistake that I make, and who sees me as some kind of representative of her. (And don't start going into your analytic grab-bag and seeing some kind of feeling about my mother. I am actually able to make a distinction between you and my mother. My mother is the one coming to see this production, and you're not. Also, my mother, for all her faults, has finally learned to stop trying to make me conform to her mode of behavior. A lesson you seem to be a long way from learning.)   Love, S.

Subj: Hi
Date: 10/19/98
From: HollyG
To: StevF

Yes, we are separate. Yes, that needs to be maintained and respected, and most people know we are separate and all that. But you're kidding yourself if you think the behavior of one half of a couple doesn't reflect on the other. (I won't even begin to go into what I think the implications are when there are children.) We are, in fact, both ambassadors of each other's lives. You certainly felt that way with your ex, and it was one of the reasons you finally

129

felt you had to get out of that marriage—because she was like a loose cannon in your life, a potential liability with personal and business contacts alike. If she had said, "What I do has no effect on you or your life and has nothing to do with it" you would have begged to differ.

As to your mother—she may have finally stopped trying to "make you conform," it's true. But she has no other choice. She can't stop being your mother and move on. I am not in that position. If we can't find a way to live with each other without embarrassing or shaming each other, then we don't have to live together. We are not yoked by blood as you and your family are. This could be a real "deal breaker" issue. For me, it goes right to the heart of a lot of the reasons I've been conflicted about us and unable to make a commitment.

Bottom line: I don't care to be "Poor Holly who is living with an asshole." That is why I bring this stuff up, and if that's being a Drama Queen, then perhaps the end of the drama should come soon, and the curtain should fall.   Love H.

Chapter Thirteen

The Question of the Rain, or
How Wet Should the Whores Get?

> Though in the eyes of the world, I am of course a disgraced
> and ruined man, still ... I often find myself strangely happy.
> —Oscar Wilde, shortly after his release from jail.

A WEEK BEFORE THE SHOW OPENED, we received a surprise visit at rehearsal (well, it was a surprise to me anyway) from three members of a Boston-based theater group, one of whom was in Joe's directing class at Yale Drama School. They all looked to be in their mid-late twenties, two women named Rebecca and a man whose name now escapes me. (For the sake of simplicity, I will call him "Rebecca" as well.) The three Rebeccas brought with them a nervous, gossipy energy, conspiratorially divulging rumors of power-plays at various large regional theaters, as well as other "secret" goings-on at Yale and the larger theater world (if there is such a thing). This kind of incestuous tattling was typical of theater programs, and of many productions, for that matter. But it had been blissfully absent from this one, and I was not at all happy to see it arrive. I was only hoping it wouldn't distract Joe or the acting company this close to the first performance.

The show was slowly but surely rounding into better shape. Part of this was simply the greater familiarity that came with repeated run-throughs, as the actors started settling into character, making the necessary connections, understanding what role they played in Yankel's downfall, and in the larger world of the play. But Joe had also succeeded in "solving" a number of staging problems, including the two difficult transitions I mentioned before.

In the first of these—end of Act I, when the Torah Scroll parade is followed by Rivkele and Manke's first love scene—Joe had devised a way to use Chip's onstage violinist to ingenious effect. He had the procession lit in silhouette, marching past as far upstage as possible, with Chip trailing the line of worshippers, providing appropriately festive accompaniment, dancing and skipping along. Then the revelers exited Stage Right, while Chip looped around, moving slightly downstage, and the violin music changed to a slower, more brooding rhythm. The lights rose on Rivkele and Sore in the family dining-room, putting the finishing touches on the celebration table while conversing about the daughter's "wonderful" upcoming wedding. Rivkele knocks on the floorboards for Manke to come upstairs to comb her hair, but Sore forbids it, saying, "It's not proper." The music then becomes heavy with erotic tension as Sore leaves the room and Manke enters, kissing Rivkele on the lips while offstage the mother describes the rabbi's son "with his black sidelocks" and the "good honest children" they will bear. (The sense of vertiginous fantasy was increased by Chip's male presence in the room, edging closer to the young girls, his bow skimming swiftly over his instrument as they embraced.)

The second transition was staged in less spectacular fashion, but still (I thought) with admirable simplicity. This is where Yankel finds out that his daughter has fled with Manke. The stage directions call for him to "scramble" up the offstage stairs, "throwing furniture and clothing around," while shaking his wife and crying out, "Your daughter! Where is your daughter?" Joe had Sore carrying a basketful of clean, folded laundry when Yankel came upstairs, crazed. The fearfulness of the moment was played out with the basket of laundry, which Sore clutched in her anxiety, while Yankel wrestled it away, dumping the clothes on the floor. (Why Sore was carrying around laundry in the middle of the night was a good question; but it made a nice metaphor for the orderly middle-class life they were aspiring to.) When the lights came up for the next morning, clothes were strewn around the room. It made the necessary dramatic point and gave the audience a sense of continuity without resorting to melodramatic excess.

But then there was the question of the rain. Ah yes, the rain. It seemed like Joe had tried everything. Sometimes he played it dry, with the brothel girls simply talking about the rain. Then he tried having just a little water splashed on the girls, to get across the "idea" of the rain. Then he doused the girls in water, having them return with hair and clothes plastered down, like kittens who'd fallen into a bathtub (or, perhaps more to the point, like contestants in a wet tee-shirt contest). On the positive side, the ghoulish trimmings on Corky's onstage lattice window had been removed, banishing sarcastic cracks about haunted houses or *Tobacco Road*. But that still didn't provide any clues on how best to convey the offstage downpour. In fact, with this distraction removed, it only put the problem itself into bolder relief.

So it was that, on the day the three Rebeccas showed up at rehearsal, Joe had the actresses run through this scene getting mildly drenched (the forecast in our Poland was looking increasingly grim), and then asked the visitors, "What do you think?"

There were a few moments of awkward silence. Then Joe's directing student from Yale—let's call her "Rebecca One"—spoke up. "I really really liked it," she said.

"Yes?" Joe said, brightening up.

"Except … I really missed not hearing the sound of the rain," Rebecca One added.

"Yes?" Joe said, his expression darkening. "What do you suggest?"

"Well … why don't you get an offstage sound effect?" Rebecca One offered.

"Yes," Joe pondered aloud, as if hearing this for the first time. He called to the stage manager up in the lighting booth, "Can we get something like that?"

"No problem, Joe," the stage manager told him.

Of course, I was sitting there biting a hole in my lip to keep from crying out, *"What the fuck? Just because I'm the playwright* (or adapter) *does it mean I'm also an imbecile? Is it just because she's going to Yale, and I didn't?"* (And, to be truthful, I *was* turned down for their playwriting program.) But really, what was the point of making a stink? Would anyone even listen?

The first sound cue they tried had an abundance of birds singing, it sounded like it had been recorded in the aviary house at the zoo. (Suddenly we were in the Polish rainforest.) But the stage manager was able to edit out most of the birds, and then it all played just fine. It wasn't the kind of adventurous, evocative theater that Joe liked to make. But with a stage set this realistic, it was (I believed) the only option.

I went up afterward to introduce myself to Rebecca One and thank her for her suggestion (and no, I didn't say anything about having suggested it first, though of course it was tempting). Rebecca One blushed slightly—she was a thin, pale girl with frizzy light-brown hair—and told me that she really liked my adaptation. (Joe had given her a copy to read.) She also confessed to not liking Donald Margulies' version.

"Wow," I thought, my opinion of her turning around more quickly than a Hollywood producer with a non-starter who sees a chance of attaching a "major star." I began imagining what our babies would look like ... lots of pale smiles and curly brown hair. They would probably come out wearing glasses, and neither of us had the whitest or straightest teeth, but maybe the children would make enough money being whiz kids to pay for the braces ...

This daydream was rudely interrupted by her disclosure that she had written her own *God of Vengeance*. More specifically, it was a hybrid, interspersing her own adaptation of the Manke-Rivkele love scenes with courtroom scenes from the obscenity trial of the 1923 Broadway production. "It was a big hit at the Boston gay and lesbian festival," she informed me, adding modestly, "though it still needs some work."

So much for the babies. I sighed, seeing the little ones disappear down a large drain, looking up at me with pleading eyes as they swirled around in inescapable eddies. Sorry guys. (Did having a play in a gay festival mean you were gay? I knew myself to be notoriously dim on the subject of sexual orientation, having made a play for several gay women. I remember one party in particular, where there were four men and forty women, and still I couldn't get any action. "Don't you get it?" one woman finally told me. "You're just window dressing here." Ah.)

In the end, Rebecca One and her fellow Rebeccas made several other useful suggestions, including having the brothel girls soak themselves with a wrung washcloth, rather than dousing them with ladled water. (Rebecca One told Joe how much she loved one character's remark in the play that the whores seem "to grow taller" in the rain, and she encouraged Joe to find a way to have this "inform" their performances.) All the Rebeccas agreed that there was a big problem in the Third Act, where Yankel seemed absolutely defeated before the end had come.

"The audience has to believe that Yankel might still be able to put the pieces back together," Rebecca Two said.

"You have to find a way to play against the inevitability of the tragic ending," Rebecca Three offered.

"Right," Rebecca One added, paraphrasing the immortal Yogi Berra, "The play can't be over until it's over."

This was (I believed) an excellent point, which I hoped that Joe and Frank Wittow would take to heart. There was no doubt that the air was already going out of the play at the end of Act II, after Rivkele's departure;

unless a way could be found to re-fill that balloon (with defiance and hope), then the production would not be successful. But just then, even such a central concern was dwarfed by something else that a high-ranking administrator at The Jewish Theatre of the South had brought to my attention.

"There is a tremendous anger among a core group of the Orthodox and Conservative Jewish community here to our involvement in this play, because it is bad for the Jews," the woman told me in a tremulous voice. She expressed fear of a backlash from "prominent business leaders" whose support their theater counted on. She also admitted to being afraid that she and Mira could become sacrificial victims, even to the point of losing their jobs.

And what was the igniting event, the taking-off point for this terrible crisis?

The woman showed me a handwritten letter from "a prominent dentist," denouncing the play as an attack on "Jewish businessmen" ("I'm tired of plays that trash them," he wrote, without specifying what plays these might be), and heaping scorn on the local Jewish Community Center for "any involvement in this project." The dentist also boasted in the letter that he had not read or seen the play, and that he had no intention of doing so. He had been "told" what it was about, and he was outraged.

I kept waiting for the woman to show me other letters, but she didn't. (The dentist hinted darkly that his views were shared by other "prominent supporters.") Instead, she told me about an Orthodox Jewish woman who worked in their office, and who was so opposed to the Jewish Theatre of the South's participation in this production that she cried whenever attempting to speak about it. "And this woman knows the play. She's actually read it," the administrator told me in a hushed voice. Yet she was also quick to add that she herself was "happy" to be involved with *God of Vengeance*. "Even if it costs me my job, I'm glad we've got the spine to go through with it," the administrator declared.

This last bit may have been said for my benefit, to let me know she was on my side. (Her reason, I supposed, for showing me the letter in the first place.) If so, I was grateful to have an ally, and I thanked her for apprising me of the brewing "scandal." But how seriously should I really take this? I mean, could a letter from some crackpot dentist (I pictured him all dressed in black, an evil Mister Tooth Decay) really derail a Joseph Chaikin-directed production at this late stage?

(It seems, by the way, that Asch himself—despite his ringing denouncement of the 1923 Obscenity trial—was not without his own conflicts about his play's portrayal of Jews. At least that's how I interpreted his refusal to allow *God of Vengeance* to be performed between the years 1933-45.)

The administrator painted a dire picture for me of the coming struggle, of pickets in front of the theater, of Rabbis railing in synagogues, of Hadassah women shaking their Hadassah arms at us. All the time she was telling me this, my inner voice was screaming out, "Yes! Please! Bring it on!" Better yet, let's have the local Jewish old age home chain their residents to the theater fence-posts in protest. Anything to stir up a little passion, to break through the ennui of "feel-good" American culture. I mean, why else do a play about a Jewish house of prostitution if not to stir up a little controversy? Why do theater at all if not to shake people up, rock their boats a little, get under their skin?

Seriously, though—while of course I didn't want anyone to lose their jobs—I was so sick of the massive indifference with which most productions (not just mine) were greeted. This was (is) the terrible plague that was (is) laying waste to the art form, not the dearth of talented people or original ideas. Theater, on its most basic level, is supposed to be exciting, give pleasure, take audiences somewhere they could not (or simply would not) get on their own. It is an opportunity to appeal to people's hearts and minds (and yes, their libidos as well), to provide the kind of visceral, present-tense experience that can make use of all other art forms and yet give something that none of the others can—at least in theory. Most of the time, of course, what you ended up with was a bland piece of cheese. The problem for me was that even when you didn't—even when you were able to make something exciting, perhaps even original—it was rarely given its due. Because, at bottom, theater no longer seemed to carry much urgency, or perhaps even "matter."

This is a big subject, of course, which has caused many innocent trees to be killed in the service of mostly-forgettable (not to mention painfully-obvious) notions. Certainly the problems of making theater in a consumerist, middlebrow culture are nothing new. They are the same ones that Joe Chaikin and his fellow experimentalists faced in the 1960s and 1970s, and that Clurman, Strasberg, Meisner, the Adlers, and the rest of the groundbreaking Group Theater faced in the 1930s and 1940s. This is a materialistic, pragmatic, utilitarian society that is hostile to new ideas (and to most old ones as well), except to the degree that they enforce the status quo. Period.

Which is a fancier way of saying that the tendency in a middle-class society is to push everything toward the middle, where it is the least threatening and can do the least harm.

The only times that theater attacking the status quo has really flourished in our mainstream has been in eras of political upheaval like the 1930s and 1960s, when middle-class values were themselves shaken to the core. (Sub-groups—like the gay "identity" theater of the 1990s—have a separate dynamic.) Otherwise, the impulse here is to push away anything—no matter how intellectually, or even personally, disturbing—that can interfere with the business of making a living or getting on with one's life.

(Which, in fact, brings me to my own reasons for wanting to write plays in the first place. Quite simply—and perhaps simple-mindedly too—I wanted to discover and dramatize the stories that could function now as Greek myths had for the Greeks, and as stories from English history and other secondary sources had for Shakespeare and the Elizabethans. What subject matter could cut across the fragmentary, compartmentalized nature of our society and provide those much-vaunted "Universal Truths," causing audiences to experience the pity and awe that Aristotle touted in his *Poetics*? After twenty-five years of searching, all I can really say is "Gee whiz, tried my best, wish I knew." The closest I've seen anyone come is probably Tony Kushner in *Angels in America, Part I: Millenium Approaches*. Yet—as tremendous an achievement as this was—its "universality" may have been largely a product of being in the right place at the right time. It will endure as dramatic literature, not drama, whereas *Death of a Salesman* and *Who's Afraid of Virginia Woolf* will be performed as long as the art form exists.)

In the spectrum of theaters that hew to the middle, the Jewish Theater (or what passes for such) may be the most "middle" of all. It is a "nostalgia" theater mostly, offering up whiffs of yesteryear, the memory of what life used to be as opposed to what it is now. It caters to an increasingly-aging, highly-conservative, mostly family-oriented audience, and the last time I looked its core idea of a hot new play was Jim Sherman's generational comedies *Beau Jest* and (God help us) *Jest A Second*. These have something to do with a woman hiring an actor to be "the perfect Jewish guy" to bring home to family. To say they're thin stuff is beyond understatement. They make Neil Simon look like Strindberg. Hell, they make Paul Simon look like Strindberg. But popular—oy! It takes a week just to sweep up all the sucking candy wrappers on the floor.

As I recall, this was exactly how Jewish Theatre of the South had gotten started—from a well-received production of *Beau Jest*. The star of the show was none other than the lovely and charming Mira Hirsch, who had built on this success by compiling audience names and addresses for future subscription and by raising money from satisfied patrons. Yet, to her credit, she had also branched out considerably since then, producing plays as varied and ambitious as Richard Greenberg's *Night and Her Stars* (about the TV Quiz scandal) and Elmer Rice's courtroom melodrama, *Counselor-at-Law*. It was Mira who had championed the co-production of *God of Vengeance* to her board, and it was Mira who would find a way to deter the rampaging dentist.

Or so I was trying to convince myself, anyway, as I lay on the gleaming white bed in the family's basement at two in the morning. The only sound in the room besides my breathing was the buzz of sleeping computer equipment. I had heard faint noises above me not long ago: the three-year-old daughter whimpering, "Mommy, I want Mommy," then the sound of a door creaking, then feet padding down a hallway, followed by the daughter's cries growing louder. Then I could hear another child whining, the son this time, something about, "I can't help it! She woke me up!" Then there was a jumble of voices and whining, which was finally overwhelmed by a deeper voice, the father's. The jumble then escalated rapidly; it sounded for a few minutes like the little girl and little boy were competing for whose whining could reach a higher pitch. Then, suddenly, it all died down just as swiftly as it had started, and five minutes later all activity had ceased—the whining and the walking and the creaking—and the house was quiet again, only the computer drone piercing the silence.

I felt like I was on the bottom of the sea, like some kind of mollusk, hearing muffled sounds overhead from a world that I wasn't a part of. Earlier that day I'd been rushing to get out of the house, late for rehearsal (as usual), when the young boy had asked me to play with him. He was playing with trucks, loading toys on the back of his dump-truck, then dumping them out. He indicated another dump-truck I could use. Say what? A part of me started getting all W.C. Fields, I could hear the voice in my head sneering, "Get away, kid, you bother me." But another part of me wanted to flop down on the floor and ram our trucks into the wall and do whatever it took to bring a big grin to that boy's face. I mean, I had three younger brothers, for God's sake, who had already made me an uncle six times over (not to mention the other six times I was an uncle through my late aunt's daughters), so all of this should be second-nature for me, right?

Except damn, I was already late to rehearsal. Sorry.

Later that afternoon I was back in the house alone, looking to fix myself a sandwich. I went to open the silverware drawer, only to have it stick partway. I kept trying to jiggle it open, without success, when I noticed that the drawer had an inner safety-lock. After pressing the inside button and extracting the butter knife, I began checking the rest of the kitchen drawers. All of them had safety locks, as did all the floor-level and countertop cabinets. "Child-proofed!" I'd heard this word before without ever attaching any specific meaning to it. My brothers had probably child-proofed, but I'd never noticed (I guess I hadn't rummaged around their kitchens). Even when my ex was pregnant, I hadn't really thought about much beyond the moment of the baby's first cry. So this was what it was like, huh? Like being in jail. Living under lock-and-key. Being a prisoner in one's own home. How could anyone ever live like this? How could I?

That's when it dawned on me: it was too late. I just couldn't do it. Not with Holly, not with Rebecca One, not with anyone. That train had left the station, and I wasn't on it. Simple as that. No matter how sweet or pleasing the fantasy of a baby might be, the reality was something quite different, and I was too far along on my particular path, too set in my ways, to adjust to things like this now. Child-proofing! Ha! You might as well say Advanced Logarithms or Mandarin Chinese.

I mean, how could I even be thinking about being a father right now? Someone's Daddy. Someone who would depend on me for love and hope and support and—money! My God! If things ended with Holly now, if we broke up (as seemed increasingly likely), then I barely had enough in my checking account to cover the security deposit and first months' rent on some dive in Mar Vista or Long Beach (please God, if you're up there, save me from Van Nuys). No, the truth was I had dodged a bullet with my ex-wife; if we'd had that baby I would have been screwed six ways from Sunday (or whatever the cliché is); I would have had a child there for the rest of my life with his or her hand out, and I would *never* have gotten away. Never.

Though I guess maybe, in some ways, that was the point at the time. I was afraid of leaving, of plunging into the unknown, no matter how unhappy I was. So great, have a baby and stay. Start the cycle all over again. (But the cycle of what? What could really be hoped for? Could anything good come out of such misery?) Except we didn't have the baby. And I did leave. Great. So was I happy now?

Well, I was happier than I would have been with her. And I was happier that there wasn't a child somewhere in the world cursing my name under his or her breath, whose final thought before falling asleep wasn't my face with the caption, "I hate Daddy."

Now if something else would just come together, make sense, emerge from the thicket of complications ...

But hadn't it though? Hadn't this production come out of nowhere, just like Goldie Hawn's psychic predicted? And hadn't I gotten the chance to work with one of my childhood idols? So what if things hadn't worked out just as I'd hoped. Ultimately, it was the experience itself that was important. And who knows where it could lead?

Except now the demon dentist and his shadowy cohorts were trying to take even that away, leaving me to skulk back to Santa Monica in shame, without even the satisfaction of a production. ("Bad for the Jews." That's what the dentist had written. Ugh! I was so sick of that kind of immigrant thinking. When were Jews going to realize that passing off self-serving public relations as Art only weakens one's image—not to mention one's spirit—in the eyes of the world, and, ultimately, in one's own eyes as well? Try telling Shakespeare, "If you don't have something nice to say, then don't say anything at all.")

I looked up at the off-white stucco ceiling, shaking my fists, feeling destitute, hopeless, despairing, like some southern-fried version of Dostoevski's *Underground Man*. (So long, Cockroach Kid. Hello gloomy Russians.)

"Yes, y'all, I do believe I can feel my liver desiccatin' in my own body. I do believe I can feel all my organs shrivelin' up in mute protest against the ways of this world. Oh, what's the fuckin' use after all, y'all? Maybe I will just lie here forever in this good family's basement, thinkin' bad thoughts—the impure to their pure, the *treyf* to their *kosher*, a victim of the metaphorical dichotomy in my own goddamn play (okay, my own goddamn adaptation) ..."

But no! Shit! I couldn't lie here forever. Tomorrow (today) was Friday, I had to be out of here by the evening.

And they couldn't cancel the play. Didn't they know that Mom was arriving on Tuesday?

(Big silent 2:00 AM Homer Simpson scream, "Aaaaaaaaaaaaah!")

Chapter Fourteen

LOL, Part 4

Subj: Hi
Date: 10/22/98
From: HollyG
To: StevF

I am not "breaking up with you" by e-mail. I know we have more to talk about and that we love and care about each other enough to continue talking and understanding in person. (And maybe with the help of a couples counselor.) My heart and innards have been heavy with pain, sadness, grief, and most especially fear. Because I don't want to lose you / us, or to lose, in general. But these, for me, are the real and the scary / painful true issues with which we're confronted, whether we like it or not.

When we first got together, I experienced you and us as a good match because, in addition to a strong understanding of each other's pain and pathology, it seemed there was also an easygoing-ness between us. I don't know if you remember, but I was always saying "you're so easy to be with" or "you're so easy-going and laid back" and that was what I needed and wanted and was looking for. My father was a difficult man. (He's better now.) I know the price of living with (and raising children with!) a "difficult" man. It doesn't mean a "bad" man or a "wrong" man. It just means a man (or woman) who is super-sensitive / delicate, someone who must be "managed" and requires a mate to "handle" them with kid gloves. Perhaps we both fit that description, I don't know. (I certainly did before medication! My experience of myself now is that I'm much more upbeat, easy-going, less sensitive in the negative sense of personally defensive or volatile, and more open to appreciating my life and the world around me. You might not agree, I don't know. And you didn't know me before, etc ...)

Anyway, you seemed the opposite of my dad in those days. You weren't controlling or judgmental. That's what I thought. I now realize there were signs I didn't want to see ...

You don't need to (and can't and won't, I'm sure) change. But you do need someone for whom that isn't a problem. It's a problem for me, and I don't know if I can overcome it. I keep thinking, "If we're going to go forward, he'll to have to change," and I guess that's not a good place to be coming from. I'm sure you think I'm being condescending or something, and that *I'm* the one with attitude problems. But my point is that I *do* have difficult and negative tendencies, as do you—but I'm afraid we may reinforce them rather than lifting each other higher. And for me, I came from *such* a dark and negative place, and now I'm happy to be alive, not depressed on a deep or daily level, feeling productive in my work, ready for parenting, and yes, I don't give a shit about traffic jams, etc.—I listen to the music on my radio, look at the ocean and sunshine, use the time to think, whatever. I'm not saying I'm "better." This is just what I need the fabric of my day to be like. Otherwise, I go down into a deep, deep hole, and miss any enjoyment in life …

I'm not saying I'm above complaining about certain things myself. I'm just getting clearer about something I knew when I met you, and which I feel has gotten lost in the time we've been together even though we say things about wanting to help each other keep growing and being open, etc. And this is: I really want to live in a space of creativity, productivity, and passion. I want to live in a space, internally, of gratitude for the ocean outside my door and the peace in my apartment and the fun with friends, etc., and not frustration, bitterness, and whatever the opposite of gratitude is. (A sense of deprivation?) I want to raise a child—a task that is joyful beyond compare, but *filled* with daily annoyances and things to "go wrong," lots of little "emergencies" and so on that can either be handled with grace, calm, self-control and easy-goingness (not a word, I know!) and thereby not become crises; or with anxiety, stress, chaos, and such, causing the crisis to escalate, or seem to—it's a choice. And I want my child to have a chance for a more optimistic life view than you or I had. But they don't learn that from what you say or intend, they learn it from your mood, your approach to people, places, and things, and especially the way you react to the "stresses" of living and caring for them. Now that I've gotten medication as well as lived through a life-threatening disease, learned a new way of being in the world through Alanon, and developed a more solid spiritual center, I just don't feel that way anymore, and I don't want to make that the fabric of my life.

I don't think you want that either. I believe you want a "higher" quality of life, spiritually and emotionally. You've said as much, and in many ways demonstrated it—and that was what made me want to be with you in the first place. I think the man I love in you is a man who embraces serenity, joy, passion, creative living, and positive problem-solving as well as creative work, and so on. But somehow together we've begun to weave a life tapestry that is too often on a lower plane than that. I'm not talking about external circumstances—most of those we don't have a lot of control over (although I maintain our attitudes contribute so much more than we are willing or able to see a lot of the time)—but ... well, I guess you know what I mean. I feel like I'm just spinning my wheels here and repeating myself ...   Love, Holly

Chapter Fifteen

It's Like Tennessee Williams Meets the X-Files, Ya Know?

I WOKE UP IN THE family's basement to a gray morning with one bird singing. It felt, to quote the great Yogi, like Déjà vu all over again. That is, in one waking breath it took me back twenty-five years to the time after my aunt's and young cousin's deaths, when every sleepless morning following every sleepless night looked just like this one. Gray. Colorless. The absence of color. Or perhaps the color that follows a nuclear winter, after the ultimate devastation has happened, when nothing is left alive in its wake. Except, it seemed, for this one bird, who insisted on singing. Why? What was there to sing about? And why always this one single solitary bird? Hadn't he gotten the memo? Hadn't anyone told him to put a lid on it, zip it, there was no longer any reason for song?

But then I took another breath, and I was back in the gray, colorless present. Just a middle-aged guy, hanging on to the most tenuous of lifestyles, still trying to make a go of it in a profession he probably should have given up a long time ago. (In the beginning, I really did want to change the world; now I was just hoping to make back my postage.)

Nothing major or terrible had happened here, no one had died. (Well, of course, people had died, many people; I just didn't know them.) I was simply a guest in the home of a family I barely knew. A guest who had to move on now, find some other place, but who had the resources to pay and wouldn't go homeless.

I stirred myself out of bed, much like the First Man must have done all those millions of years ago, when he too probably looked around bleary-eyed and wondered what the hell was going on. Unlike him, I assumed the heroic posture of Homo Erectus (that's progress, folks!), hobbling to the bathroom naked, hair covering selective portions rather than all of my body. I looked in the mirror at my familiar, bespectacled face—comforted that I was still here. I took off my glasses so I could blur the edges and imagine myself looking more like Mel Gibson. (That's civilization, folks!) Somehow I had a bad hangover without having debauched or otherwise accumulated any nasty but enjoyable memories I could barely remember.

I did manage, however, to put on a sufficiently-public face (not to mention sufficient clothing) to enter the breakfast room and thank the family for all their help. (I didn't say how much I'd learned about what it would be like to have children). The children, as if sensing what was on my mind, took no notice of me at all, behaving as if I was already gone.

The grayness of the day entered my mood and followed me to rehearsal, no matter how much I tried to shake it. I felt like a veritable fountain of negative vibes, spewing out desolation and melancholy from every pore. It was exactly the wrong time for such a mood swing; this was a sensitive point in the rehearsal process, when good cheer—no matter how phony—was sorely needed. (Really, there's never a good time for the playwright to get bitchy; he / she has had plenty of time for that during the months and years of malingering it took to string all those speeches together.) I sequestered myself in a far corner of the theater, sucking on some green health food concoction in the desperate hope it contained some brilliantly vernal ingredient that would brighten my outlook.

And the truth was, yes, the show was getting better. The actors were picking up their cues, laying down the lines, finding some kind of reality they could relate to. The seduction scene had some sexual tension to it, Chip the violinist was stroking up a storm, and Frank as the brothelkeeper was chewing up the scenery, looking and sounding like Orson Welles before he ate Joseph Cotton and the rest of the Mercury Players. Joe—wearing a faded purplish-blue tee-shirt and the black jeans he'd bought at the mall—presided over everything, seemingly unfazed by ill-wishing dentists or anything else.

More likely, though, no one had told him about the dentist. I didn't have that luxury, nor did I have the Ritz-Carlton to go home to, so I sat in my out-of-the-way place, sucking down green stuff and wondering what fleabag motel I'd be resting my head in that evening. Finally I saw Mira Hirsh enter the theater and walk down the House Right aisle, taking a seat next to Joe. I saw her turn and flash him a smile. He smiled back. (He seemed to be having a really great time, at the top of his game.)

As soon as there was a break, I approached Mira. She, in turn, was locked in conversation with Joe. (About the dental menace? I wondered. But nothing in Joe's expression reflected that kind of concern.) I stood off to the side, looking cool and blasé, like I could stand here for a hundred years if I had to without breaking a sweat. Joe kept glancing at me (though Mira rarely did). After awhile he turned and asked if I'd join him and Mira at a local Indian restaurant that evening.

"Gladly," I said.

Joe then moved on to speak with Frank, while Mira turned to face me.

"Look, I don't know what you've heard," Mira told me, barely able to contain her impatience, "but this production will be going on without a hitch. The situation is under control. So you don't need to worry."

Okay then. Just as I was walking off to reserve my own little piece of paradise (Motel 6), Del Hamilton strode by and clapped me on the shoulder.

"Have a place to stay tonight?" he asked. I shook my head. "Go see Faye in the office. Pronto," he added.

I made my way to the office, moving swiftly, as if the opportunity might evaporate before I got there. The small staff was hard at work, sending out flyers. (Oh Andy Suggs! How could you?) Faye was on the telephone; she nodded when I approached, motioning for me to wait. I noticed a magazine on a nearby table, an English-language publication about Yiddish culture called *Pakn Treger*. I was familiar with the magazine, though not with this issue from 1996, which included a section devoted to ... yes, you guessed it, the Donald Margulies version of *God of Vengeance*.

I picked it up, already feeling the white-hot lava bubbling up in my belly. Surely there was some mention of the Jewish Rep's 1992 production, of my adaptation. But a quick perusal of the section made it all too clear that there wasn't. I did, however, run across this paragraph, from the oh-so-glib director of the Margulies version:

> Running the whorehouse is an act of assimilation, and Yankel regrets that, or realizes that it has been at the expense of his Jewish roots ... [This] Yankel, trapped between two worlds, wonders whether he is a Jew or "other."

"Act of assimilation"! "Trapped between two worlds"! Puh-leeeze! What the hell did that have to do with *God of Vengeance?* I thought, erupting into a full-blown playwright snit-fit. I mean, Asch's brothel was located in the Polish-Jewish ghetto, *where it was frequented only by Jews.* Yankel was alienated from his fellow Jews by virtue (so to speak) of his profession, not because he catered to gentiles. Yes, Margulies may have had a superficially clever idea in transposing the action to New York's Lower East Side in 1922. This enabled him to explore *his* issue of choice, assimilation; but it had nothing to do with Asch's play, or with anything that interested Asch. It wasn't an adaptation, it was a *rewriting*, and he had no business using Asch's original title. (Say it was "inspired by *God of Vengeance*" or whatever, but please call it something else.)

"So," Faye said, putting down the phone. "Does the name 'Hartsfield Manor' mean anything to you?"

"What?" I thought, "What?" Trying to snap out of my Lear-like rage, huffing at the theater gods from my own private heath, I could barely manage to shake my head no.

"Well," she said, smiling, "get ready for a nice surprise."

"Surprise? What? What is she talking about?" I thought, still caught up in the massive injustice of a world in which I was not the king.

A short time later, however, I was up to my eyeballs in lace doilies and spotted beige wallpaper, in faded off-white divans and sepia postcards of old Atlanta. The Hartsfield Manor is a solid stone structure that reminded me of something that Sherlock Holmes might come across on the Scottish moors, except here it was in Little Five Points, a few blocks down from 7 Stages, on a lazy side street surrounded by white-blossomed catalpa trees. I was here because the theater had already paid a night's lodging for some silly bloke who hadn't shown up; so I—lucky fellow—was reaping the benefit.

Walking inside, the parlor was cool and dark in a way that let you know it would be like this on even the hottest and brightest day. I had a brief meeting with Sandra Hartsfield, herself a cool blonde beauty, who had converted the house to a bed-and-breakfast with her husband some years before. She told me that the place was a favorite of visiting blues musicians (I could readily see why, given the funky decor). Then she handed me the key to the room and went on her way.

The room was on the second floor, down a narrow hallway. It was like an old New Orleans roominghouse, like something out of *Streetcar Named Desire*, all dark wooden railings and worn carpets and frilly things tacked to the walls. Then I turned the heavy metal key in the heavy metal lock and opened the door and—stepped into what looked like the set for a Tennessee Williams play, an impossible room crowded with mirrors and memorabilia, with silhouettes of semi-nude women and velvet chapeaus nailed to the walls. The room was so overwhelmingly *feminine*, so filled with frilly and lacy things (not to mention the semi-nude women), that I got a hard-on just walking in.

But hey, there wasn't really time to think about that (he lied). Besides, there would always be time to dwell on this later. (I was not really a bath type of guy, but in a room like this, with its own elaborately-wallpapered bathroom, that could easily change.) I was meeting Joe and Mira for dinner in less than an hour, and this was a room in which an hour could pass really slowly and really fast.

Dinners with Joe—three or four times a week—had become an unexpected benefit of the gig. My experience with celebrity directors is that they usually wanted to maintain very clear boundaries of where your authority ended and theirs began. With Joe there was none of that, something that was probably largely unchanged from his pre-aphasia days. He was a democratic, supremely non-authoritarian spirit, who loved the companionship of making theater and had no use for petty power plays. The big difference now, after the stroke, was that Joe's conversation was limited. I gathered from friends (and my own acquaintanceship confirmed) that Joe had loved nothing more than to mull over moments from that day's rehearsal, to examine them from every angle. Now that was pared back to a few well-chosen words, but he was still a fun guy to bat things around with over chicken biryani.

One peculiarity, though—which never ceased to catch me off-guard—was Joe's tendency, every now and then, to blurt out embarrassing information about well-known people in the theater. The main subject of these remarks was his long-time friend and co-writer, Sam Shepard. I've already mentioned my own interest in Shepard, compounded equally of respect and envy. At a certain point in my life, I might have lapped up these unbidden morsels; now they just made me uncomfortable. (I'm sure you don't expect me to pass them on, reader.) And it wasn't just Sam the Man either. One time, apropos of nothing, he had remarked, "Herbert Berghof and Uta Hagen had a house in the country. When they were there, she liked to suck on his penis." (Whatever you say, Joe.)

On this particular evening, the conversation turned for some reason to my own family background. I told Joe and Mira about being the oldest of four boys in an upwardly-mobile Jewish family, and some of the problems entailed as the only son with artistic yearnings. "It would have been *so* much easier to be the baby," I said. "The oldest has to deal with so much stuff about being responsible, setting an example, and making good. By the time they get to the youngest, I think everyone's a lot less uptight."

Joe—the baby of five children, and still very much fussed over by his sisters—said, "I just hope you have a good therapist." Mira seconded this.

This wasn't something I really felt like discussing (okay, I admit that Joe's habit of divulging the occasional secret may have contributed). I turned to Mira, asking about her plan for thwarting the dentist. Now it was her turn to squirm. She stammered a bit, reassuring Joe that there was nothing to worry about. "I'm simply having a prominent member of the Jewish community come to see a run-through on Sunday." (Oy. Now we had dueling "prominent members of the Jewish community.") Mira turned to Joe, "That's okay with you, isn't it? I promise he won't get in the way."

"Sure. Why not?" Joe said.

"I'm absolutely sure there's not going to be any problem," she said again.

But by this time Joe was already standing up and moving over to a nearby table where two men were eating, one of them in a wheelchair. Halfway there, Joe turned and motioned for me to follow.

By the time I reached the table, Joe had already launched into a halting description of *God of Vengeance*, as a prelude to inviting the men to our first public performance (technically a dress rehearsal) on Wednesday. "And this is the playwright," he said, nodding in my direction. I could tell from the men's glances that I looked a little young and untroubled to have written something with the Old Testament grimness with which Joe had invested the play in his summary.

(Quite honestly, I'm not sure how to make Asch's play sound more light-hearted. "Well, it's this frolic about a small business owner who raises his daughter as a pure virgin, while conducting his business downstairs … oh, I did mention that he's in the *brothel* business, right? Oh, and there's some folderol about God and fate and the Torah, but you can fall asleep for those parts. Basically it's a big screamfest! And there's girl-on-girl sex too! Whoopee!")

Joe's invitation had been addressed almost exclusively to the man in the wheelchair, a burly man of around forty with thick lips, a beefy complexion, and a full head of slicked-back black hair. It was painfully apparent that the man knew why he'd been singled out for this special treatment. I'm sure that in Joe's mind, this reaching out was being done in solidarity, in brotherhood, to a fellow handicapee. But to the man, it was an insult, a mark of condescension and pity. I tried to squeeze something in about what a famous guy Joe was, what a great director, etc. The man in the wheelchair just looked up with fish eyes, he muttered some excuse about being out of town all next week. Then he went back to eating his curry while we were still standing there.

Joe seemed unprepared for this response, and he might have continued standing there until the man had paid his check and wheeled off into the night if I hadn't grabbed his arm and steered him back to our table.

"What was that all about?" Mira asked.

"Just trying to spread the gospel of *God of Vengeance*," I said.

"He said he was busy," Joe mumbled.

Mira nodded. I could tell she understood right away what the purpose of Joe's mission had been, and how the man had responded. "There's nothing to worry about, Joe," she said. "We'll have a good audience. We have a good show."

Joe nodded, smiling slightly.

We finished our meal in short order and were heading out the door when Joe suddenly disappeared from our side. Mira and I looked at each other and shook our heads, then both of us stopped and looked around. Joe was again at the table of the man in the wheelchair, speaking with great animation. I walked over there swiftly, just in time to see the disabled man's face turn various shades of mottled scarlet and purple.

"... And anytime you want to see the show, just mention my name, and they'll give you free tickets," Joe said, taking a flyer out of his pocket and putting it on the table.

("Oh yeah, that *flyer* will do the trick," I thought to myself.)

"You can come to any performance, it doesn't have to be Wednesday," Joe added.

I thought the wheelchair-bound man was going to haul off and smack Joe into someone's vindaloo. Instead he turned to me and pleaded, "Why can't he understand that I'm not going to be here for the next month? I can't come to the show."

I apologized to him, grabbing Joe's arm. "Have a good evening," I said.

The washtub in my bathroom at Hartsfield Manor was a huge four-legged porcelain thing, of a size and girth I'd rarely come across outside of Henry Miller novels. (The shower-nozzle attachment also seemed vaguely European-decadent to me, which only strengthened the connection to Miller.) It was a perfect fit for two people, and while I was at the restaurant my spicy Indian food had been accompanied by even spicier fantasies. These started

151

out with my flowing-haired girlfriend, who really would have been my bathmate of choice. But then I recalled some of the things she'd written in her e-mails, and how she could have come down here but had chosen not to, and how we were very likely going to part ways when I got back to the west coast … and she was swiftly replaced by Salma Hayek. After Salma and I had splashed around for a while, her place was taken by the raven-haired girl who worked in the Olive Café and was always smiling and waving at me. My thoughts had then entertained a swift succession of other women (too numerous to mention) before I finally left the land of vindaloo and made my way back to my hothouse lair and the tub in question.

Much to my surprise, there was a bath partner laying in wait for me when I opened the door. It wasn't exactly what I had in mind, though. No, this was a big brown waterbug, one of the largest I'd ever seen—the size of a small rodent, I swear—who was valiantly trying but failing to scale the high porcelain walls. I immediately took it as a reference to my recent Kafkaesque sojourn on Ben's workout room floor, and I sort of chuckled as I turned on the faucet full-blast and watched the struggling bug get washed back where it came from. I then filled the bath up with steaming-hot water and eased myself in.

Aaaaaaah. I closed my eyes, letting all worries about the show and the dentist and where I was going to sleep tomorrow night and even my future with Holly just follow that bug down the drain. Then I opened my eyes again, glancing around the ornate john.

My God! It really was like being *in* the play, *Streetcar Named Desire*. (Either that or a New Orleans cathouse.) I half-expected Blanche Dubois to walk through the door. (Okay, yes, she *was* one of the women I had imagined playing water sports with.) On the far wall hung a small mirrored shelf with ceramic white and pink slippers frozen in mid-dance step. There was also a woman's disembodied ceramic hand holding a ceramic rose. Though I could imagine much better use that the hand could be put to.

This is probably as good a time as any to repeat how it had been *weeks* since I'd had sex. I suppose, given the subject matter of Asch's play, it would have made sense if I'd been Whoring It Up In Atlanta—which would have made a helluva title for this book, by the way, much better than *Best Revenge*—but my limited experience with ladies of the night had left me less than enthusiastic for actual whoring (Henry Miller notwithstanding).

No, I was currently making do on a diet of pathetic double-entendre scenes like the following:

PLAYWRIGHT enters, sees DARK-HAIRED WOMAN TECHIE WHOSE NAME HE CAN'T REMEMBER eating a large chocolate muffin.

PLAYWRIGHT approaches, chuckling in a "knowing" way.

DARK-HAIRED WOMAN TECHIE: What are you laughing at?

PLAYWRIGHT: (more chuckling) You have a very large muffin.

DARK-HAIRED WOMAN TECHIE: Fresh. Do you want a bite?

PLAYWRIGHT: (takes an exaggeratedly long, sensual bite of the woman's muffin) Mmmmm. That's very buttery.

DARK-HAIRED WOMAN TECHIE: I'm glad you like it. Maybe you should go buy your own.

PLAYWRIGHT: Mmmm. Maybe I'll do that.

PLAYWRIGHT watches the DARK-HAIRED WOMAN TECHIE walk away, swishing her lovely behind in a way that turns the chocolate taste in his mouth to ashes, but is sure to earn her a place in the playwright's bath fantasies.   THE END.

And so the curtain once again comes down without the playwright getting laid. Which begs the question: what-the-hell use is Realism anyway?

But wait a minute—we were in Blanche DuBois country now, right? As the lady herself said, "I don't want realism. I want magic! Yes, yes, magic! I don't tell the truth, I tell what *ought* to be truth." Yeah. So let's wave our wand (so to speak) and put some magic in that realism, have the Dark-Haired Woman Techie stay, have the Playwright eat that muffin down to the last crumb, have them BOTH race down the center aisle of the theater, leap on to the stage—and end up here in Dame Blanche's bathtub, sloshing up the floors, steaming up the gilt-edged mirrors, the smell of buttery chocolate filling the room ...)

I emerged from the bathroom, the spirit of Blanche still singing in my ears. I suddenly remembered this Tennessee Williams anecdote that someone had told me years ago. It seems that Tennessee and Truman Capote were hanging out in some local Key West dive. A man in a flowered shirt approached Tennessee, handed him a felt pen, whipped out his dick, and asked for an autograph. Tennessee looked down at the size of his writing surface and asked, "How about if I just put my initials?"

Hmmm. Looking around the room, I saw several framed prints of porcelain-white, semi-nude women in provocative poses. There was a *Saturday Evening Post* lady named "Gladys," powder-fresh, in a black broad-brimmed hat with an orange flower; there was "Marguerrite," who might have been modeled on the character who seduced Faust, or might just have been a pouty-lipped vixen of the same name with designs on all members of the male sex; and there was an unnamed lady with a come-hither look, wearing a clingy transparent garment, and reclining alone on a mound of soft white pillows ...

Oh my God. Now I understood why nobody ever seemed to sleep in Tennessee Williams plays. There was just way too much *stimulus*, way too much going on. Hey, it was 24/7 Mardi Gras in the dark places of Tennessee's soul! But it was only 8:58 PM here. How the hell was I ever going to get through the night?

(Yeah, I know: if I'd been a wild-eyed, libido-driven character from one of his plays, I would have been on the phone an hour ago to an escort agency, ordering up a few southern belles to play out my *Streetcar* riffs, to put the Tennessee in my Williams. Or else I would have seduced all of Atlanta by now, raising the temperature of the women-folk—and yes, some menfolk as well—to the point of igniting another burning of the city. But wow, that was just way too exhausting. At forty-five, I was lucky if I could raise my own body temp. And I'd already tried many times to sing along with the siren song of my own dick, and it was a song that just never ended, a rhythm I grew tired of dancing to.)

I neglected to mention it before, but there was also a more "high-tech" component of the room, consisting of a mini-fridge, a microwave, and an old but fairly large color TV. Aesthetically, this trio offended me (which is why they had gone unmentioned). They were really a violation of sorts, sending all these harsh Stanley Kowalski vibes into the lace-and-frills Blanche DuBois aura. But now I found myself surrounded by the Eternal Feminine (or *Ewige Weiblichkeit,* in the words of horny old Goethe), with no flesh-and-blood woman to hold onto. So I flicked on the tube, as a Kowalski-like revenge against beauty.

And there it was, like magic—"The X-Files"! That hymn to paranoia, that pet obsession of the conspiracy-obsessed everywhere. And what was "conspiracy" anyway (when you got right down to it) except the new Religion, the source of Truth in an age of Spin and Cover-ups, the means of finding Order and Purpose in a world that increasingly seemed to have neither?

So here were Mulder and Scully once again chasing down the unexplainable mysteries of this world and many others. To be honest, I don't remember that particular week's intrigue, though I'm sure it was one of those episodes in which Mulder—that Hamlet of the post-Roswell, post-Watergate universe—went in search of the truth about his own murky family history. And the deeper Mulder dug, the more his discoveries seemed to merge with the spirits in this room. So he would open a door, and there would be Gladys lying naked in bed, the sheets twisted around her powder-fresh limbs, the broad-brimmed hat with the orange flower lying beside her. (Didn't she know that a hat on a bed was bad luck?) And then he would open another door, and there was Marguerrite in the bath, lathering up her vixenish torso, her ruby-red lips whispering offers of pleasures—of exotic sexual practices and erotic delights—that Scully could never (would never) bring him. And finally, behind door number three, was the still-nameless mystery woman by an open window, smoking a cigarette in the dark, moonlight caressing every inch of her body through the transparent gown. "Young man," she whispered. "Young man. Come over here ..."

And after Mulder had slammed every door and run through every corridor, after he had followed every clue to its logical and illogical conclusion, he ended up in a barren, windowless room, surrounded by hulking men, each with his hand out. And who were these men? Aliens? Androids? Unkillable replicants? No. They were all-too-earthly creditors, and they had to be paid.

Mulder fell to his knees and cried out for mercy. "Why did You make me a playwright?" he wailed to his Creator. "What were You trying to get at? What was Your point?"

"Hey, Spooky, nobody ever told you to be a writer," some wise-ass creditor shot back. "It's a crapshoot, and you got crapped on. So what?"

"But I can't even remember why I wanted to do this in the first place!" Mulder anguished (as if any of the guys with their hands out could have cared less).

Yet even as he said this, Mulder knew that it wasn't quite true. He could feel the memories seeping back into his brain, could see momentary flashes of scenes: him racing toward a craggy tree in the middle of a blinding rainstorm, feeling one with the storm and the poem he was writing about it; reading *Brothers Karamazov* in one sitting, forty-eight hours straight, the words striking him with the force of revelation, until he thought that his heart would leap out of his body; his making love with a girlfriend on the beach one moonlit night, moving in harmony with the planets, knowing that nothing in the world really mattered, nothing would last, except that this mattered somehow, this and his writing …

Mulder realized that these were old memories, laughably outdated. The world had moved on, spinning its wheels over and over and over, until it had nearly wiped out all traces of footprints, of any tracks leading back to or away from these (personally) primal events. It was a different decade, soon it would be a different century, a different millenium. Wasn't it time to give up these ghosts and move on too?

But move on to what?

Mulder posed this question to himself, and suddenly he knew the answer, knew what he had to do. He rose to his feet, drew himself up, stretched out his arms away from his body, and offered himself up to his creditors. The hulking men descended like vultures, tearing off handfuls of clothing, tearing, ripping, until all the clothes were torn away, and he was naked, stripped bare. But the hulking men still weren't satisfied, they were in a frenzy now, a feeding frenzy, and they had to be fed. They started tearing his flesh, ripping the very skin from his bones, until soon this was gone too, until there was nothing left, nothing, except a mass of blood and protoplasm staining the floor.

Then, and only then, were their appetites sated, and they shuffled out of the room, looking down at their shoes, their hands and mouths stained a bright red.

As soon as they were gone, Dame Blanche emerged from behind a closed door, she put her lips together and blew. Then Gladys and Margueritte and the Mystery Woman opened their doors and walked in, looking at the mass without form that had once been Mulder. On a cue from Dame Blanche, these Three Graces, Three Sirens, Three Witches gathered up the pieces and dumped them into the large bathtub. Then they gathered up Mulder's primal memories (which lay formless and scattered about) and dumped them in too. At a sign from Dame Blanche, this girl group from the great beyond began moving, these metaphysical Supremes began bobbing and weaving around the huge tub, chanting their pop incantation:

> "Nose of Malden, Hunter's tooth,
>   We don't want the true,
> We want what ought to be truth.
>
> Brando's pubics, Viv Leigh's too,
>   We don't want the truth,
> We want what ought to be true."

And before you could say "Stella!!!!", there was Mulder again, good as new. No, better than new, much better, his skin was gleaming like a newborn child's, and his manhood was flowering, in full bloom.

"Young man. Oh, young man," Dame Blanche whispered.

"Scully? Is that you?" Mulder asked, looking around.

The women all tittered, their laughter hanging in the air for a long pause, then silence. Then they descended to their Orpheus, long limbs flowing, merging with the revised playwright where he lay soaking in his unconscious.

"Sometimes there is God so quickly," Mulder gasped, before going under.

And Blackout.

Chapter Sixteen

LOL, Part 5

Subj: Hi
Date: 10/24/98
To: HollyG

Personally, I think the connections between us are deeper than you think, that your ties to me and mine to you are stronger than you're aware of. I know that's why I stay with you, why I keep hoping for better things to come. I know how devastated I would be without you, how much I love you at the bottom of everything and despite all the differences between us. If I felt you were talking to me from that place, then I could respond more calmly and collectedly to it. But I don't feel your love at those times, only your anger and resentment. And I feel like the good things get lost in the process.   S.

Chapter Seventeen

Up in the Air with Mom and John Glenn

THE LEADING THEATER CRITIC of Atlanta, Dan Hulbert, had touted our production in the *Atlanta Journal-Constitution* as a "blue-chip prospect," and it was beginning to look like he might actually be right. (Of course, he'd also done cartwheels over Elton John's *Aida*, burbling like a little girl on her first visit to Disneyland, so what did he know?) The *Sturm and Drang* of this brothelkeeper's battle with God was starting to gather some heat, perhaps even to cook. It still seemed a little soft to me in places, wearing its heart a little too openly on its grease-stained sleeve, but maybe this was just what it took to put the play across to the good Jews of Atlanta, including the disapproving dentist.

And, oh yes, speaking of him—on the last Sunday before opening night, we received a visit at rehearsal from a local "heavy Jew," a solemn man in a well-tailored suit who was not only a high-ranking official of some sort but also a Holocaust survivor. After viewing part of a run-through, he gave the show his thumbs-up. (And what if he hadn't? Could this one man Hayes Commission have boiled our chicken?) We got three-and-a-half out of a possible four Yarmulkes. So it was lights out for the other side. They could grumble into their kasha as much as they liked, but take on a Survivor—no, I don't think so. They might be piously outraged, but they weren't nuts.

I was, to tell the truth, a bit disappointed. The specter of a swarm of *alte kochers* screeching out Yiddish epithets, insulting each other ("Who you callin' a *meshuggeneh* Litvak?") and jostling for better position on the picket line—well, it did my heart good. Also, my Mom was due to arrive Tuesday evening, and I would have liked nothing better than to give her a good protest. (Like a little flashback to the Eugene McCarthy antiwar days.) I found myself lying awake Saturday night, murmuring lines like, "Watch out Mom, those wheelchairs are headed right for you!" Or "Duck, Mom!" as a stuffed derma sailed right past her head. But now there would be no duck and no derma. Just a production that may or may not hit the mark.

Not that I was holding my breath or anything about Mom's opinion. I mean, we had a history—an often-rocky one, as might be expected. (Politically-ambitious mom + perenially-"aspiring" black sheep eldest son = well, you do the math.) But I was a professional writer, not a kid. If she liked the show, fine. If not, that was her business.

I had to admit, though, that I had not felt so sanguine the first time my adaptation had been produced. The Jewish Rep's production had taken place during the height of Mom's political power, when she was a Deputy Mayor of New York City under David Dinkins. I was happy for Mom's success, which came after many years of working for the election of Liberal Democrats of conscience and integrity who always finished out of the money. (Much like her political "first love," Adlai Stevenson.) Mayor Dinkins seemed like a good guy, even if he could never remember my name. (I was just one of countless people whom he addressed by the all-encompassing title of "Buddy.") I cheered loudly for New York's first black mayor (and for Mom) on election night, mingling with the crowds at his headquarters, where people chanted, "It's about time!"

Friends of mine were convinced that Mom's rise on the world's stage would have a coattail effect of sorts for my scripts, causing them magically to rise to the top of slush piles everywhere. I wasn't so sure. I had grown up knowing many family friends who were powerful and influential people in the New York theater scene. Their general reaction to my pursuit of the bright-lights was to keep me at arm's length—humor me wherever possible, but don't get in bed with me (so to speak). Of course, it may be as simple as no one thinking I had any talent. But what I observed more than that were people who feared social embarrassment, either by (a) having a public flop with my work; or (b) having their private behavior reported. (Either way, it meant having their autonomy compromised.) I couldn't see how this would be any different now.

And, to be honest, it wasn't. Having a Mom in high places did enable me to hobnob with the occasional star or cadge a meal at Gracie Mansion with Mary Tyler Moore and Gregory Hines (enjoyable, but not what I was after). It did make it possible to strike up a conversation with theater legend Joe Papp, which led to our meeting every few weeks for a talk in his office—until Joe succumbed to cancer a short time later. ("Nobody understands that I've got this thing licked!" he told me, thumping the table, in our final encounter.) But it didn't get my scripts produced. Nor should it have. I'm a firm believer in the work speaking for itself. The problem was, there were all the old familiar reasons for people *not* to do my work, only now the stakes were much higher, the risks of being accused of currying political favor or worse that much greater.

Which is why the Jewish Rep gig was so important for me. Here was a chance to grab a little spotlight and show something of what I could do, independent of any "connections." It all would have been a much bigger deal, of course, if F. Murray had stayed with the show. Even so, there was a fair amount of pre-show publicity, including the lead Theater article in the "Arts & Leisure" section of the Sunday *New York Times*.

Now it's true that the impact of such things tends to be way overstated, and that 99% of the people who actually *read* the article—which is a very small percentage of the *Times* readership, not to mention of the larger world—had completely forgotten about it by the time they ordered-in Chinese that night or put little Billy to bed or whatever. Nevertheless, in my parents' world having an article about something you've done in the Sunday *Times* ranks right up there with being mentioned by name in the Old Testament. ("And Esther begat Stanley Silverman, who begat the firm of Silverman, Saltzman, Steinberg, and Klein. And God looked down from heaven, and He said that they were good. Very good.") So I had what I think was a reasonable expectation that Mom would be proud, in the way that Jewish mothers are justly famous for. Except, in this case, not.

Now it's only fair to say that Mom was never big on the playwriting thing—mostly for very good, if obvious, reasons. She was more diplomatic than Dad, careful not to make statements (like "You're going to be a bum!") that could be quoted or thrown back at her later; nevertheless, the subtext was clear. She kept waiting for me to grow out of it. When several years' worth of rejection slips didn't bring this about, she cut off all supplementary funds (things like "birthday money," whatever) in the hope of hastening the demise.

Of course, any student of Behavior 101 could have predicted what effect her actions were going to have. And it may in fact have been true that if she'd been lovingly supportive of my career choice, I might have had second thoughts. (All you parents out there, take note.) As it was, I had dug my heels in more firmly than ever. And now I finally had something to show for it that would translate into the circles she moved in: an "Arts & Leisure" piece. (Of course, I had written for "Arts & Leisure" before, but—sadly—hardly anyone notices an arts byline; anyway, nothing beats being *written about*.)

I thought this little "accomplishment" would carry enough weight to tip the scales of her judgment, at least momentarily. But when I stepped into the back of her large black chauffeur-driven Town car on the afternoon before the show's first preview, I could see right away I was very mistaken.

Truth to tell, Mom in a chauffeur-driven vehicle was not something I ever felt that comfortable with, any more than Mom on the Evening News filled me with joy. It wasn't that I begrudged her the trappings of power, it was just that I'd had enough trouble dealing with the Mom I grew up with. This new Mom was some weird hybrid of Eleanor Roosevelt and a Mafia don. She always had invitations to twelve different events on any particular evening, usually things like raising money for Kurdish children and a sickle-cell anemia square dance. But she sat in the black car's backseat like Carmine Galante on the way to a hit. She would motion with her head for me to get in more quickly, as if she couldn't stand even a moment's delay from getting on with her whacking. But on this particular occasion, Mom seemed even more harried and annoyed than usual.

"Tell me again when your show opens," she said.

"In a week," I told her.

"I don't see how I can possibly be there," she said. "There's a big breast-cancer fundraiser at the New York State Theater that night. Dave was supposed to host it, but he had to back out, so now they want me. There's also a big auction at Christie's to benefit Filipino flood victims, and they want me to wield the gavel. And there's a 10:00 PM run through Central Park to kick off Literacy Awareness week at the New York Public Library, and they want me to shoot the starter's pistol."

(Note: Just to be clear, these are made-up examples, standing in for real events. Happy now, Mom?)

"Okay, Mom, that's fine, you don't have to be there," I said.

"It's also opening night at Lincoln Center, Manhattan Theatre Club, and Playwrights Horizons, and they all want me to host their after-play parties."

"Yeah, Mom, fine, whatever," I said.

(Oh, did I mention that Mom was the official liason from the Mayor's office to the Arts community for the whole goddamn city? You might think that having a son who was a produced playwright would fit right into that "community" thing, but naa. It only seemed to make things more awkward, like I was a "spy" for the "other side.")

"Also, your Dad is very busy these days. He has a big deal which is about to come through at any moment, and he can't be away from the phone."

(Did I mention that Dad had sold his business and become a Venture Capitalist? Now his office hours went from 4:00 AM until ... well, 4:00 AM. He hadn't been away from the phone in three years.)

"So, Mom, how did you like the piece in the *Times*?" I asked.

She looked at me quizzically, as if I'd just said something in Serbo-Croatian. "You know, about my adaptation of the play ...?"

"Oh, it's too bad you couldn't have kept F. Murray Abraham," she said. (Which made me feel oddly as if I'd done something to lose him.) "Who are these actors again?"

I explained what a talented group the actors were, even if they hadn't yet become household names. "So, Mom, you told everyone about the piece in the *Times*, right?"

(By "everyone" I meant my three younger brothers, of course. I had told each of them when the article was coming out, but it had seemed kind of pathetic to phone them that Sunday and make sure they read it. Still, I hadn't gotten any calls, which surprised me. My two middle brothers had young children already, so perhaps they just had their hands full. But I had certainly expected to hear from my youngest brother, almost eleven years my junior and less conflicted by sibling rivalry.)

"No. I didn't tell anyone," Mom said. "I didn't realize I was supposed to."

Okay, *now* my mind was officially blown. Mom had always been the family conduit for information of any general importance at all. ("Oh, you know Joel is having a cyst removed from his back on Tuesday. We're all gathering at Klingenstein Pavilion at 5:30," is one that comes to mind, mainly because who the hell tells anyone they even *have* a cyst, much less that it's being removed?) It was a role she had fulfilled faithfully during her tenure in the Manhattan Borough President's office (as Senior Advisor to Dinkins), and it was one that I thought was still in operation, despite the sickle-cell square dances and the gavel-wielding for Filipinos at Christie's. But I guess I was wrong. Or else this just didn't qualify as "news." (Hey, it's hard to compete with cyst-removal. And to think, I had a boil lanced and didn't tell anyone!)

Mom looked at her watch, frowning. "I'm late for three appointments," she muttered. "Can I let you off here?"

Before I could say anything, she had already motioned to her driver, who swerved over to the sidewalk and dumped me out among the rest of the mass-transit-taking pedestrians. "Call my secretary and make an appointment for sometime next week," she said vaguely before zooming off.

Mom did eventually come see the production, accompanied—miraculously enough—by Dad. (These were the days before cell phones, or else he would probably have spent the entire time in the lobby venting his wrath or waiting for that one call from Tokyo or Bombay or Dubai that could not be missed.) Mom and Dad tore off in unison when the play was over, as if they themselves were runners in some public event and had just heard the starter's pistol. I managed to catch up with Mom, running breathlessly alongside her. "Oh, that lead actor of yours," she said, shaking her head. "He looks just like Ed Koch!"

Cut to six years later, and Mom was no longer in political office, courtesy of Rudolf Giuliani. (Just before the re-election, the biggest question on Mom's mind had been whether to stay with Dinkins for two or three terms; then a black kid got run over in Brooklyn, a Jewish man was killed for payback, and the question was suddenly moot.) She now had a job in academia, running a department in one of the branches of the State College. She no longer had to choose nightly between twelve invitations. She was no longer asked to shoot starting guns or wield auctioneer's gavels. And she was far more supportive of my writing ventures than she had been before.

How had this come about? Well, removing the mask of Power had helped, returning Mom (at least in my humble opinion) to human form. And then, partly, it was the (highly) unwitting work of my ex-wife, when she made her desperate attempts to go after my parents' money. This had forged a union of mutual interest between the folks and myself that hadn't existed before, and that might never have otherwise happened.

But mostly, I think I just wore Mom down. Just plain broke the poor woman's spirit, to the point that she got sick and tired of fighting me. Just like I was trying to do on a larger scale to The World . . . not very successfully so far, as I'd be the first to admit. But hey, guys, it wasn't over.

As for the more immediate question of my lodgings, well, fate or luck or whatever you choose to call it had once again intervened to keep my freeloader status intact. The morning after my *Streetcar* soiree, I went down the long, narrow, atmospherically-musty ground floor hallway to the rear kitchen area, to get the second "b" of my b&b. There, among the steaming coffee and sticky buns, was the mistress of the Manor herself, Sandra

Hartsfield. We began speaking about the upcoming production, about Del and Faye and Joe, all of whom she cared about deeply. The more we spoke, the more I had this nagging feeling that—corny as it sounds—I had met Sandra before. But how was that possible? This was my first time in Atlanta, and we hardly traveled in the same circles. I tried to dismiss the idea from my mind. But it stubbornly lingered.

Then she started telling me about having seen *God of Vengeance* before, in a 1992 production at Playhouse 91 in New York City—and it came back to me. Yes! During the run of that show, there was exactly one non-Jewish couple (or individual, for that matter) who had sought me out and complimented me on the adaptation. "Last night we saw *Les Miserables* (or *Miss Saigon* or *Tommy* or whatever the mega-hit musical of that season was), and we enjoyed this so much more," they said, adding, "It was such a well-told, deeply-moving story." They were both such blonde, healthy, good-looking people . . . I remember wishing that we'd had one of those TV ad campaigns with testimonials from real audience members, just so we could make use of their gentile enthusiasm. "You see," I could tell everyone, "if such long-legged white people could identify with these characters, then so could you."

There was a framed 8 x 10 photograph of Sandra and her husband on a nearby cherrywood table. Looking over at that, then back at Sandra . . . My God! What were the odds? I felt like I was back in Hollywood, or at least in a typically far-fetched and improbable Hollywood movie. Or else in one of those pieces of bad southern fiction, those generational sagas of families torn apart by antebellum hysteria, then reunited years later through accidental meetings in places like, well, Hartsfield Manor. I told Sandra, and her face lit up. "I knew that I knew you from somewhere!" she said.

Sandra went on again about how deeply-moved they had been by the Jewish Rep production. ("How had you ever ended up there?" I asked. "We read a review, and it sounded interesting," she told me. "Why aren't there more people like you in the world?" I lamented.) She suddenly stopped in mid-sentence and looked right at me, her expression changing. "How long are you here for?" she asked.

"Another week," I said. (It was Saturday, our opening night was this coming Friday.)

"How would you like to stay here next week?" she asked.

I told her that I'd love to, but I couldn't afford it.

"No, no, for free," she said. "You'd be my guest."

Wow. I was bowled over by her generosity, thanking her profusely. "Hey, that's real southern hospitality," I said in my best Yankee accent.

"You better believe it, honeychile," she countered. "That's how we do things here in the south."

It turned out that Sandra's offer was for Monday-Thursday of the coming week (alas, in a more modest, less sensually-provocative room), which meant that I still needed a place to stay for this weekend and my final night (Friday). After another round of thank-yous to Sandra—she was leaving that night for two weeks, so I wouldn't see her again—I walked the few blocks up Euclid Avenue to 7 Stages, a jaunty skip in my step. I felt so good with this unexpected turn of events that I walked right past the "Best Humus in the World" store, waving to the proprietor. He waved back at me, nodding, though I'm not sure he remembered who I was.

I crossed paths with Joe's assistant, Scott, in the theater lobby, and he said there was a message for me in the 7 Stages office. This turned out to be a call from Lois Overbeck, the nice Beckett lady who worked out of the clapboard shack at Emory University. When I reached Lois back (in her shack), she offered me a place to stay for the rest of my time in Atlanta, starting tomorrow. (She lived only a mile or so from 7 Stages, in the opposite direction from Hartsfield Manor.) I thanked her, accepting for Sunday and Friday. This left only tonight to account for.

I wouldn't have minded staying in some cheap motel for one night, except it was Saturday night, and in my experience Saturday nights at cheap motels were hard to get, being reserved for whoring, murder, suicide, drive-bys, and crank parties—really, anything except sleeping. I wasn't particularly in a mood to battle these determined revelers and devotees of darkness for a room, so I went online, hoping to make a last-minute appeal to Amy S. for some relative whom I hadn't already pissed-off. And lo and behold, what do you think I found when I opened my e-mail program? Only a message from Amy herself, letting me know that her Aunt Delilah could put me up for a few nights, if I was interested. Wow, talk about serendipity. I called up Delilah—that evening's saving angel—pronto, and made the arrangements.

And so there it was: a place to rest my head for the rest of my time here. In fact, for some nights I had *choices*. It made me giddy just thinking about how lucky I was.

Mom rolled into town on Tuesday night, and of course she had the most expensive digs in Atlanta. Seriously. The Ritz-Carlton, Buckhead. *Fodor's* guidebook described it as "among the finest hotels in the country." They put four dollars signs ($$$$) next to it, which translated into my world as a high-pitched, hyena-like laugh. Actually, *two* dollar signs translated into a high-pitched, hyena-like laugh. Four was like a really *long* high-pitched, hyena-like laugh, followed by one of those awful jaw-dropping, tendon-stretching, bored-to-tears yawns.

In any case, I wasn't paying, so there was no reason to sweat it. And why shouldn't Mom travel in style if she could afford it? I mean, somebody has to stay in all those $1,000 a night (or whatever it costs) rooms, right? Just like somebody has to eat the overpriced hash they serve in those places. (Not that it doesn't taste good, mind you; even the bellyache afterwards gets four stars.) Otherwise where would Donald Trump and Bill Gates hang out when they came to town?

And on the upside, I was getting to spend some quality time in Buckhead, which could only be a good thing. I mean, right off the bat I saw more guys with sweaters tied around their necks in one hour than I had seen in the entire time I'd been down here. And I saw real debutantes in action, prancing around the cocktail lounge area in their flouncy gowns (at least they said they were debutantes). Who knows, maybe if I hung out long enough, I'd actually get to see Elton John. (Well, he said that he liked to hang out with the kids, right?)

But for all her Lifestyles of the Rich and Famous, Mom was not really a "shop 'til you drop" type of gal. I mean, she would have been in heaven if she had been. For Buckhead—from what I could see—was just like one big Niemann-Marcus, where people's happiness seemed to be in proportion to how big the mark-ups on and how small the usefulness of the items in question. ("Oh, twelve hundred dollars for a life-size stuffed alligator that sings the theme from *Titanic?* I'll take *six* of those!") No, Mom was pretty practical. And she didn't get to travel all that much. Even as a Deputy-Mayor she hardly got to go anywhere, only one fact-finding trip to Africa, I think, where the only facts she found out were that the people were poor, hungry, and hot, and wanted to know if they could come back on the plane with her.

I would have liked to show Mom the sights, but there wasn't really time, and, besides, I hadn't really seen them myself and didn't know where they were. Anyway, Mom only seemed interested in two things: the upcoming production (we opened in three nights) and John Glenn's "Return to Space," as all the commentators were calling it. (They made it sound as if his thirty-six years in-between flights had been like one long layover in an airport bar.)

Mom also wanted to see Hartsfield Manor, which I'd been raving about. (I was back again after stopovers at Delilah's and Lois Overbeck's.)

It was too bad that I was no longer in the Tennessee Williams room, as I would have loved to introduce Mom to the spirit of Dame Blanche. My current room was nothing special, more like a really great dorm room, with high ceilings and lots of closet space. I was sure Mom would flip for all the antiques and crazy doodads and gewgaws in the parlor—more ladies' chapeaus tacked to the wall, along with framed programs from cotillion balls that Mom would have been too young to attend.

"Look at this," I said, showing her an honest-to-God stereoscope, that offered 3-D views of various sepia slides like "A train chugging through the countryside," "A Sunday couple out for a walk," and "The Strange Toymaker." (What exactly *was* that toymaker doing with those toys? Hmm. Maybe that wasn't something I should have shown Mom.)

Mom was polite enough, looking at everything I pointed out, without showing a whit of enthusiasm. "It's very bohemian," she said, in her best politician's manner. Then she sniffed her nose agitatedly, as if trying to breathe in a dust storm.

We were soon out the door, making our way up the few lazy blocks to 7 Stages. There was a movie-style marquee above the theater entrance, with the kind of block-style black lettering that I always associate with church signs for "Jesus Saves." As we strode up Euclid Avenue, this emerged from behind a swaying poplar tree, proclaiming, "*God of Vengeance* by Stephen Fife," along with the dates of the show and box office number. (This was unfair to Joe and truly insulting to Sholem Asch—like saying *The Three Sisters* was by Stoppard or Jean-Claude van Itallie instead of by Chekhov. But what could I do? Do you think anyone asked my opinion?)

Of course I knew this marquee was coming up, and I plead guilty, your Honor, to arranging our position on the sidewalk so that the black letters would emerge suddenly, with the maximum visual impact. I mean, hey—it wasn't like I was David Mamet, but it compensated a bit for not having my photo in the paper. Truth to tell, it was the closest I had ever come to having my name up in lights. Why wouldn't I want Mom to see that?

And yes, the next few minutes were spent taking the predictable photos: Mom pointing up at the marquee, me pointing up at the marquee, Mom and me pointing up at the marquee (we waylaid some poor guy coming out of the wrap store to take this shot). It was as corny as some Neil Simon schmaltz about a struggling playwright who, having wiped out on various

170

speed-bumps of life, finally gets his name up in lights, even if it is at East Podunk community theater. This was certainly better than that—7 Stages and Jewish Theatre of the South were pretty great places, and Atlanta was a long way from East Podunk. But I *was* a struggling playwright, rather long in the tooth to still be playing the part, and the moment was ... well ... nice. (What can I say? I guess that's why Simon has sold a few scripts.) When it was over, we walked through the cool dark theater lobby, as I steered Mom away from a table that held a pile of the show's flyers.

The actors were in the middle of a very intense run-through, in preparation for tonight's invited dress—their first taste of public opinion. Everyone involved with the production was here, from Faye Allen and Mira Hirsch to the dark-haired techie with the large chocolate muffin. Everyone except me, of course, who was now the least necessary person in the mix. All I could really do at this point was be a model audience member, providing some feedback, hopefully of a constructive nature. Accordingly, Mom and I took a seat towards the back of the theater, out of everyone's way.

It was excruciating. Not the show so much—though that did seem kind of slow—but no, it was just the feeling of everything being out of my hands, of it being too late to do anything to fix what was wrong, patch up all the leaks, plaster over the cracks, etc. On the upside, Chip's violin sounded pretty snazzy. And someone had finally figured out to put a few family photos and knickknacks on the shelves in the brothelkeeper's house. (Only a note I'd been giving for two weeks.) I mean, hey, the guy keeps talking about what a rich man he is, how he was able to purchase a Torah scroll, but his own digs looked like something out of Sing-Sing. Hello! Has anyone tried reading the script?

I noticed Barbara LeBow (Frank Wittow's significant other) sitting nearby. She was watching the run-through intently, taking copious notes. Since Mom had seen *A Shayna Maidel* (hadn't every Jew in New York City?), I thought she'd get a kick out of saying hello. Accordingly, when there was a break, I guided Mom over and introduced her.

Barbara managed a smile, but she was preoccupied, even grim. "Should I tell these to Joe?" she asked, waving around a thick sheaf of notes. "I guess so," I said, even though Joe seemed pretty preoccupied himself at the moment, surrounded by actors and designers and just about everyone else. Barbara nodded, joining the crowd around Joe.

It had been my intention of approaching Joe myself at this point, to introduce him to Mom. But Mom had second thoughts.

"He's so busy," Mom said. "Let's do this later on."

"Don't be silly," I said. "He's dying to meet you."

Mom made a face, clearly casting her vote against the idea. This wasn't a democratic process, however, so I guided her in Joe's direction. I leaned close to Joe, just as he was telling Barbara LeBow to please not give him the notes, but to go over them with Mira Hirsch.

"Joe, this is my Mom," I said quickly, as if Joe was a bartender at a great bar, and I was trying to get in my drink order before all those ahead of me could.

"Yes?" Joe said, smiling, his gaze shifting from me to Mom. They shook hands and exchanged so-glad-to-meet-yous, as the camera in my brain went click. (The headline over the photo read "Mom shakes hands with Son's Youthful Idol! Is Black Sheep Status Endangered?") Desperate shouts of "Joe! Joe! Joe!" then propelled us out of the inner circle.

Mom had decided that she would skip tonight's invited dress and instead would see the play "with the rest of the paying public" at the first preview tomorrow. She also made it known that she would prefer not seeing any more of the run-through. ("I want my perceptions to be fresh," she said.) She offered to browse the curio shops on Euclid Avenue while I remained at rehearsal.

"No, let's go," I said, happy to have an excuse to duck out.

Mom and I strolled around Little Five Points (and yes, I did take her to meet the "Humus" master, but sadly he was out of his store that afternoon), and then we took in a few sights like the very fine art museum, etc. Around 3:30 or so, I started driving back to Buckhead, hoping to miss the traffic. No such luck. It was bumper-to-bumper for the next hour, and when I finally reached the Ritz-Carlton, it was practically time to come back for the invited dress. But Mom prevailed on me to park the rental and stay for a bite at the hotel.

And so I found myself on the verandah of this four-star luxury lodging, slurping down some $10 concoction, spooning down ice cream and *shlag*, and looking down on the multitude of people happily buying overpriced items that they didn't need. What place did I have in this world that so many people aspired to, that defined some popular ideal of "the good life?" No place really. But so what? It was an old question, and it somehow didn't really matter anymore. A little ice cream and *shlag* was fine in its place, just as it was a nice thing when Moms dropped in from out of town to show an interest in their sons' endeavors and remind them of how the other five percent lived.

172

Chapter Eighteen

The Secret of My Success

I WOKE UP ON THURSDAY morning with this quote from William Blake ringing in my head, "If the fool would persist in his folly he would become wise."

This had been something of a mantra of mine for many years, though I hadn't thought of it much for a while. I mean, it was a great motivational tool in my youth, prodding me to follow my heart down one uncertain path after another, hoping to hell it would all lead to something like wisdom. And there had certainly been moments along the way where I had reached some minor sense of revelation, either about myself or about the world and its many pitfalls and traps. But the heart is a deep and often-fathomless place, whose signposts are not easy to read. And the world is an unforgiving task-master, that has little use and even less pity for fools. (Unless of course they managed to become Presidents or CEOs.) I'd come to wonder if perhaps the fool who persisted in his folly only became more foolish.

Then again, reading over Blake's *Marriage of Heaven and Hell*, I noticed that he'd also written, "The road of excess leads to the palace of wisdom." So does that mean that the fool persists in his folly *on* the road to excess—all leading to that wise place—or are we talking about two completely separate roads? (Or is that just a foolish question?) I mean, if the road of excess does indeed lead to the palace of wisdom, then the king of wise men would be Keith Richards, right? And what about all the other purveyors of excess, whose crushed hearts, minds, and bodies lay strewn along that cruel pathway?

No, in the end the only reliable guide, it seemed, was an unreliable and unpredictable heart. In my case, this had counseled me—quite against common sense—to marry my ex-wife, write two plays about Vincent van Gogh, and a post-Holocaust comedy. So far I think you'd have to say it was Common Sense 4, Heart 0. Then again, maybe not. I mean, who knows where all these things fit into the Big Picture? Maybe I needed to marry my ex when I did, for reasons that I can't see now (and doubt I ever will). Maybe I needed to write those plays, whether successful or not, in order to write this book, or whatever else will come after. To quote the Scribe from *God of Vengeance*, "Who could tell?"

Who can even say if I'd have been happier or healthier if I'd made more "common sense" choices? (Hopefully I would have been wealthier.) And that's where the "persisting in folly" part comes in. Because we don't know where the road leads (however much we think we do), and it could just as well lead somewhere wonderful, that we could never have imagined before, as it could lead to ruin.

(Common sense may get you a house in the suburbs, but it will never get you bliss, ecstasy, crazy joy, or any of life's sweet intangibles; on the other hand, this argument will never carry much weight with your creditors, and believe me, I've tried.)

Where it led on this particular morning was to the first and only preview of this Joe Chaikin-directed production, after last night's invited dress. The theater had been around half-filled last night for that performance, which had brought together such recent friends and acquaintances as Lois Overbeck, the solemn "heavy Jew" who gave us the thumbs-up, and Amy's cousin Ben (who delighted in the few actor goof-ups he was able to spot). The show seemed to come off fairly well, which meant there were no major technical gaffes, and the audience appeared to be drawn in, leaning forward on the edge of their seats for the seduction scene (how it should be). Yet the applause at the end was more subdued than I had hoped for. I mean, what's the point of an invited dress if you don't hear a "huzzah" or two at curtain call? These folks are presumably your amigos, and besides, they got in for free. If they can't manage a real orgasm at climax, then they should fake one. Isn't that what friends are for?

Of course, Asch's drama wasn't really a "stand up and cheer" sort of play. Everything falls apart at the end, turns to shit, so it was understandable if the audience felt a little shaken. But to my mind there was a bigger problem: Frank Wittow, the lead. Frank was giving a powerful performance, full of gravitas and old-fashioned angst, but it belonged in a different production. Joe had directed the rest of the show to play against the melodrama, something that his major innovation—the agile Chip on his violin, commenting musically on the action—particularly underscored. Then along would come Frank, our own personal "heavy Jew," shaking his humorless fists at the heavens.

174

(No wonder God was unmoved. "Would it kill you to smile, laugh, maybe do a little jig now and then?" the Big Guy was probably thinking.)

No, when Frank zigged, the production zagged; and never the twain seemed to meet. It was so painfully apparent, even Joe was grumbling. "So slow, so slow," he lamented, shaking his head. He cautioned me to keep this between us, but the bigger issue was how we could keep it from the audience, much less the critics. (That imagination-killing set was yet another element that didn't fit with either Frank's performance or the more poetic brothel scenes, but don't get me started.)

So what could be done at this point? Exactly zip. Nada. Nothing. Just grin and bear it. (Of course, affecting the hip I-could-give-a-shit attitude of the modern artiste also worked nicely too.) Then again, it helped if you could lie to yourself convincingly. "On some level, all these conflicting elements really get underneath the audience's skin in a powerful way and bring out the underlying tensions already present in Asch's play." (Yadda yadda yadda. I knew all that lit-crit self-stroking would come in handy someday.)

After awhile, you ended up sounding like one of those drunks in O'Neill's *Iceman Cometh*, sitting at your corner table in Harry Hope's bar. "Come here, leedle monkey-face. Buy me a trink. Loan me a dollar. Give me a good review." (The funny thing was that the critic—instead of being Hickey the truth-teller—would more often be just another drunk spinning his own little pipedream, and he'd give you the dollar, the drink, and the review. Or else he wouldn't when you deserved it.)

In any case, I was resolved to say nothing about it to Mom. If she didn't like the production, then fine. But let her reach her own conclusions. I wasn't going to start apologizing for what was onstage—not until after she'd seen the show anyway.

(In general, if I could extrapolate one lesson from all my experience to tell the young playwright or artist of any stripe, it would be this: *Never apologize. Never make excuses.* It doesn't do any good, and it only pre-disposes the reader / viewer negatively toward your work. Of course, this book would have been a helluva lot better if my NEA grant had gone through, and I hope those yahoos at Yaddo choke on their high-flown Georgia O'Keefe sensibilities, but that's another story, okay? Never apologize. Never make excuses. Just follow those simple dictums, kids, and you'll never go wrong. Now if you wouldn't mind lending me a few dollars ...)

When I turned up again at the Ritz-Carlton veranda in Buckhead, it was apparent that Mom had much bigger fish to fry than my little fears about the production. No, Mom—to change metaphors—was in the middle of a full-fledged bout of John Glenn fever. Newspapers were spread all over the table, displacing the remnants of a breakfast. (Can't you get any service at this dive?) There was *The New York Times*, *USA Today*, and *Atlanta Journal-Constitution*, all vying for space (so to speak) to tell the same story: at two o'clock today, Glenn would be shot out of an interstellar canon, back into orbit again.

"I just can't believe it's been thirty-five years!" Mom cried, waxing nostalgic. "I mean, everyone writes in their columns about how small his space capsule was in 1962, how it looks more like a tin can now than a rocket ship. It's just amazing that he made it back."

"Yes, Mom. You're right. It's amazing," I said. (Hey, I wasn't about to start competing with an astronaut, to do some Smothers Brothers routine of "Mom always like John Glenn best.")

Mom and I lingered at the table a while—I probably ordered some humongous breakfast, the Ritz-Carlton Buckhead equivalent of Denny's Grand Slam (minus the sausage and bacon, of course)—and then we drove across the street to the high-fallutin' shopping mall, where I was more than happy to have Mom buy me some overpriced duds that I would probably never wear. (We'd been carrying on this clothes-buying ritual for many years; I think I can say with some certainty that it was highly satisfactory for both of us.) In any case, the point was simply to waste some time in an entertaining fashion until 2:00 PM, when we adjourned to Mom's hotel room to watch Glenn blast off.

This is where I'm supposed to set the scene, providing the kind of detailed description of a $1,000 a night (or whatever) hotel room that makes you feel like you've been there yourself, like you know every inch of that room, like you can close your eyes and see yourself there, perhaps lounging beside Mom and me in one of the white Mies van der Rohe chairs, facing the twenty-five inch Sony Trinitron. Unfortunately, though, I forgot to write anything down in the little notebook I carry around, and I have no memory of the place whatsoever. (That stuff about Mies van der Rohe chairs and Sony TVs was pure malarky.) I have a vague image of hunting scenes on the wall, of bleeding chickens and some deer buck with huge antlers nailed to a cross. But maybe that was some other room.

Sadly, I can't say I remember much about the liftoff of the Discovery either. I do recall thinking something about how phallic the space shuttle looked, and then having an extended fantasy about space being this giant vagina, and how maybe someday we'd all be able to take a Jules Verne-like voyage to the planet G-Spot ... but I had pretty much this same fantasy at every launching, even of things that didn't look like giant cocks. So it may not have been John Glenn's takeoff that I'm remembering now. I really can't say.

I can report that Mom was pleased with the outcome, clapping her hands together and smiling girlishly. I was pleased too, don't get me wrong. Ever since the misfiring of the Challenger ... Well, I'm sure anyone who's old enough to have been around then (and probably many who weren't) still holds their breath at a shuttle count-down, fearful of any reprise. I was in the process of getting my Master's Degree from Columbia when that event happened, and the death of teacher Christi McAuliffe was very real to me. While I may not have been afflicted with "John Glenn fever" like Mom, I was very relieved not to have little pieces of the hero senator washing up at some fraternity's beach party. I'm sure he's a very nice man, and besides, there is nothing quite so boring as reporters droning on endlessly about how we're all "united in grief," "a nation in mourning," etc. After awhile, you just feel like picking up a pair of maracas and dancing down the street like Carmen Miranda. (Or Charo. "Coochie-coochie-coochie." Take your pick.)

Anyway, by the time Glenn had blasted off, shed his booster rockets (or whatever it is they shed) and was safely in orbit, it was already around 3:30 or so, and—oh yeah, there was something else I meant to tell you. Mom and I were supposed to meet Joe and his sister Miriam for a pre-show dinner at a restaurant near the theater called Terracotta. Then Mom had heard about some fabulous place she wanted to try ... I think Ted Turner's personal chef cooked the food, or Jane Fonda danced on the tables, something like that. So I had called up Joe and told him to join us at this other place, but he'd said no, he and his sister were going to keep the reservation at Terracotta's. Then Mom changed her mind again after the shuttle takeoff (a woman's prerogative, so they tell me) and decided she'd like to revert to the original plan. While I had no luck reaching Joe or his assistant, there didn't seem to be any problem. Joe and his sister were coming to the restaurant anyway. We'd just meet them there.

So Mom and I took in a few more sights—Mom's area of expertise was urban planning, so she loved "examining" city buildings, hanging out in city parks, and other thrilling things like that—and then we made our way to Terracotta's. But there was no sign of Joe or his sister, and indeed, they never showed up. (No, they didn't go to that "Ted Turner-fabulous place," but good try; that kind of plot twist has spiced up many a narrative.) This was very disappointing, as I was looking forward to getting Mom and Joe together. And Terracotta had been the scene of one of my best nights in Atlanta, when Del and Faye had treated everyone in the show to a "get-to-know-you" dinner. It was a wonderful party, with great food and fun conversations, of the kind that only happens in the theater (it may happen with movies as well, but writers are rarely invited). I was hoping to conjure up the spirits of that previous meal, but it was like the second night of a production, after a glorious opening: everything just reminds you of how much better it was before.

Still, Mom said she had a fine time, and I tried not to take the mix-up with Joe as a portent. We saw him briefly when we got to the theater, but he was way too involved in the various complexities of the moment for me to say anything more than, "Hi, break a leg," and all that crap. There was, of course, that super-charged feeling in the air that comes with people paying actual cash money to see your show: now it finally counts, now it's for real. Faye was in front of the theater greeting her 7 Stages patrons and friends, Mira Hirsch was there greeting her Jewish Theater of the South patrons and friends, and there was a line at the box office. Glory be. (And nary a protester in sight, not even a lone Mister Tooth Decay. Damn.)

I introduced Mom to Faye and Mira and a number of other people in the bustling crowd. Mom was at her politician's best, smiling and shaking hands, saying how much she was looking forward to seeing the show, how proud she was of me, etc. Then I said a little silent prayer to Sholem Asch—"Oh thank you, primogenitor, for being enough of a pissed-off Jew to give this pissed-off Jew the chance to have his name on a marquee"—and Mom and I went inside and took our seats in the nearly-full theater.

There was more excitement in the air tonight, and the actors seemed to catch hold of this, giving a more urgent and self-assured performance. Frank, in particular, seemed more energized, and scenes started coming alive that had just lain there before like a lox. There was one very difficult scene, with Yankel and the temple Scribe and Reb Elye (Del's character), that was a real challenge. The three older men essentially sat around for a number of minutes while the Scribe answered Yankel's questions about whether God could forgive a man who had done terrible things. (This is where the Scribe says, "Who can tell?") This scene tended to drag down the entire First Act,

178

Del Hamilton, Frank Wittow, and Jim Weiss perform the "Who can tell?" scene.

but for the first time it showed some signs of quirky life. (Even if Del—who was a very nice actor—still seemed about as Jewish to me as Buffalo Bill.)

The applause was encouragingly spirited at the intermission break. While Mom went to the Ladies Room ("It's really going well!" she said convincingly), I took the time-honored route of the playwright / adapter and mingled with the crowd in the hope of catching some revealing off-the-cuff comments. "It's good! It's good!" I heard, often laced with as much surprise as Mom's version had had. The seduction scene didn't take place until after the break, but there was that big kiss between Rivkele and Manke early on, accompanied by Chip's sinuous violin. A few people said things like, "Well, there's something you don't see every day." (Actually, you do, just not in the theater.) And I saw some other people respond with raised eyebrows or semi-lewd smiles. But in general everyone seemed to be having a rousing good time.

This level of audience involvement was ratcheted higher in the brothel scenes that began Act II (my act break was different from Asch's), as the brothel girls played in the rain and reminisced about the "normal" lives they had left behind; and it reached something like a fever pitch in the seduction scene, which had become much more playful, the girls teasing out the beats, allowing the sense of sexual taboo to simmer. I definitely got the feeling that many people in the audience knew about this scene beforehand and were waiting for it. Looking at the faces of people around me, I saw slight smiles of recognition, as people seemed to be thinking, "Oh ho! So this is what all the talk was about!"

Yet as soon as Yankel found out about his daughter and trashed his living quarters, the play once again went into as deep a funk as Yankel himself. This didn't have to be the case. There was still a great deal at stake—can Yankel get Rivkele back in time to salvage her marriage to the rabbi's son?—but the immediacy seemed to have drained out of the play. I felt the problem had everything to do with the way Frank was playing it, as a man already defeated by life and disappointed by God. Humpty Dumpty had fallen off the wall, and pity the fool who tried to put him back together (or who even believed that such a thing could be possible). Accordingly, the audience response at the final curtain was more measured than at intermission, the enthusiasm more muted.

Mom, however, was aglow with superlatives. "Really well-done," she said. "Very substantial." She thought it was better than the production at Jewish Rep (not that I believe she really recalled it). And, regarding the "seduction scene," Mom didn't think it was a seduction scene at all. "It's about a young girl coming of age, discovering her own sexuality for the first time."

"But it worked for you?" I asked.

"Oh yes. Absolutely," Mom said.

Mom and I were pretty much the only people left in the theater now. We were soon joined by the cast of the show, who had gathered to hear notes from Joe.

Joe wore a red-and-green striped long-sleeved polo shirt and green shorts, looking a bit like the Spirit of Christmas Past. The notes he gave were of the small-details variety. ("Chip—relax more onstage. When moving, don't dance ... Manke—when you sit next to Rivkele, after coming back in from rain, put your face next to her hair. Breathe in the smell ... Rivkele—don't turn your head away when you're talking to mother. Keep looking right at her.") He didn't give a single note to Frank Wittow, which I thought was wise. Frank had received many notes. To say anything more would simply serve to make him more self-conscious (and even slower) in his performance.

There was a party afterward, but Mom had an early flight to catch, so I drove her to Buckhead. I parked the rental and went up to the cocktail lounge area with Mom for one farewell toast. (Drinks in my world were a helluva lot more fun than in hers.)

Our conversation went pretty much as you'd suppose: I thanked her for coming, she told me how much she'd enjoyed seeing the show, etc. There were things I might have liked trying to say, about wounds inflicted or received in the past, but it wasn't easy being emotional with Mom. A few years before, I had come across that poem I'd written at her sister's graveside, after having put it away in a drawer a long time before. (It's the one that begins "Touch us with noble anger / To cry so the dead may hear ...") I touched up a few words and gave her a copy when I came over for dinner that evening. I guess I expected some expression of gratitude, or at least recognition, a shared moment of something. Instead she slipped the lone piece of paper off the table as if it was an unspecified threat or gave off a toxic substance. She soon spirited it off to a drawer of her own, where it was locked up, entombed, never to be mentioned again.

But then, it was simply too easy to pick others apart for not being the people we need them to be. (If I hadn't known this before, I had certainly come to learn it from my marriage's breakup and subsequent hashing-over in court.) Mom was a powerful person, a successful politician who knew where the liberal bodies were buried and would never tell. (An astrologer once told me that Mom was going to write a political memoir; that's when I knew that nothing this woman predicted would ever come true.) Mom's armor had served her well in her chosen profession. Far be it from me to try to pierce it.

Chapter Nineteen

Meshuggeneh Litvaks of the World, Unite!

T HE DAY OF OPENING Night started interestingly with a congratulatory e-mail from Holly in glowing pink and green.

> *You have a great opening!!!* (and I should know)
> Or if you prefer ...
> *Knock 'em dead!!!* (but don't lay 'em in the aisles).

Hmm. Lots of messages to decode there. "Nice gender-bending twist," I e-mailed back. Okay, yes, I was wussing out, but there would be plenty of time to decode later. For the time being, our communiques were becoming civil again, and that gave me hope I'd be able to sleep in one bed for a while. After my recent stint as the "Wandering Jew," that wasn't a possibility I wanted to squander.

The rest of the day swiftly devolved into a muddle, as I had to gather all my possessions and move from the Manor into Lois Overbeck's house for one night, in preparation for my departure tomorrow. This should have been routine, after all the moving I'd already done; but it wasn't. Maybe I was still pondering the hidden meanings in Holly's message, I don't know. In the end, I just threw everything in the trunk of my rental and took off for 7 Stages, where I hung around all day like a bad cold.

Though my experience with this is limited, I still feel some confidence in describing the hours before Opening Night as an exercise in mass (self-)delusion—Jonestown without the Kool-Aid. Everyone involved with the show, from the actors and producers to the poor soul running the lightboard, knows very well that the production has serious flaws. They know that three or four weeks of intensive rehearsals have not solved these, but in many ways have only deepened them. And yet there is this irrational but unquenchable optimism that, come Opening Night, everything will be okay. "All we need is a good audience," people will say (as they did that day at 7 Stages, myself included). The truth is that all we need is a good play performed by well-cast actors in a well-directed and well-produced production. But, barring that, a good audience is pretty nice too.

(Perhaps it's different with a big Broadway show, I don't know. My guess is that the raised stakes would only ratchet up the degree of delusion. My only real experience with something like this came with the World Premiere of Edward Gorey's *Dracula* at the Nantucket Stage Company. That seemed to my very young self to be a pleasantly campy show—entertainingly silly, but hardly groundbreaking—that people had all these inflated expectations about; then the play opened, and the audience went nuts, stamping their feet, screaming, exceeding what anyone had expected. I remember an older actor named Jerry Dempsey wandering around the stage later that night, crying. "I've waited twenty-five years for something like this," he kept saying. "Twenty-five years!" I didn't really understand what he was babbling about at the time. I think I do now.)

Not only did we have a good audience for Opening Night of *God of Vengeance*, we had something better—one that was good and *soused*. Oh yes. You may remember that one of the sponsors of our show, listed above the title on the flyer, was Absolut Vodka. Well, they showed up big-time at the opening, dispensing free shots like they were little buckets of water to put out a fire. (Of course, they'd have the opposite effect on fire than water would, but you get the idea.)

I vaguely remember downing somewhere between eight and ten shots. (Or maybe twelve. Who could tell?) I'd done something like that once before, when I was Best Man at my youngest brother's wedding. Then they had to use the Jaws of Life to pry me loose from some woman's cleavage. I was doing my best to keep that from happening again, though it wasn't easy. I saw several low-cut blouses that I was sorely tempted to jump down. It was only the memory of Sholem Asch, and the unique place in the universe I occupied as his adapter (give or take a Margulies), that kept me from taking the plunge. (My inner frat guy kept yelling out, "Screw Sholem Asch, let's just get the boy laid!")

Eventually I was able to stagger to a seat in the theater (it was probably somebody else's, I really can't say). At some point either Faye or Mira made a welcoming speech (whomever it was, she looked very foxy). Then the lights went down, and all I wanted to do was curl up and go to sleep (preferably on some obliging woman's breast). But then the lights came up again (damn!) and actors started talking, and there went any chance for a good nap. This pissed me off for a while, but I gradually found myself looking at the play through new eyes (bleary and besotted, but new). "Hey," I found myself thinking, "this isn't half-bad." And when Rivkele and Manke had that first kiss, with Chip stroking the strings right beside them—man alive! That was really sexy! (Sad to say, but that's an exact transcription of my thoughts.)

Intermission was a blur. I seem to remember consuming a few more shots, and then the absolutely fabulous Absolut lady turning a bottle upside-down, just to prove to me that it was empty. Then I wandered down toward the sidewalk, where I found a few other solid citizens who were as Absolutly smashed as I was. I think we engaged in some kind of hugfest, dancing around awkwardly like circus bears. Our scintillating dialogue went something like:

THEM: Oh, I love your play! I really love it!

ME: Oh, thank you! Thank you! Thank you!

Then we all staggered back to our seats, though how the hell we got there, and whether they were the same seats that we'd been in before, are questions I will never be able to answer.

The Second Act plunged me into a serious question: how could I get into Yankel's brothel? Seriously. How could I make my way through the fake rain to Yankel's house of horrors? Because that seemed like the solution to all my problems. I mean, I wouldn't be sleeping with the actresses—which was morally questionable at best, and could have consequences—I'd be doing it with the *characters*. And that was okay, right? Because I was partly responsible for their existence. (Okay, it seems creepy and kind of incestuous now, but trust me, it made sense at the time.)

And then it suddenly came to me, how it could happen. I could be the unseen *meshuggeneh* Litwak! Yes! Manke even says, "when he kisses me, he hides his face in my breast and closes his eyes, like a baby sucking on his mother's nipple." Perfect!

So Asch hadn't made a mistake after all by not getting the Litwak off-stage, he was merely providing his future adapter with an opportunity to have sex with his characters. Great! What a prince! I was overwhelmed for a moment by all this thoughtfulness. But how to make it happen, how to get in position onstage? How to vault over everyone else in this damn row, sneak backstage unnoticed, and be waiting there for Manke when she came back? But just in that moment, Manke grabbed Rivkele's hand and dragged her off to some other place, where nothing good was going to happen. And it was too late.

Soon Yankel came in, threw his tragic fit, and went into his funk. "I'm with you, brother," I thought, my funk deepening as I realized I could have taken the Litwak's place at the start of Act II. What was I thinking? And of course I was leaving tomorrow, so I wouldn't get a second chance to make a *meshuggeneh* impression. What a dunce!

When Yankel was railing at God, I railed at Sholem Asch. Why couldn't you have given me a clue to your higher purpose any sooner? But already the vodka was wearing off, my gray adapter-consciousness coming back into focus, just in time for the house of cards to fall apart. Soon it was over, the audience clapping with great gusto (I swear I even heard a huzzah or two).

("And what happens to Rivkele?" I found myself suddenly wondering. The actress playing the part had asked me that question during rehearsal, and I had given her the obvious answer: she becomes a brothel girl, as the sins of her parents are repeated. But now I saw another possibility. She could get her money back on the Torah Scroll. (What was the return policy on those anyway? Was there a restocking charge?), and she'd use the cash to book herself transit on a boat to the New World. Once here she would work in a sweatshop, join the suffragette movement, and end up marrying an abortionist. She would have a large family (naming her eldest girl "Manke") and escape the darker fate of the real Manke and the other girls, along with that of her spiritual "coming of age" sister, Anne Frank—all of whom never made it back from Camp Hitler. So, in a way, the play really did have a happy ending. Who knew?)

This time I went to the after-play party (of course), though I stayed away from vodka and mixed drinks. Everyone was excited, upbeat, triumphant. I mean, I knew there were problems, as I'm sure Joe and Frank and Del and Mira, and pretty much everyone else did too. But it was Opening Night, and the audience seemed to like what we'd done, and everyone had had a few drinks, and it was okay. Yeah. The show was okay.

Chapter Twenty

Terminal

JOE'S SISTERS MIRIAM AND Shami had done everything possible to insure that the trip to the airport terminal would go smoothly. They named a particular pickup spot, saying over and over, "Get Joe there by exactly 11:00 AM, and a red minivan will come pick him up." So of course the car was a lime-green town car, it arrived ten minutes late, and it parked a hundred yards away from the spot. It took us another ten minutes to figure that out ("Um, Joe, do you think that's the car?" "Maybe. But Shami said red, so …" "It's true, she did say red, but …"), by which time we were no longer in such great shape for the departure. This was especially true for me, since I still had to return my trusty Neon to the rental place, which was a ten-minute ride from the airport proper—

Hey. Wait a minute. Something is not linking up, folks. Now I have that mix-up about the airport car in my notes. And I have a very detailed—and, if I don't say so myself, very amusing—description of how Joe and I made our way through the sprawling and confusing Atlanta airport, taking a transport train to the right concourse, then walking a very long distance to the right terminal, while carrying lots of carry-on baggage … but I don't understand where that airport car fits in. I mean, wouldn't I have driven Joe to the rental place, then taken a cab from there to the airport? That only makes sense. And I do vaguely remember having Joe there while I paid my rental bill. ("$422? For a lousy Neon? Yikes!" "Um, Steve, don't you think we should be going?") The sad truth, however, is that I was so hungover that morning, so whoozy, so dead on my feet—well, it's amazing I could drive at all, much less remember anything about it.

(Not that I want Miriam or Shami to know that. No, please, ladies, there was no effect at all from the vodka, or if there was, it only made my senses sharper, more able to cut through the complexities of freeway traffic

Joseph Chaikin

Leaving Atlanta, I appear to be still under the influence of opening night.

patterns like Stephen Hawking slicing through unsolvable riddles of Time and Space.)

(Hear that, kids? Don't do what I did. Unless I didn't do it.)

Unless I didn't drive Joe at all, but only met up with him later at the airport check-in counter, after dropping off the rental myself. In which case you won't really care how I almost forced that Coca-Cola delivery truck off the road, or almost collided with that CNN Tour Bus, right?

Well, in any case, I know that we reached the takeoff gate in plenty of time. (Because it's right there in my notes, only slightly smudged from the seltzer water I was drinking to calm my stomach. Or is that hangover drool? Yecch.) And yet there was one more obstacle to overcome, one more hurdle to clear, one more twist in this twisted saga, before our weary selves would be safely winging their way back to northern climes.

It happened like this: Just after the omniscient announcer had let us know there was ten minutes until our flight's boarding, Joe told me, "I go to the bathroom. Right back." I wasn't too pleased about this, and I would have suggested he wait until we got on the plane, but Joe was gone before I could speak. So I waited. And waited. And waited. My eyes were glued to the Men's Room doorway, to make sure that Joe didn't turn the wrong way or otherwise wander off. (Well, if his mind wandered while driving, then it could wander here too, right?)

Soon the first boarding announcement was made. Then the second. Then the final boarding announcement. And still no Joe.

At this point, you may very well be asking yourself, "What is this guy's problem? I mean, what is he waiting for? Why doesn't he just go in the bathroom and tell Joe to get on his horse before it's too late?"

The problem, my Friend, was that I was looking after all this carry-on baggage, and these were the days—remember?—when a person could carry on a piano, or perhaps a few cases of scotch, and it was okay as long as you could cram them into an overhead rack (pianos were a little difficult that way, though not after you'd taken a few swigs from the scotch). I did attempt to deal with the situation by calling over a gate attendant and asking her to look after our piano and our scotch while I went to the Men's Room to tell Joe to hurry.

"Sorry, sir, we're not allowed to do that. Security regulations," she told me.

I explained our current dilemma, deepening by the moment. "You'll be able to hold the plane for us, right?"

"Sorry, sir, we're not allowed to do that," she said. (See, even then they weren't allowed to do much. Though in our memories, it may seem like the sky was the limit.)

Up to then I'd been telling myself, "Stay calm. Don't panic. He'll be here any moment." But now that reasonable self was drowned out, it was being bitch-slapped and otherwise manhandled by the demons of doubt, who cackled demonically, "He's not coming back, you fool! He probably slipped out when you weren't looking! So not only are you going to miss your flight, you've probably lost him as well! And how are you going to explain that to poor Miriam and Shami, who put all their trust in you?" I suddenly had this image of Joe wandering back to the concourse, stepping on a train to another concourse, being trampled by the teeming hordes who were late for their flights.

"Aaaah! Aaaaah! Aaaaah!"

I let out three inner Homer Simpson screams, then I started stuffing our baggage under chairs, where they seemed the least stealable. (Not pianos or cases of scotch perhaps, but still things we had been more than willing to drag through several miles of airport.) Just as I was about to walk off, I closed my eyes, took a deep breath, and told myself that he was going to come walking out at that very moment. Then I opened my eyes, and there he was.

"Long line," he said, walking up to me. We picked up our stuff and boarded the flight, just as they were about to close the escape hatch. (Or whatever the name for that door is.)

(Oh, wait a minute! Something just came to me! Yes! The red minivan that Miriam and Shami had sent to pick us up—the one that turned out to be a lime-green Town car—that was for *after we'd landed in Newark!* Of course! It picked us up (late) outside the arrival terminal and drove us to

Westbeth in downtown Manhattan, where Joe lived. Which means that I really did drive Joe to the Atlanta airport ... So no, Miriam and Shami, there never was any Coca-cola delivery truck or CNN Tour Bus or van full of schoolchildren. It was just a little joke, ha ha—oh, wait a minute, did I mention the children before? Anyway, I was sober as a judge, and a look of sheer unadulterated terror never crossed your baby brother's face. (Hear that, kids? It never happened.) If I'm lying, let God strike down my agent. Right now.)

I was a little afraid that once we got on the plane, Joe was going to divulge more secrets to me, probably something else about Sam Shepard's love life. (What more could there be? Had he been screwing Marilyn Monroe when he was eleven? Was he Jackie O's secret lover? And hadn't I heard enough on this subject for one lifetime?) But no, there were no further revelations, just some small talk about last night's opening, and what lay ahead. I suddenly felt badly about having distrusted Joe before, about having been anything less than candid with him.

(Just as I feel badly now, Reader, for having disclosed this quirk in Joe's character—but then I would have been less than candid with you otherwise, right? Of course, for all I know this was a complete aberration on Joe's part, and he's never made such disclosures before or since.)

What lay ahead for Joe was a full slate of directing jobs. First there was a mainstage production at Yale Repertory Theater of *Glass Menagerie* by Tennessee Williams (who felt like an old friend to me now). Then there was a workshop at the Mark Taper Forum in LA of an Open Theatre-style experimental theater piece about aging. Then it was back to Atlanta and 7 Stages for a revival of an anti-war play by his old buddy Sam Shepard called *States of Shock*.

Joe had actually cast this short play—it was more like an extended one act—and done a first read-through while we were in Atlanta, a few days before *God of Vengeance* opened. I was "shocked" to hear Joe say with some conviction that this was his favorite Shepard play. (For me, it was a dead-heat between *Tooth of Crime* and *Curse of the Starving Class*, with much admiration as well for his little-known play about Howard Hughes called *Seduction*, at least as I'd seen it performed by the great Rip Torn.)

A friend of mine had stage managed the original production of *Shock* at the American Place (NYC), and he told me how depressed everyone was when they first sat down to read the script, which my friend described as "forty-five pages of incoherent blather." My friend was, however, duly amazed by the degree of rewriting Shepard was able to do during rehearsals, essentially constructing something powerful out of near-nothing. I have to admit that I didn't think that much of the show when I saw it—it seemed to have gone from incoherent to coherent blather—but it did feature a mind-blowing ego trip of a performance by John Malkovich.

I'm afraid I have to stop the presses one last time, and—in the spirit of my forebear Al Jolson—go into a dance about this well-known but often under-appreciated performer.

William Redfield, in his book *Letters From An Actor*, does some provocative musing about "the perfect actor," positing this to be a hybrid of Laurence Olivier (pure technique) and Marlon Brando (pure instinct). In my experience, John Malkovich may be the closest I ever witnessed onstage to that actor. Now I know he drives many people (especially some fellow actors) crazy with his vocal mannerisms, and he can be quite affected, it's true. To me this is part of his charm, as it was Brando's. And like Brando he possesses enough charisma to blow legions of more "believable" actors right off the stage. His work as the homeless brother in *True West* and as "Biff" in the Dustin Hoffman production of *Death of a Salesman* had such primal force, such present-tense electricity, such a fusion of mind, body, and spirit—okay, I may be going a little over the top here, but I can't help it, it's the dance talking, not me—that they went straight into my bloodstream (as Dustin's overly thought-out performance didn't). Even his work in such plays as Lanford Wilson's *Burn This* elevated minor outings into mythic occasions. Yet the film roles that have been able to harness his odd and somewhat ungainly powers are few and far-between. And—like Brando again—he has largely abandoned the theater, except in his case for rare forays (mostly as a director) with his native Steppenwolf troupe in Chicago.

Truth to tell, I spared Joe this dance (it was for your eyes only, dear Reader, unless you're John Malkovich—in which case I hope to hell I've brown-nosed you into "being" in one of my plays), not wanting to express any negative feelings about *States of Shock*. In fact, I didn't want anything negative between us at all. Was it because I was harboring hopes of working with Joe again, perhaps on a new version of *Kaddish?* Well, I loved the poem, but it didn't seem to me like something that "needed" to be a play. And there was a certain spark between Joe and me that, for one reason or another, hadn't been struck. But there had been good times and good feelings, and I didn't want those to be sullied. Maybe it was a Karma thing, but I already had enough crap in my life, and I wasn't looking to add to the pile.

Oh boy, did I have enough crap. I was going back to a relationship that might already be over. I had no real money or source of income to speak of. And, while my divorce may have finally come through, I still had no financial settlement, which meant that it didn't make much sense for me to get a day job, since she'd only try to attach my wages (the fight over this would cost more in legal fees than I could make). Same problem with selling a movie script, though I could probably hide that income more easily (if only I'd get the chance). And I couldn't get any money from family, since they were all terrified of falling under the scrutiny of my ex's attorney (ultimately it was their money that she'd been after). Yet here I was, a forty-five-year-old man, and it amazed me that I couldn't snap my fingers and make something happen that caused all these problems to just go away.

I looked out the window of the plane, at the seemingly-infinite blue skies, and the sun shining brightly on the thick cloud cover below. Of course I had that predictably sappy moment of self-pity—oh, everything looks so dark now, but above those gray clouds of legal and personal troubles the sun is shining, and it's always darkest before the dawn, and did Bill Clinton come up with that finger-wag to accompany his "I never had sex with that woman" all by himself, or did Paul Begala or some other handler tell him, "Oh Bill, it's so much more convincing if you treat the nation like naughty schoolkids who tried to look up teacher's skirt" (while of course his head was up Monica's skirt)?

But then that moment passed, and I was somewhere else. (In general I was appalled by the taxpayer money being spent on a sexual peccadillo, but that particular act of presidential hubris outraged even me. Then again it was nice of the man to distract me from my own messy life. Yeah. Come to think of it, that finger-wag could almost be called—dare I say it?—witty.)

I looked out the window again. This time I really tried to send my gaze outward, to lose myself in the endless and depthless blue. ("Oh, Dame Blanche and your Three Graces, hover around, give human form to this vastness, kiss my thoughts with your ruby red lips!" I invoked.)

Soon, images began to come back to me from a time when I was fifteen and swimming naked in the ocean off Madaket beach in Nantucket. I had just started writing poetry in earnest, and I felt so powerful, so empowered, slicing easily through the waves with my swift strokes. "I have everything inside me that I will ever need!" I suddenly thought. "Just give me pen and paper, and I can do without all the rest!" That was a turning-point moment for me, the moment when I took my vow of poverty or whatever else would be required to pursue the particular destiny I sensed for myself. (Little did I think at the time that the Taker of Vows would be so literal about the "poverty" part.)

Looking back on that now, I had to admit that deep inside I still felt pretty much the same way. "I have everything inside me that I will ever need." Yes. Of course, even back then I had needed a few other things. I needed my glasses so I could see the two large women on a nearby sand-dune looking down at me with keen interest. And I needed a bathing-suit so the approaching Beach Police wouldn't arrest me. ("Yes, sir, I know that this is public property, sir.") And eventually I needed food and shelter and family and lovers and friends, and a car would be nice too, and of course what was life without books and music and pictures? But then I needed bookshelves and music-players and picture-frames, and somewhere to put them, and somewhere to hang them, and somewhere to *live*. So of course I needed money. (Of course.) So I got a job teaching other people to do what I wanted to do but no longer had the time or energy. And my sense of destiny dwindled away until it was the size of a small fetish, like a rabbit's foot, which I would take out when I was alone and rub for good luck. But there was no good luck anymore, or anything else good. Because I had betrayed the only thing I had ever really needed, myself. And, what was worse, what was really unforgivable, I had done all this in the name of not betraying me.

But then I kept looking at that unchanging blue, and soon the memories I conjured up had receded, dispersed.

In the end, what did it really matter? Good people like my aunt died, and bad people too, and it didn't really make any difference. One did the best one could, one played the verbal detective following the trail of words, the clues, to wherever they led ... which inevitably was back to the sand and the ocean and this unchanging blue. It was a mystery that couldn't be cracked (Stephen Hawking notwithstanding). Many great minds have lamented this, but really, it was more of a circumstance to take comfort in. Might as well make the most of it for as long as one can.

What other choice was there?

Chapter Twenty-one

Okay, Now I'm Really Ending It. Really.

Rᴇᴠɪᴇᴡꜱ ᴏꜰ ᴛʜᴇ ꜱʜᴏᴡ didn't come out until a week after the opening. (Morning-after assessments in Atlanta were reserved for mainstage shows at the Alliance (the city's largest regional theater) and touring companies of Broadway shows.) But I had already received some telling critiques from people associated with 7 Stages at the after-play party and even on the morning of my departure. (Apparently my juiced-up state wasn't sufficient to act as any deterrent.)

"It's good, but I would have directed it differently," said Emily, the young woman whose father's fortunes sank with the demise of Tammy Faye Bakker and the PTL.

Philip B., a playwright whose drama was next up for 7 Stages (and who was currently installed at Hartsfield Manor), was somewhat less cryptic. "We need to see Yankel stuffing food in his mouth, drinking gallons of booze, living high on the hog—in general, enjoying the worldly life that money from the brothel has allowed him to have. We need to see more of the upside of his ill-gotten gains, not just hear about this, before his terrible fall."

Bingo. The production lacked texture and forcefulness, just as I'd thought. Thanks, Philip, for confirming my worst fears. Leave it to another writer to know just what to say.

(Just a quick note here. After more than three decades of receiving critiques from other writers—and of dispensing more than my share—I caution everyone who's ever put pen to paper to beware of these comments: "Nice writing" or "There was some good writing in it" or "There's some pretty strong stuff in there." These gems of wisdom often masquerade as encouragement, trying to pass themselves off as "positive reinforcement" of some kind or another. Bullshit. They are condescending comments meant

195

to wound by implying problems without being specific about them. Much better to have someone tell you what they're really thinking, to be entirely candid and up-front. On the other hand, if you ever hear me use any of those phrases, then I'm being absolutely sincere.)

The reviews were faxed to my parents' apartment—where I was staying while in the glittering city—on the day before my return to LA. Like most reviews, they both hit the nail on the head and missed it by a country mile.

My old friend Dan Hulbert—he of the Elton John infatuation—wrote in Atlanta's daily paper that Joe's production was "tentative." "Judging by Stephen Fife's adaptation, it's not a strong script even by melodramatic standards," he asserted. (Ouch.) But he loved Corky's set and Frank's acting, and he probably would have loved Andy Suggs' flyer too if he'd reviewed that. He did admit that "Act I is often effective, especially in its gathering sense of foreboding." And I had to agree with him when he lamented that the tension "diffused" and that "Yankel seemed resigned to his fate [before the ending]." But then he lost me in his sentence's hind parts: "As if the playwright himself became bored before reaching his long-telegraphed climax." Yeah, right. That's why the play has lasted a hundred years. Brilliant.

The critic for *The Atlanta Press*, that city's alternative weekly, was far kinder. (Her name was Rebecca, and I imagined her secretly being one of the "Three Rebeccas" who had dropped in on our rehearsals.) "While opening the doors of the 7 Stages Theater," she wrote, "you must also open your mind." (Love this gal.) She used words like "dynamic," "entertaining," and "thought-provoking," though she had problems with the male characters, whom she found "abusive" and "crude." (Hey, honey, it's a whorehouse,

Miriam Chaikin

Joe and me in downtown NYC, our "Vengeance" behind us.

196

okay?) "You have to ponder deep into the core of this play to find its message," she concluded. What really delighted me, though, was that she singled out the staging of the seduction scene, calling it "so strikingly-innocent that we begin to understand Rivkele's search for herself in the abusive environment created by ... "Papa.'"

There were a few other reviews, all very mixed, most expressing dissatisfaction with Joe's direction. (One thing all agreed upon: they loved Corky's set and made little or no mention of Chip's violin-playing. In fact, Hulbert even complained that there wasn't "more incidental music." What happened, had he slept through the show?)

Ultimately, though, the reviews were beside the point for me. I mean, I had hoped they were good for Joe's sake and for the sake of the actors, and for publicity purposes for everyone involved in the run of the show, but they certainly weren't going to affect me one way or another. Of course, it's nice to have people say nice things about you, so you can show them to Mom or Aunt Bessie or maybe some person you're trying to sleep with. But unless it appears in *Variety* or a New York-based publication—preferably the Friday edition of the *Times*—then it ain't gonna make a whit of difference to your career. And, honey, it's a rare day on this earth when you *learn* something from a theater critic.

(Okay, that's not entirely fair. I studied with Harold Clurman, perhaps the greatest American critic of all, from whom I learned quite a lot. Harold always complained that, with a few exceptions—like the much-loathed John Simon—there were no critics anymore, only consumer advocates who told the reader "thumbs up" or "thumbs down." And that was in *1979*. No, the sad truth is that most reviewers are knowledgeable folk, passionate about the art form, who are as stifled in their development as most playwrights are, victims of the same numbers crunch. ("Don't give me ideas, just tell me if I should plunk down $100 for a babysitter, $30 for parking, $80 for dinner, and $150 for tickets, so the wife and I can go hear some English couple talk about why they want to split up.") Yet even so, I didn't feel much fellowship with their plight. I mean, at least reviewers get paid, while most playwrights I knew were out on the street with a dog and a tin cup.)

No, I had formed my own opinions about what had taken place in Atlanta, and that's all that really mattered to me. In the end, I think it was as simple as *God of Vengeance* not being a "Joe" type of show.

Asch's play was a melodrama (as Hulbert, master of the obvious, took

197

great pains to point out) with a metaphysical twist, and it demanded a ferocious energy and sense of urgency to make it work. That was its strength, the source of its potentially-mesmerizing power, the reason why it was still being performed after so many heartwarming, sensitive, and uplifting Yiddish plays had fallen by the wayside. (Only *The Dybbuk* and *The Golem* could match it for staying power, and both of those were based on folk tales; Asch created his own myth.)

To put it crudely, this play was like an old-fashioned stud in a live sex show: it came out from the wings, displayed a huge hard-on, and proceeded to use it. Subtle it wasn't. The payoff was in the rhythm, the relentless forward momentum, which was ancient and tribal and (hopefully) hard to resist.

Joe, on the other hand, was one of the most sensitive artists ever to grace the American Theater. His specialty was in creating indelibly poetic moments onstage, full of feeling and nuance, and then stringing these together to create a strong emotional impression, a very personal and irreducible collage. Of course, I'd seen another side of Joe (or so I thought) at that rehearsal for his Winter Project—coarser perhaps, more slyly joking and sexual—who might have treated the play with more brashness, more daring. But that other Joe was long gone. He might have disappeared by now in any case, even without the aphasia, if indeed he had ever existed.

When I got back to LA, I ran into an old friend and associate of Joe's, who described his essential impulse for making theater as "anti-dramatic, or at least anti-narrative . . . Joe is all about capturing the floating moment." Well, there weren't many floating moments in Asch's play. It was narrative with a vengeance—excuse the pun—and it had to be done pedal-to-the-metal to have any chance of working at all.

No, the amazing thing really was that the show hadn't been a total disaster. And it hadn't. (Even Hulbert reluctantly agreed.) But even if it had, I would still have treasured the opportunity to work with a man such as Joe. It may sound sappy, but it just does a body good to be around a true artist like that, a person of such inner strength and spiritual resilience.

And then there was the matter of my having put that wish out into the Universe when I was a kid, a fresh-faced actor, to have the chance someday to work with the great Joseph Chaikin.

Well, my wish had finally been granted.

End of story.

Coda

Every Ending Is a New Beginning (or So They Say in LA)

WELL, MAYBE NOT THE end. Not quite yet.

On a balmy December evening in Santa Monica, six weeks after Opening Night, I found myself at another party with Joe ... except this time I was hosting it, along with my life partner, Holly.

Among the actors, writers, artists, and friends who crammed into our informal digs near the ocean were Jean-Claude Van Itallie, Joyce Aaron, and Tina Shepherd—all original members of Joe's Open Theatre, and all here in LA for the workshop production of *Still Alive—Teasing Time*, their collaboration-in-progress about growing older, which was a part of that year's Mark Taper Forum New Works Festival.

Also present was another guest, a mystery guest, unseen by everyone, but very much on my mind, at the top of my list.

I was eager to give Joe the lowdown, but didn't have a chance until some hours into the party, when we finally had a few moments to talk.

"So Joe," I said, conscious of a broad smile rising to my lips. "Gonna have a baby."

"Yes?" Joe said, caught off-guard.

"Yep. How about them apples?"

We both glanced over at Holly, who was talking animatedly with a group of friends, though without her usual glass of red wine. She was forty-two years old, and it was early in the pregnancy yet, but ... I had a strong feeling that this was going to happen. (And no, none of the psychics or astrologers had predicted it.) A bigger question was: was it a good idea?

To which I could only answer, along with the Scribe from Asch's play, "Who can tell?"

It certainly didn't make much logical sense, but then neither did anything else these days. I could only hope that—persisting in my folly, as I was—it would indeed end up making me wise. Or, failing that, happy.

We'll see.

Fringe Benefits

Joseph Chaikin (1935-2003)

Joe Chaikin died while this book was in its final edit. I hadn't seen him since late 2001, when I'd attended a workshop performance at New York's Public Theater of a new piece he was working on about disabilities. Joe looked back at me quizzically then; he seemed to have trouble placing me. I tried to broach the subject of this book, but he just shrugged, smiled, walked away. I resolved to surprise him with a published copy. Instead he surprised me.

The following tributes all appeared in the *Village Voice* shortly after Joe's death. They were gathered and edited by Michael Feingold, the *Voice's* lead theater critic. Some appear here in abbreviated form, solely for reasons of space.

Michael Feingold

Joe Chaikin was for four decades as significant a figure as the American theater has yet produced. Actor, director, writer, and founder of the Open Theatre, he influenced the lives of innumerable artists worldwide. Plagued his whole life by chronic heart disease, in 1984 he suffered an aphasic stroke from which he recovered sufficiently to direct, write, and even perform for two decades more. Joe once said that, since he had not been expected to survive past puberty, he considered every further day of his life a miracle. *Michael Feingold is a playwright, dramaturg, and theater critic.*

Edward Albee

When you've known and admired someone for over forty years they develop a kind of permanence and it shocks you when they cease. Losing Jack Gelber and Joe Chaikin within a month of each other was a double whammy, but this piece is about Joe, gentle, soft-spoken, eagle-minded Joe.

A sequence of memories crowds in: Joe in Jack Gelber's *The Connection*; Joe working with Jean-Claude van Itallie to make a new idea of theater; Joe alone in a chair in a spotlight on the stage of the Royal Court Theatre in London, reading Beckett; Joe in Alaska—just last year—performing Sam Shepard before an audience of eager young playwrights who, after, crowded him to pull from his presence nourishment, knowing they would get it; these and much more. Thank you, Joe.

Anders Cato

In his work as well as in his life, he embraced dark and difficult questions. Often Joe would cut through any kind of small talk when meeting people, and immediately ask them, "What do you believe?" The big questions were not asked to make people nervous or challenge them, but rather part of his own ongoing search for the joy and wonder of being alive. Once when we were on an airplane, crossing the Atlantic, Joe was listening to music on his Walkman. He handed me one of his little Post-it notes on which he had written, "Mozart 90% percent happy."

On several occasions during the last couple of years, Joe told me in his simple and beautiful way, "No need living longer." I remember asking him if there wasn't a part of him that was still afraid of dying. Joe responded with his particular, light tone of voice, his face completely open, "No."

Anders Cato is a director who served as Joe Chaikin's assistant and co-directed Arthur Miller's All My Sons.

Jean-Claude van Itallie

When I met Joe at the Open Theatre loft on 24th Street in 1963, he looked like an attractive curly-haired kid with startling blue eyes. Listening to him drop philosophical "pebbles," as he called them, as if into a pond around which we, young theater people, sit, Joe seems like a mildly spoken guerrilla fighter, using theater to unmask the lies with which we've grown up in the 1940s and 1950s. Perhaps because Joe started creating theater games when he was ten, incarcerated in a cardiac home for children who might die any day, death was always present for him, and making theater was life itself. In the Open Theatre industrial loft, with its peeling dark blue plaster walls, I'm struck by the intense quality of everyone's attention as Joe talks about feelings taboo to express publicly—grieving, joy, and fear. No one here is paid; everyone chips in to pay the rent. We're all alarmed by the escalating Vietnam War. Joe plans improvisational exercises to show how the facade painted for us by our parents, by politicians and advertisers, is so different from what we feel. Curiously, as we listen to Joe talk, everyone's ego seems to have dropped. Because of this the room feels lighter. After the workshop I feel exhilarated and inspired. I want to show my plays *War* and *Motel* to Joe, and to talk with him about Artaud and Gordon Craig. I say excitedly, "Your work is wonderful but how do you make your acting exercises into plays?" Joe's sweet face lights up, "I've been waiting for someone to come along and ask me that question." Our collaboration, our deep friendship, has begun. It will last forty years.

Jean-Claude van Itallie is a playwright who was among the original members of the Open Theatre.

Tina Shepard

The thing was, working with Joe, it was always an adventure: If you thought you knew where you were headed, you were wrong. We worked from our imaginations, our impulses. Joe was interested in devising a means for getting at those impulses before they were tamed. We were working toward what we *didn't* already know. The work we made was held together by the tension between the demands of theatrical presentation on the one hand and the wildness, the lawlessness of the human spirit on the other.

Tina Shepard is an actress who was in the original company of the Open Theatre.

Susan Yankowitz

When Joe talked about the stroke that left him aphasic, he said, "I couldn't say anything, only the word *yes*, I couldn't say *no*, only *yes yes yes*." That *yes* wasn't calculated, it was a spontaneous reflex of his spirit, the same affirmation of possibility—*possibility* was an important word in Joe's lexicon—that gave birth to the Open Theatre; that anatomized death (in *Terminal*) so all of us would pay attention to the ordinary act of our breathing, which reminds us that we are alive; and that later enabled him, after much anguish, to accept the limits on his speech and reinvent himself as he had reinvented the theater. In the last years of his life, he wanted more "comic," he said, and what I will remember best, I think, is his chuckle when he found it.

Susan Yankowitz is a playwright who wrote the performance piece Terminal *for the Open Theatre.*

Joyce Aaron

I last worked with Joe in October 2002, in the revival of Beckett's *Happy Days* at the Cherry Lane Theater. I felt enormously privileged to work on this play with him: He loved Beckett and had wanted to direct *Happy Days* for many years. He was a master at plumbing the depths of the text, all its details, its humor, and its rhythms. He never stopped exploring. He never stopped giving notes—at the last performance I received notes from him. His devotion to the material, to the work, to the actor, was relentless. I will miss his presence, his eye, his enormous talent.

Joyce Aaron is an actress who was in the original company of the Open Theatre

Paul Zimet

At the end Joe's failing heart made each breath a great labor, and then his breathing stopped. The breath was always key to Joe's work as an actor and director. The breath was a more powerful tool than psychological analysis for discovering "the parts of yourself which have not lived yet." He told us to play each moment on stage as if it were the only chance we would get. Don't assume the present breath will be followed by countless more. This was not an abstract thought for Joe. It shaped the intensity of his work and the work of those who were fortunate enough to collaborate with him. It determined his aesthetic: Pare an event down to its essential emblem—an image, a phrase, a gesture. It governed the choices he made: Only work on what is important to you. Yet for someone so influenced by thoughts of mortality, Joe's theatrical work was anything but grim. He knew the darker the subject, the more important it was to find the humor in it. When we found it, he would break out in an infectious smile, an irresistible giggle. In 1996, when we were rehearsing the revival of the Open Theatre's *Terminal*, a piece about death and dying, Joe was afraid we were getting too gloomy. To make his point—with the eloquent brevity of his aphasia—he said, "Sarah Bernhardt. Slept in a coffin. Too much."

Paul Zimet of the Talking Band was in the original company of the Open Theatre.

Arthur Miller

Joe inspired those who could quiet their souls long enough to listen to him, or more accurately, observe him. He seemed to bear happiness into his art and world, irony and laughter and respect for living things and ideas. Long ago, he composed a scene around a Thanksgiving dinner in which eight or ten actors "talked" by simply vocalizing sounds and gesturing and using their faces to convey attitudes and character while uttering a nonsensical no-language. It was hilarious and conveyed a crippled poetry that backed one into a corner where the view of humanity was devastating—suddenly we were all fools and simultaneously gallant enough to go on struggling to climb out of our fatuousness and ignorance and vanity; and it somehow ended up in some kind of tragic space. Joe, I suppose, lived so close to death that it was for him simply the part of life one had to give the nod to and fend off at the same time. And it all came down to a kind of artistic decency, for he was a servant of truth, which is not at all as easy as it sounds.

Sam Shepard

I died the day I was born
and became an angel on that day
since then
there are no days
there is no time
I am here by mistake

These were Joe's own words and became the opening lines of *The War in Heaven* back in 1984 when we sat down to work in his New York apartment. He was recovering from a stroke suffered during his third open-heart surgery, which had left him with a kind of left-hemisphere aphasia (a fancy term for the loss of language). This was a devastating setback for Joe, whose language was such a profound aspect of his work. As always, Joe responded to this terrible dilemma with a bright, energetic courage, as though life had again presented him with a rare and mysterious challenge ... I was in the presence of an extraordinary man, reinventing himself on the brink of disaster, and realized that this had always been the case with Joe and his work. His whole life had been in the constant company of death, and this reminder of his own mortality informed everything he did in the theater and in life. It characterized the atmosphere surrounding the early Open Theatre days on Spring Street. It was the sign by which we all recognized him as a true teacher and seer into the terrible predicament of our modern era. And it was, finally, the root of his inspiration, which he transferred to us with such amazing generosity and sweetness. Joe liked to quote from Brecht in his early workshops. One line I remember in particular was, "You can make a fresh start with your final breath," and I believe this is truly the way he lived and died.

The Boomerang and the Jewish Dentist

by Stephen Fife

At the beginning of this century, the controversial Jewish playwright and novelist Sholem Asch wrote derisively of "The Jewish Play," which for him was "a play where Jews are specially characterized for the Gentiles." He went on to proclaim, "Jews do not need to clear themselves before anyone. They are as good and bad as any race."

At the close of the century, it has become clear that, in large part, The Jewish Play has become The American Play. From Clifford Odets, Paddy Chayevksy, Arthur Miller, Neil Simon, and Woody Allen to Wasserstein, Mamet, Alfred Uhry, and even Tony Kushner—these writers are no longer defined by their outsider status, they are part of the American mainstream. They don't need to "clear themselves before anyone" because their sensibilities have helped define what it means to be American. In fact, throw in Jules Feiffer, Philip Roth, Mel Brooks, Saul Bellow, and Jerry Seinfeld, and you have covered a large swath of contemporary American culture, high and low.

So, in America, the Jew has finally *become* the Gentile. Right? And in that case, is the fact of a writer's Jewishness even relevant anymore?

"Very much so," was the answer recently given by Ellen Schiff, a noted scholar and anthologist of Jewish plays, as she addressed a Jewish Theater conference in Atlanta.

"We are, I believe, seeing a phenomenon which Isaiah Berlin called 'the boomerang effect,'" Ms. Schiff stated. "This is the way in which ideas belonging to one culture are absorbed by a second culture, where they become transformed and vitalized, and then they're reclaimed by the original culture, which shapes these reinvigorated ideas to their own measure."

Toward this end, Ms. Schiff hailed the way that Jewish artists were now "extracting Jewish elements from the melting pot," where they had become "homogenized and dejudiaized," in order to make art that—"while intended for the broad, postmodern theater audience"—was also explicitly Jewish. By this, Ms. Schiff said, she meant that the plays "demonstrate ... a fierce commitment to traditional Jewish values and to the society where these ideals can operate."

She went on to divide these "boomerang" works into two categories: "Diasporism" and "Neo-Shtetelism" (the terms come from a 1995 J. Hoberman *Village Voice* essay). Plays of the first type examine the ethical dilemmas of Jews in the modern world; Uhry's *Last Night at Ballyhoo* and Jon Robin Baitz's *Mizlansky / Zilinsky* were cited as examples. Plays in the second category return to the European ghetto (or *shtetl*), in order to re-examine those values; her examples included Kushner's version of Ansky's *The Dybbuk* and my own adaptation of Sholem Asch's *God of Vengeance*.

I was, in fact, in attendance here because of my adaptation. It had been co-produced a few months earlier by the Jewish Theatre of the South, who was hosting this conference of the Association for Jewish Theater, an organization of sixty or so theaters in the US and Canada that operated out of JCCs (Jewish Community Centers). But this production of *God of Vengeance*—which was directed by Joseph Chaikin, of the Open Theatre—almost hadn't happened.

A week before the show was to open, I was told by a high-ranking theater official that "There is tremendous anger among a core group of the Orthodox and Conservative community to any involvement in this play, because it is bad for the Jews." The official went on to express fear of a backlash from "prominent business leaders," whose support their theater counted on. As proof, she showed me a letter from "a prominent dentist," who denounced the play as "an attack on Jewish businessmen" ("I'm tired of plays that trash them," he wrote) and lambasted the JCC for its "involvement in this project." In the end, the theater had had to bring in a highly-respected Jewish leader (who was also a Holocaust survivor) to see a rehearsal. This man gave the play his thumbs up. The show completed its run without incident.

I must confess to some slight disappointment at this outcome. Asch's play depicts a Polish-Jewish brothelkeeper's search for salvation, as he raises his daughter "purely" upstairs, while running a brothel in his basement. It is a lower-depths tragedy that criticizes religious hypocrisy and dares to place a lesbian love scene downstage center. But it is also a ninety-five-year-old classic which has been a part of the European repertory since 1907 and has been widely anthologized as one of the "three great Jewish plays" (along with

The Dybbuk and *The Golem*). Could it really still be seen as so threatening, as "bad for the Jews"?

I have to admit that these thoughts kept coming back to me during Ellen Schiff's discourse. While she spoke fervently of the "reclamation of Jewish source material," I couldn't help thinking about that Jewish dentist. He admitted in his letter that he hadn't actually read or seen the play. He should have been dismissed as a crank; but he wasn't. His letter—probably the only written protest the theater received—became the basis for controversy. What if the local religious authority had turned thumbs down? Would the show have simply been cancelled?

It's comforting to think that elements of the community—artists, liberal Jews, defenders of Freedom of Speech—would have rallied to the play's defense, as they did, say, to Terence McNally's *Corpus Christi* in New York, or as happened regionally with Christopher Durang's *Sister Mary Ignatius* and Kushner's *Angels in America*. I would like to believe that would have happened.

Then again, once the question of "Is it good or bad for the Jews?" is introduced, it tends to have a freezing effect on open discussion. It is, of course, a public relations, not an ethical, question. It is the kind of question that immigrant groups ask, but which most Americans never do. But perhaps it is just the "boomerang effect" in action.

Ellen Schiff concluded by saying, "The future of American Jewish theater appears enormously promising." Could be. But only if the theaters and their subscribers demonstrate the same courage that is being asked of the writers.

God of Vengeance

by Sholem Asch
Adapted by Stephen Fife

TIME: Early 20th Century. (March-May, 1905).

PLACE: A large provincial town in Poland, not far from Warsaw. The action unfolds in the home of Yankel Chapchovich, which consists of two levels: the upstairs living quarters of Yankel and his family, and the downstairs brothel.

CHARACTERS

YANKEL CHAPCHOVICH—proprietor of a brothel, a man of some power and influence in the town.

SORE (pron. Sor-ra)—Yankel's wife, a former prostitute.

RIVKELE—Their daughter, around 17.

HINDL—A prostitute, around 30; the years have taken a toll.

MANKE—A prostitute, around 20; she becomes Rivkele's lover.

BASHA—A prostitute, 18, newly-arrived from the country.

REYZL—A prostitute, 19. She also has an occasional life upstairs, as a helper for Sore.

SHLOYME—A pimp, early 20s. Works for Yankel, but wants to set up his own house.

REB ELYE—A "*macher*" or middleman who hangs around the local synagogue; obtains the Torah Scroll for Yankel and serves as a matchmaker for Rivkele.

REB ARON / FATHER—The scribe who has copied the Torah Scroll, he is the only true moral authority in the play. This role can be double-cast with the bridegroom's father.

A NOTE ON INTERMISSION: This play was written to have two intermissions. For today's audience, one intermission is best. Ideally, this should come in the middle of Act II, after Yankel's exit. This will only work with a unit set. If a set change is needed, then intermission can be taken after Act I. But the Act will only be twenty-five minutes long.

Script History: This play was commissioned by the Jewish Repertory Theater (NYC) in 1992. It was produced by the Jewish Rep in the fall of 1992 at Playhouse 91 (in association with the 92nd St. Y). It has subsequently been revived by 7 Stages in Atlanta, as well as by various academic and community theaters. I would like to acknowledge the important contribution of Nina Warnke, the Yiddish consultant on this project.

ACT I

(March, 1905. Yankel's home on the first floor of an old wooden house, located above a brothel in the cellar.

(Lights come up on the main room, a large space with a low ceiling. The street entrance is at the rear (Upstage). The room looks very public, decorated more to impress others than to express any personal preferences of Yankel or Sore.

(It is afternoon and company is expected. SORE and RIVKELE are cleaning the room, putting more decorations around and laying out food on a wooden table. SORE is a confident woman, attractive, SHE moves with the air of someone whose authority on domestic matters is rarely questioned; the finery and jewelry she's wearing are a little too gaudy, the wig customary for an Orthodox Jewish woman can't completely conceal her own coquettish tresses. RIVKELE is in her late teens, though SHE's been made to look younger. Her hair is in braids, and her short dress would be appropriate for a girl of 13. SHE pins a handmade Jewish star to the window curtain)

Rivkele: There Mama. How do you like it?

SORE: (not looking; arranging the food on the table): Very nice, dear.

RIVKELE: Mama—look!

SORE: Please, Rivkele—hurry! The guests will be here soon.

(RIVKELE pins another Star on the second window curtain):

RIVKELE: What fun this will be! How many people are coming, Mamale?

SORE: That depends on your father.

RIVKELE: There will be music and singing, won't there?

SORE: Yes, dear. It's a dedication ceremony, a great celebration. Believe me, not everyone can afford to have their own Torah Scroll copied. Only the best people can do it.

RIVKELE: And will there be girls coming too? Will there be dancing? Really, Mama?

(SHE claps her hands in joy and hugs SORE)

SORE: Rivkele, please. The people will be arriving soon.

RIVKELE: (suddenly concerned about her clothes): I must buy a blouse, Mama. And a pair of white slippers. How am I going to look, dancing in high-button shoes?

SORE: You'll look like what you are, a lovely young girl.

RIVKELE: But Mama!

SORE: When—God willing—you become a bride over the Holidays, then you'll get your long dress and your shoes. Girls will come here, fine upstanding girls, and you'll be just like them.

RIVKELE: You're always putting things off 'til the Holidays. I'm grown up now.
        (SHE stands before a mirror admiring herself)
Don't you think I'm grown up, Mama? Look at how long my braids are. Manke told me that—And Manke will be there too, right Mama?

SORE: No, my sweet. Only good girls.

RIVKELE: Why not Manke? She drew these stars, and she did another one for the Torah Scroll cover—oh Mama, it will be so pretty! I'm embroidering it with silk thread and—

SORE: Whatever you do, Rivkele, don't tell your father about it.

RIVKELE: But it's for the Torah Scroll, Mama.

SORE: Just don't bring up Manke at all.

RIVKELE: But Mama!

        (Offstage noises are heard from the street)

SORE: Hush now. Your father is coming.

        (SORE looks over the serving table, then opens the door:
        YANKEL hurries in, muttering aloud)

YANKEL: Who do they think they are? They think I'll go down on my knees to them? Who cares? Who needs them? (pause) Yankel begs nobody.

        (YANKEL slams the door shut. He is a formidable man, not the kind of person anyone would want as an enemy. Yet there is an appealing frankness about him.)

SORE: Nobody's coming?

YANKEL: Who needs them?

SORE: But Yankel—

RIVKELE: Papa—

YANKEL: Don't worry, we'll have people here when the time comes.

SORE: Who?

YANKEL: Don't worry about it.

SORE: Nobody's coming. I thought so.

YANKEL: You'll have plenty of customers for whatever's left over, don't worry. There are lots of empty stomachs around, they don't care where the food comes from.

        (He sits, calls softly to RIVKELE)
Come here, my beauty. Come here.

        (RIVKELE doesn't move)

SORE (serving the food, very angry, banging around):   You'd think they were dragging their names in the mud just to show up here! But when they need a hundred

211

on credit, or contributions to charity ... Oh, our house may be tainted, but our money is kosher.

YANKEL: What are you getting worked up for? Reb Elye and the Scribe will be here soon! You want them to see you like this? (To RIVKELE) Your Papa loves you, Rivkele. Come here.

(Pause: RIVKELE approaches slowly, warily)

RIVKELE: What is it, Papa?

YANKEL: What are you so afraid of? I'm not going to hurt you.

(YANKEL reaches out with his hand. RIVKELE comes toward HIM)

YANKEL: You love your Papa, don't you?

(RIVKELE: nods)

YANKEL: Then why be so afraid?

RIVKELE: I don't know.

YANKEL: Never be afraid of your Papa. He loves you more than life itself. There is nothing that he wouldn't do ... (Pause) I'm picking up a Torah Scroll today that I ordered for you. Did you know that? It cost a lot of money, a lot, yes! But I pay it gladly for you.

(RIVKELE says nothing)

YANKEL: And, with God's help, when you're a bride, I'll buy your husband a gold watch and chain weighing half a pound. What do you think of that? Don't you know that your Papa loves you?

(RIVKELE looks away, embarrassed. YANKEL continues)

YANKEL: What—are you blushing? But it's a good thing to be a bride, Rivkele, everyone should, God decreed it. (Pause) So do you love your Papa?

RIVKELE: Yes.

YANKEL: What would you like me to buy you? Go on, tell me, don't be afraid. If you could have anything in the world, anything ...

(SORE is still busy with food and arranging the table)

SORE (To Rivkele): Your father is talking to you. Why don't you answer?

RIVKELE (To Yankel): I don't know.

SORE: She wants a silk blouse and a pair of white slippers.

YANKEL (To Rivkele): You want a silk blouse and a pair of white slippers?

(RIVKELE nods. YANKEL smiles and hands her a gold coin)

YANKEL: Give this to Mama. She'll buy it for you.

(RIVKELE walks over and gives the gold coin to SORE:)

SORE (To Yankel): Should I leave out the vodka?

YANKEL: Of course. They're people too, aren't they?

SORE: But what if they're insulted?

(Pause)

YANKEL: Alright, take it away.

(SORE takes away the tray with bottle and glasses. YANKEL turns to RIVKELE)

YANKEL: This is a great day for our family. A great day. You won't let me down?

RIVKELE: No Papa.

YANKEL: I know it. (Pause) Let me see you walk across the room.

RIVKELE: But Papa!

YANKEL: Go on.

(Pause. Then RIVKELE takes a few uncertain steps)

YANKEL: No, no! Not so stiffly. And smile.

(RIVKELE tries again, but YANKEL shakes his head)

YANKEL: Sore, you show her.

(SORE walks grandly across to YANKEL and stands beside him.)

YANKEL (To Rivkele):   Alright now. You do it.

(RIVKELE tries again. YANKEL sighs)

YANKEL: Fine, fine. That will have to do.

RIVKELE: Should I try it again?

(YANKEL shakes his head)

RIVKELE: Can I wait in my room then? I'm sewing a star on the Torah Scroll cover.

YANKEL (smiles):   Give your Papa a kiss first.

(RIVKELE kisses him)

YANKEL: You're my good girl.

(RIVKELE exits.

SORE places a tray on the table.)

SORE: It doesn't seem right. There should be music and dancing when the Rebbe arrives.

YANKEL: You expect "decent" people to come? You must have forgotten who we are.

SORE: "Who we are?" Who are you? Are you a robber, a thief? No. You have a business. You don't force it on anyone, do you? Just try giving away some of your money, you'll see how much they take.

YANKEL: Oh, they'll take alright, then they'll toss you right back in the dirt. "Let him stand by the synagogue door, let him come in the door—but no further." (Pause) Do you think they'd ever ask me to bless the reading from Torah?

SORE: Do you really think they're better than you are? This is how the world is today: if you have money, then even a "respectable man" like that Reb Elye will come to see you, he'll do you the very big favor of taking your money. He couldn't care less where it comes from—if you stole it or did something dirty—just as long as you've got it, the cash.

YANKEL: Watch out who you slander, you hear me? Don't try pushing in where you're not wanted, or they'll push you right back, six feet under! (pause) You have a house? Then you stay there. You have food on the table? Then eat. But don't try nosing in where you're not invited. Every dog must know his own ditch.

(HE moves away)

I wish we'd never started this "Torah" business. It will come to no good.

SORE: And you call yourself a man! Even I can say: The past is over, it's gone—fffft! We have nothing to be ashamed of. The rest of the world is no better. (Pause) If you have money, who cares about anything else? Right? Am I right?

(SHE moves closer)

Of course, once we've made enough, we can close up shop, and no one will be any wiser. Who cares about what used to be?

YANKEL: Do you really think so? Oh, if only I could start over, I would buy a stable of horses and go sell them abroad like my father, God rest his soul. And no one would laugh at me there, no one would stare at me like a thief ...

SORE: The only thing, Yankel ...

YANKEL: What?

SORE: I hear that it's hard to turn any profit selling horses ...

YANKEL: We wouldn't need much.

SORE: The overhead, Yankel, the overhead ... Whereas here you have money in hand, you can see it ...

(Pause: SHE works)

And thank God we have a daughter who is as sweet, genteel, well-behaved—I wouldn't trade her for any other girl in this town! You'll see, she'll get married to a respectable man, have respectable children, and not have anything to do with our life ...

YANKEL: Yes, and you'll show her the way, won't you? (Pause) Letting Manke come up from downstairs. Why don't you ask her to eat at our table and sleep with us too?

SORE: Just listen to him! I brought Manke up once to show Rivkele how to embroider. What's wrong with that? Our child's a girl, after all, we have to think about her marriage trousseau. And who else does she have to be friends with? You never let her go out. (Pause) But if it makes you unhappy, then Manke won't come.

YANKEL: Unhappy? Unhappy? From now on, I will not have my home mixed with downstairs. Do you hear me? They must be kept apart, separate, the way kosher food is kept separate from treyf, the way "pure" is kept apart from "polluted." Do you understand? Down there is a brothel, a house, while up here a young virgin lives, who will someday make a pure bride. There must be no mixing, none!

(Footsteps are heard on the outside staircase)

SORE: Shhh! Someone's coming. It must be Reb Elye.

(SHE pushes her stray hairs under her wig and takes off her apron.
YANKEL adjusts his clothing, etc.)

SORE: To think how you were shouting just now! What if he heard?

(The door opens wide and SHLOYME and HINDL enter. They are a couple, the pimp and a whore from downstairs. SHLOYME is insolent, mocking.

214

HINDL is the oldest whore in Yankel's stable. THEY breeze in boldly, making themselves at home.)

YANKEL (To Sore): And you thought we wouldn't have guests! Aren't we lucky? (To Shloyme and Hindl) Downstairs! Everything downstairs! I don't do business up here anymore. Go on, I'll be right down.

SHLOYME: Look how he talks to us, Hindl. My feelings are hurt.

YANKEL: Downstairs I said!

SHLOYME: Can it be that you're really ashamed of us?

YANKEL: Alright, quickly: what's on your mind?

SHLOYME: We heard you were throwing a party. Isn't that so, Hindl?

HINDL: We just stopped by to wish you good luck. (To Sore) We're old friends, right?

SORE: Is that what you'd call it?

YANKEL: All of that's over. You hear? From now on, you want to speak with me—fine, we do it downstairs. Up here, I don't know you.

SHLOYME: So that's how it is?

YANKEL: Yes.

SHLOYME: How about one drink, for old time's sake?

SORE: The liquor has been put away.

SHLOYME: But you can get it out, can't you? (Pause)

YANKEL: Alright, just one drink.

SORE: But they could be here any—

(YANKEL orders her to go off. SORE grimaces, but then goes)

SHLOYME (taking out Hindl's wage book): This whore has a complaint against you. Since she's my fiancee, I'm complaining.

YANKEL: Downstairs I said! Everything downstairs.

SHLOYME: Not until we get some money.

HINDL: I want a new hat.

SHLOYME: That's right. She wants a new hat.

YANKEL: Out of here now.

SORE: The nerve of some people! (To Yankel) It's not worth letting garbage upset you.

SHLOYME (approaching Sore): You can't talk to my wife-to-be like that!

HINDL: If Madame doesn't think I'm a good whore, why don't you go down yourself?

YANKEL: That's enough!

SHLOYME: Or send that daughter of yours down. She would be great for business.

(YANKEL knocks SHLOYME down with a swift blow)

215

YANKEL: You can insult me. And you can insult her. We're in the life. But if you even mention my daughter's name ...

SHLOYME (smiling):   You still pack quite a punch, huh? For an old man ... (HE stands) It seems we're not welcome here, Hindl. (to Yankel) Just give us our money. We'll go.

YANKEL: Downstairs!

(The voice of REB ELYE can be heard on the stairs)

REB ELYE (O.S.): This way, Scribe. He lives right up here. Not much further.

(REB ELYE, a greasy little man, pokes his head in the door)

REB ELYE: What's going on? I heard *shouting*. When a man has a Torah Scroll written, there should be music and dancing. (HE withdraws from the room, O.S.) This way, Scribe. Don't tire yourself.

SORE (seeing the liquor is out, frantic):   Oh my God!

(SHE runs out with bottle and glasses, returns soon)

SORE (to Yankel):   I told you this would happen, didn't I?

(SORE grabs some paper money out of her stocking, slips a few bills to Shloyme, pushing HE and HINDL toward the door, just as REB ELYE and SCRIBE enter and stand in the doorway: THEY regard Shloyme and Hindl, take a step back)

SHLOYME (to Hindl): Isn't Yankel getting up in the world? He'll go into politics soon.

(SHLOYME and HINDL exit smiling, their noses in the air)

REB ELYE: Just come in, Scribe. Come in.

(The SCRIBE is an elderly man with a white beard, his gaze is inner-directed, only vaguely aware of what goes on around him. REB approaches Yankel.)

REB ELYE: Have you no idea of how to behave? (To Scribe) This is the man.

(SCRIBE examines Yankel with a keen gaze; then extends his hand)

SCRIBE: Sholem Aleichem.

YANKEL (shakes the Scribe's hand):   Aleichem Sholem.

(REB ELYE sits down at the table, pushes out a chair for the Scribe)

REB ELYE: Won't you sit down, Scribe? (HE indicates a chair for Yankel) The sooner we can get started ...

(SCRIBE sits, YANKEL stands to the side. REB scans the table, points to kettle)

REB ELYE: What is this?

SORE: Why, it's tea, sir. We made it special.

REB ELYE (looks at tea, shakes his head):   Is this how you celebrate a holy occasion?

(Pause: then SORE runs inside, brings out the vodka, etc. REB ELYE pours glasses for himself, Scribe, and Yankel; turns to SCRIBE)

REB ELYE: Since this man had no son, he wishes to serve God by purchasing his own Torah Scroll. It is a custom, and if he wished to observe it, why then he should be encouraged. Lekhayim, Scribe!   (REB drinks, pours another; to Yankel) Lekhayim, Patron! Today you've performed a great deed! (drinks) Drink up, Scribe. You too, Patron. This is a day for rejoicing. God has chosen to help you.

SCRIBE (holds his glass in his hand; to Reb, looking at Yankel):   What does this man do?

REB ELYE: What difference does it make? He's a man. Not a learned man, but everyone can't be a scholar. (To Yankel) Drink up, rejoice!

SCRIBE: Will he know how to handle a Torah Scroll?

REB ELYE: He's a Jew, isn't he? What Jew doesn't know? (pours himself a third glass) Lekhayim, Lekhayim, may God grant the Jews better times. (HE drinks)

SCRIBE (To Yankel):   Lekhayim, Patron. (Stands and drinks. Looks directly at Yankel) Just remember, the Torah is holy, the entire world rests on it, and every Scroll is exactly like the tablets that were given to Moses the Prophet at Mount Sinai. In the house where there is a Torah Scroll, there God resides. But the Scroll must be protected from every uncleanness, from every—

YANKEL: I am a sinful man, Rebbe! I want to tell you the whole truth! I have to, I must!

REB ELYE (interrupting):   This man wants to repent his past life and should be encouraged. The Talmud says we have to help him. (HE continues, to Yankel) The Torah Scroll must be revered, just as if a great rabbi were there in your house. (HE addresses Sore, *not* looking at her) A woman must never uncover her hair in the presence of the Torah Scroll. She must never go near the Torah Scroll with bare arms.

(SORE pushes some stray hairs under her wig, tugs down her sleeves, etc.)

REB ELYE: If these rules are followed, then no harm will come to your house. Prosperity and good luck will abound, the keepers of a Torah Scroll will be protected from all misfortune.

SCRIBE (To Yankel):   Do you understand? The entire world rests on each Scroll, the very survival of Judaism! With a single word, God forbid, with a single word you could disgrace the Torah Scroll, and a great misfortune, God help us! A great misfortune might fall on all Jews. May heaven preserve us.

YANKEL: I'm not worthy, Rebbe, that you should be here, under my roof. I know you're a holy man, Rebbe, and I am sinful and weak. So is she. We do wrong even to talk about something so holy. But in there, Rebbe— (points to Rivkele's room) In there . . .

(HE goes into the room and leads RIVKELE out. SHE is holding the Torah Scroll cover, a Star of David embroidered in gold.)

YANKEL: She is as pure as the Scroll itself. For her, Rebbe, for her it is proper. I, Rebbe—I won't touch your Torah Scroll. My wife won't touch it. (Points to Rivkele)

Her hands are pure, Rebbe. Look at them: her hands are pure. The Torah Scroll will go in her room. And when she marries—(To Rivkele) Out of my home. Take the sacred Scroll with you to your husband.

REB ELYE (prompting):   That is, you intend to give the Scroll to your daughter's bridegroom as part of the dowry, right?

YANKEL: When my daughter marries, Reb Elye, I'll give her a dowry—it will be a lot of money, a lot! And I'll say to her: forget your father, forget your mother, just have good Jewish children, like a good Jewish daughter should. That's what I'll tell her.

REB ELYE: You see, Reb Aron! And to think how you doubted this man. He has a daughter, so what does he do? He has a Torah Scroll written for her bridegroom. What a fine gesture! It touches me, Reb Aron. It touches me deep down in my Jewish soul. Akh! Akh!

(YANKEL escorts RIVKELE back to her room, closes the door; turns to Scribe)

YANKEL: Rebbe, we are sinful people. I know that God will punish us. Let Him. Let Him take my legs away, let Him cripple me, let Him make me a beggar. Who cares? But not her. (HE lowers his voice) If you have a son and he disgraces himself, then out! Out of the house! Let him drown in his vomit. But a daughter, Rebbe, a daughter. If a daughter should sin ... That's why I went to the synagogue and sought this man out. (Points to Elye) "Get me something to protect my home from sin!" I said. Then he tells me to have a Torah Scroll written. (Pause) We are beyond help, I know it. We have gone too far. But for her, Rebbe. For her.

(Pause: REB ELYE leans over, whispers in Scribe's ear, points to Yankel. There is a pause, the SCRIBE closes his eyes, nodding once. ELYE smiles at Yankel.)

SCRIBE (opening his eyes):   But where are the people to help honor the Torah?

REB ELYE: Just leave that to me. I'll have no trouble finding a minyan for such a happy occasion. (HE rises, fills glasses again. To Yankel)   Cheer up! God helps him who repents. So you'll marry off your daughter to some poor boy at the yeshiva, and you'll support him while he studies the Torah. For that alone, God will forgive you. (Pause) In fact, I've already got my eye on a scholar. He comes from a very good family. You're giving a large dowry, right?

YANKEL: Take the shirt off my back, Reb Elye. Everything. Take everything from me. (HE addresses an imaginary Rivkele and her future husband:)   And as for you, my daughter, don't even think about your father or mother. Here's your food, here's your drink, I'll take care of everything so no one will know. And as for you, my son, just keep studying those holy books. We don't know each other.

REB ELYE: You see, Reb Aron? A Jew, even if he takes the wrong path—he still has a Jewish soul, for his daughter he wants a student! (Aside to Scribe) And believe me, he doesn't come from a bad family. I knew his father, a hardworking man. (To Yankel) Because if you're not one for learning yourself, then you must support those who are, because "Al hatoro ho-o-lom omeyd"—"The world rests on the Torah." So you must give up your old ways and help out the yeshiva.

YANKEL (To Reb Elye): Just let me put away a little more money, just a little more, just for the dowry, alright? Then I swear to God I'll close up the shop. I'll go to the market in Lovitch and deal in horses just like my father did, rest his soul. And when I come home for Sabbath, I'll sit down right here and listen to my son-in-law studying the Talmud. May God strike me dead if I'm lying!

REB ELYE: Of course, of course. God will help. Won't he, Reb Aron?

SCRIBE: Who can tell? Our God is a God of mercy and compassion, but He is also a God of Vengeance. (HE stands up) It's getting late, I have to get back to the synagogue.

(The SCRIBE walks to the door, exits)

YANKEL (To Reb Elye): What did the Rebbe mean?

REB ELYE (shrugging): That's just his way. He's a little old-fashioned. Come and get your Torah Scroll, we'll have a big celebration.

(REB ELYE heads toward the door, but YANKEL hangs back)

REB ELYE: What's the matter? You want to tell the little woman to make something for when we return?

SORE: It's all prepared, Reb Elye. Everything's ready.

REB ELYE: Then what's the problem? The Scribe has gone on ahead.

YANKEL: Me? In the company of the Rebbe? There, on the street?

REB ELYE (nods): If God forgives you, then why can't we? Come along, come along.

YANKEL (very happy): Reb Elye, you're a good man, a very good man.

(YANKEL spontaneously opens his arms to embrace REB ELYE; then stops)

YANKEL: On my life, Reb Elye, I thank you.

(YANKEL shakes REB ELYE's hand. THEY leave together.

It begins to darken outside.

SORE cleans up the table, preparing for her guests. SHE calls O.S. to RIVKELE)

SORE: Rivkele, come here and help! They'll be here with the Torah Scroll soon!

(RIVKELE enters warily from her room, carrying the Torah Scroll cover)

RIVKELE: Is father gone?

SORE: He'll be back soon, and they're bringing some people.

RIVKELE (holds up Torah Scroll cover): I sewed a star on, you see? How do you like it, Mama?

SORE (nods): Comb your hair and get dressed. Our guests will be here soon.

(SORE works busily, not hearing what RIVKELE is saying)

RIVKELE: I'm going to call Manke up to comb my hair. I love it when she does my hair. She combs it so beautifully. Her hands are so cool. (SHE knocks on floorboard, calls) Manke! Manke!

SORE (horrified): Rivkele, stop! You mustn't be friends with Manke anymore. Haven't you heard your father? (Pause) Anyway, you're too old for that now. Nice young men are being proposed for you. Yeshiva students.

RIVKELE: But I love Manke.

SORE: It's not proper. You'll be friends with good girls now. Why, your father just went off to have a look at the young man who will be your husband. Reb Elye said …

(SORE goes off to an adjoining room, keeps speaking to Rivkele from there)

SORE (O.S.): Time to get dressed. The people are coming.

RIVKELE: A husband for me, Mama? What kind of man will he be?

SORE (O.S.): Oh, a student, very gifted I'm sure. From a good family.

(MANKE, a young prostitute, pokes her head in the front door, wags her finger at Rivkele. RIVKELE winks at Manke and moves stealthily towards her, trying to keep from laughing. The room begins to get darker. RIVKELE falls into MANKE's arms.)

RIVKELE (speaks to O.S. Sore): Do you think he is good-looking, Mama?

(MANKE kisses her)

SORE (O.S.): Of course, my sweet. A handsome bridegroom with black sidelocks. He's a rabbi's son, so he'll dress like a rabbi. Reb Elye said.

(RIVKELE is in MANKE's arms, caressing her cheeks)

RIVKELE (To O.S. Sore): Where will he stay, Mama?

SORE (O.S.): Why, in your room, of course. Where the Torah Scroll will be. He'll live there with you and study the holy Torah.

RIVKELE (To O.S. Sore): Will he love me, Mama?

SORE (O.S.): Very much, my child, very much. The two of you will be very happy together, and you'll have good honest children, you'll make us all very proud …

(RIVKELE and MANKE are kissing passionately.
Lights fade slowly to Blackout. End of Act I.)

ACT II

(Downstairs. The brothel in the cellar. It is six weeks after Act I, a rainy spring night in early May.

Wind and rain are blowing in through the curtains of two open windows SL, with flower pots on both window sills. At the rear is a Dutch door, the upper part of which is open, rain blowing in. The space is largely taken up by several cubicles, each separated from the others by thin partitions and each fronted by heavy black curtains. One curtain is drawn, revealing a bed, a washstand, a mirror, vanity table with makeup, etc., a nightlamp with red-tinted gel. The room is lit by a lamp hanging from the ceiling.

Lights come up on SHLOYME asleep on a sofa DSC, snoring, his long legs hanging over the end. Behind one of the closed curtains, MANKE (unseen) is attending to a client. We might hear occasional whispers and moaning, etc.

HINDL enters from the street, pausing briefly to look at SHLOYME. SHE covers her head with a light shawl and is wearing a dress too short for her age. SHE walks around the room, purposely making noise to wake up Shloyme.)

SHLOYME (still groggy): Is that you? You're supposed to be outside.

HINDL: It's raining.

SHLOYME (sits up): So we're on speaking terms again, huh? You're not mad anymore?

HINDL: Who said I ever was?

SHLOYME: So it's like that, is it? Well, stay mad if you want to. Who cares?

(SHLOYME lies back down. HINDL goes to Manke's curtained cubicle, listens)

HINDL (to Shloyme): Tell me, and be honest for once: are you really going to marry me?

SHLOYME: You don't want me, you want a new hat, remember? Isn't that why you told Yankel I was stealing from you?

HINDL: I was hurt. What do you have to run after that red-headed bitch for? I give you the shirt off my back, then you give it to her. How can you stand her? Her breath stinks.

SHLOYME: You're asking for a beating, you know that?

HINDL: Go ahead. Hit me. Tear me apart. I'll get you started.
(SHE rips the sleeve off her dress, throws it down)
You've already made me black and blue. How else can you hurt me?
(SHE rips off her other sleeve)
Go on, if that's what you want. (Pause)
I demand that you tell me right here and now if we're going to be married.
Swear on your dead father, swear on his grave.

SHLOYME (yawning): I wanted to once. But not now. How about bringing me a glass of tea, Hindl?

HINDL: Alright then. That's it. You want my money? Here. You want my coat. Take it. Just don't play games with me.

SHLOYME: Don't worry, you don't look that bad yet. You'll hook some other fish.

(HINDL brings him a glass of tea, sets it down)

SHLOYME: That's a good girl.

HINDL: You'll have to buy yourself a street organ and lead that red-headed bitch around by a leash. You'll make a fine organ grinder, I'm sure. I'll throw you a few pennies myself.

SHLOYME: Shutup!

HINDL: And what if I don't?

SHLOYME: Then you'll have hell to pay.

221

HINDL: Just watch out. Blows can be repaid with knives.

SHLOYME (getting up):   Oh yeah?

(SHLOYME walks over to Hindl's cubicle, sees HER conceal something)

SHLOYME: What's that you're hiding away?

HINDL: None of your business.

SHLOYME: Come on, let me see it.

HINDL: Are you threatening me?

SHLOYME: What if I am?

(SHLOYME and HINDL struggle, HE tears a red blouse from HER)

SHLOYME: Let's see what we've got here.

(HE rips the blouse apart with great satisfaction, a picture falls out)

SHLOYME (looking):   Oho! Moyshele the Locksmith. Since when are you two so cozy?

HINDL: Why should you care?

SHLOYME: I'll show you why.

(HE slaps her around. SHE falls on the bed, crying.)

SHLOYME: So it's you and Moyshele, huh? When is the wedding?

(SHLOYME tears up the photo and tosses the pieces on her. Then HE returns to his table, drinks tea)

SHLOYME: Come here, Hindl. Hindl! Come here!

(HINDL goes to him, covering her face with a handkerchief)

HINDL: What do you want?

SHLOYME (in an undertone):   Did you talk to Manke?

HINDL (still sobbing):   Yes.

SHLOYME: What did she say?

HINDL: She'll come with us, when our "house" is all set.

SHLOYME: Are you sure?

HINDL (wiping tears):   She doesn't want to go by herself, though. She'll bring a friend.

SHLOYME: All the better! You think we could pay the rent with only one whore? Where is she going to find her?

HINDL: I've got my eye on a girl. A real budding flower.

SHLOYME: Can she bring in the money?

HINDL: And how.

SHLOYME: Where'd you find her? A house?

HINDL: Oh no. She's a good girl.

SHLOYME: Really?

HINDL: She comes to Manke every night. No one sees her. She's drawn there.

(RIVKELE knocks on the outside window)

RIVKELE (pokes her head in):   Is Papa here?

HINDL (signals back):   No.

(RIVKELE disappears from the window)

SHLOYME: Her? (HE smiles) A treasure!

HINDL: Shhh. Here she comes.

(RIVKELE enters wrapped in a black shawl. SHE is nervous, on edge)

RIVKELE: Where's Manke? Tell me. (SHE sees that Manke's curtain is closed.) In there? With a ...?

(HINDL nods. RIVKELE listens at the curtain.)

SHLOYME (To Hindl):   Let's take a look at the place on Pivne Street tomorrow. It's good, huh? Right around the corner.

HINDL: When are we getting married?

SHLOYME: First we need a place to stay.

HINDL: No, first we need to get married.

SHLOYME: And then there's furniture too.

HINDL: Not until we get married. Who knows how much the Rabbi will charge for the wedding?

SHLOYME: We need something impressive, not junk like this.

(The door is thrown open: YANKEL enters.
RIVKELE desperately tries to conceal herself in a corner)

YANKEL (shakes rain from his hat):   What a night! Who needs it? (Sees Rivkele) What?

(YANKEL grabs RIVKELE by the collar and shakes her)

YANKEL: Down here?

RIVKELE: (crying):   Papa, don't hit me! Papa!

YANKEL: How could you ...? How could you ...?

RIVKELE: Mama ... Mama sent me ... to—

YANKEL: Mama sent you ... down here? (HE shouts upstairs)
Sore! Sore! (HE drags Rivkele out)
She'll ruin everything yet.

RIVKELE: Papa, don't hit me, please!

(YANKEL drags RIVKELE O.S. HER crying and screams can still be heard after THEY exit)

SHLOYME: Look at this bastard. What else should his daughter be?

(Noise is heard from O.S., above: feet stamping, SORE crying, etc.)

HINDL: A mother should watch over her child. You'll see, with God's help, when we have our children, I'll know how to raise them. My daughter will be as pure as a saint, I'll make sure she gets married—

SHLOYME: We'll see about that. Just keep working on Rivkele now, or else everything's lost.

HINDL: I'll take care of her, you take care of our marriage.

SHLOYME: As soon as you have her, take her over to my place, you know . . .

(YANKEL comes in out of the rain)

YANKEL: We're closing up! This night isn't fit for animals! (calls out) Reyzl! Basha! Come inside! Bedtime!

REYZL (O.S., calling):   Coming!

BASHA (O.S., calling):   Coming!

YANKEL (muttering):   They don't even have enough sense to come out of the rain. (To Shloyme and Hindl) What are you two whispering about? Can't you wait until you get married?

SHLOYME: What business is it of yours?

YANKEL: This is my business. Everything that goes on here. And don't you forget it.

SHLOYME: Go to hell.

YANKEL: Oho! (Makes a fist) So you're asking for it again?

(HINDL pulls SHLOYME away)

HINDL: Go home, Shloyme! You hear me? Go home.

SHLOYME (to Yankel):   You old fool. (HE spits on the ground, turns away)

YANKEL: Go on! Who needs you? And take this old witch with you too. Set up your own shop! You wouldn't last for a week.

HINDL: Not if we had a surprise. A real attraction.

YANKEL: You trying to scare me? Ha. (calling out) Rezyl! Basha! Come on now! (To Hindl and Shloyme) I've looked God in the face without flinching. So stay out of my way.

(YANKEL turns, walks upstairs, exits.

SHLOYME exits to the street.

HINDL goes to her cubicle, shuts curtain.

RECOMMENDED INTERMISSION.)

(HINDL is in her cubicle, the curtain open.

REZYL and BASHA run in, giggling. Their clothes are wet, water drips from their hair.)

BASHA: How the rain smells! (SHE shakes the rain from her hair) Just like the apples at home drying in the attic. It's the first May rain.

HINDL: You're crazy to be out there tonight. What fool is going to walk by in this downpour?

REYZL: Who needs them? I paid up my book yesterday. (giggling) We were standing under the drainpipe. The rain smells so fresh. It washes the whole winter away. (SHE goes to Hindl) Smell how fresh my hair is.

224

BASHA (tying her hair back):   Back home in my village they must be having the first Schav. You know, when the first rain of May comes down, they cook sourgrass soup. And the goats are probably out in the pasture. And the freshly-cut logs are floating downstream. And I'm sure Franek is there, rounding up all the young girls for a dance at the inn. And the women are probably baking cheese buns for Shevuos. (Pause) You know what? I'm going to buy myself a new summer dress and go home for a visit.

>   (SHE dashes into her cubicle, puts on a new summer hat with a long veil;
>   emerges)

What if I were to show up in this hat on Shevuos and take a long walk down to the railroad? Oh, I can see their faces now. Turning so many colors with envy. (SHE smiles. Pause) I would do it too, but I'm afraid of my father.

REYZL: Why, what would he do?

BASHA: He'd kill me right there. In a moment.

REYZL: Come on.

BASHA: He's looking for me all over with an iron bar. Once he found me dancing with Franek, and he hit me so hard—(SHE displays her arm) I have a scar to this day. (Pause) I'm from a good family, you know. My father's a butcher. Oh, the matches I could have made! (Pause) Once they wanted me to marry Notke the meat cleaver. I still have the gold ring he gave me. (SHE displays the ring) Oh, he wanted me badly, you could see it in his eyes, but I didn't want to.

REYZL: Why not?

BASHA: He smelled of blood. He stank from it. Brrr. They called him "Beef Breath." How could I marry "Beef Breath" and every year have another little "Beef Breath." Brrr.

REYZL: And what's so good here?

BASHA: Here I'm free. I've got my basket of pretty linens. I have much better clothes, let me tell you, than the wife of our local merchant. (SHE goes to her cubicle, holds up a dress) If I walked down Marshalkovska Street wearing this, boy, would their eyes pop! They would burst a blood vessel! Yeah. I'd take a casual stroll down to the railroad.

>   (SHE slips on the dress and walks around, playing this out)

I can see it all now. They'd have a stroke on the spot. Oh, if only I could!

>   (REYZL straightens the folds in Basha's dress, adjusts her hat)

REYZL: Don't lower your head, raise it up. No one has to know you were in a house. Just say you're in business. Or a rich man adores you.

HINDL (from her cubicle):   And what's so bad about a house? How are we any different from other girls who go into business? That's how the world is today. Even respectable girls are no better. But if one of us marries, well then! We're more faithful than they ever could be. We know how men are.

BASHA (continues to strut back and forth): How I wish that were true! But they know. They know in their hearts. That's why my mother died. She couldn't bear it. I've never even been to her grave. (SHE stops strutting suddenly) I see her at night, in my dreams. She comes in her white shroud, covered with thorns and briars, and she tears at my hair.

REYZL: Dear God! You mean you actually saw her? What is her face like?

HINDL: Shutup! Talking about dead souls at night! The dead can't get in here, didn't you know? Our boss has a Torah Scroll upstairs. (Pause) So what if his wife was in a house for fifteen years? When she got married, didn't she make him a good wife? Didn't she give him a good, decent daughter? And isn't our Yankel a good man? He makes the largest contributions to charity. And he paid for his own Torah Scroll.

REYZL: They say men like him aren't supposed to have something holy.

HINDL: Who says so?

REYZL: My old granny told me. She was a witch.

HINDL: Where is she, the gypsy? I'll scratch her eyes out. God's still in heaven. We have a great God who loves us.

(MANKE emerges from her curtained cubicle, wearing red stockings, half-dressed in night clothes, a light shawl around her)

MANKE: Why is everyone sitting around?

REYZL: Am I glad you're here. She's trying to put the fear of God in us. (Pause) Where's your fool?

MANKE: He's asleep.

REYZL: So does he have money? Is he good for a few rounds?

MANKE: He's a meshuggeneh Litwak. Keeps coming back to me, asking me questions. Who's your father? Who's your mother? Where do you come from? You'd think he wanted to make me his wife! (SHE laughs) When he kisses me, he hides his face in my breast and closes his eyes, like a baby sucking on his mother's nipple. (To Hindl) Has Rivkele been here?

HINDL: I'll say! And so was her father.

MANKE: When?

HINDL: A while ago. He's probably asleep by now. (Pause) I'm sure she'll be back.

REYZL (To Manke): Let's go outside. Come on. It's the first May rain. Who wants to come out with me in the rain?

MANKE (goes to the window): My God, how sweet it smells! Let's go.

BASHA: When it rains like this back home, the drains overflow and flood the narrow streets, we take off our shoes and socks and dance in the rain. Who wants to dance around barefoot? (SHE flings off her shoes and stockings) Come on, Manke, do it. Let's dance around in the rain.

(MANKE takes off her shoes and stockings, loosens her hair)

MANKE: The rain will soak us from head to toe. You grow taller if you stand in the rain in May, don't you?

BASHA (runs over): Come on, let's pour water over each other, handfuls and handfuls of water! (SHE loosens her hair) We'll wash our hair as the trees do. Come on.

HINDL: Wait a minute. Yankel may not be asleep. What if he hears you?

(Pause: ALL listen towards the ceiling)

REYZL: Let's go. I'm sure he's out cold.

MANKE: I want to let Rivkele know.

(BASHA and REYZL exit O.S. MANKE picks up a stick and taps lightly on a corner of the ceiling. We can hear the GIRLS splashing around outside, laughing)

BASHA and REYZL (O.S.):   Come out! Come on out!

(RIVKELE pokes her head in through the same window as before. SHE is wearing night clothes, wrapped in a shawl, as before)

RIVKELE: Manke? Was that you? Did you call me?

(MANKE puts a chair under the window, steps up, takes Rivkele's hands)

MANKE: Come, Rivkele. Let's stand under the May rain and pour water over each other. We'll grow taller.

RIVKELE: Shhh. What if he heard us?

MANKE: My little Rivkele, don't be afraid of your father. He won't get up so soon.

(SHE undoes Rivkele's braids)
There, now I'll wash it for you in the rain.

RIVKELE: I'm only wearing a nightgown. (pause) I've been lying in bed all night, waiting to sneak out. I stole out so quietly, barefoot, I don't think he heard me.

MANKE: The night is so sweet and the rain is so warm. Come.

RIVKELE: Papa locked the door and hid the key near the Torah Scroll. I stole the key from the Ark of the Scroll. My heart is still pounding.

(RIVKELE pushes her chest forward. MANKE feels her heart)

MANKE: I'm coming, Rivkele. Wait.

(MANKE jumps off the chair and exits.

RIVKELE's face disappears from the window, the Two GIRLS run off.

HINDL has observed this entire scene, standing at the edge of her cubicle. Now SHE paces around, going over her plans)

HINDL: Here's bread and butter. Now rent a place. Get married. You can be somebody. As good as anyone else. (SHE stops pacing and prays)   God in heaven, You are the God of orphans! Mama, help me from beyond the grave! Give me good luck for once! Let me get what I want! (Pause)   If You grant me this, God, we'll go to the synagogue and have a Torah Scroll written, I promise! Three pounds of candles for the synagogue every Sabbath. You are a good God, I know it. I'm just as good as they are. Don't I love you just as deeply? Father in heaven, I won't let you down!

(HINDL goes to her cubicle, packs her belongings.

MANKE and RIVKELE enter, both dripping wet.

HINDL closes her cubicle curtain)

227

MANKE: Are you cold, Rivkele? Snuggle up close to me. Come, let's sit on the sofa.

(SHE leads Rivkele to the sofa. THEY sit.)

MANKE: That's right, let your body caress me. So cool, like water running between us.

(SHE coos like a serpent in Rivkele's ear)

I uncovered your breasts and washed them with the rain water that ran into my hands. Your breasts are so white and so firm, the blood in them cools under my hand like white snow. They smell like fresh grass in the meadows. And I loosened your hair, like this—

(SHE runs her fingers through Rivkele's hair)

And I held it so in the rain and washed it. Its scent is the scent of May rain.

(SHE buries her face in Rivkele's hair)

Cool me with your hair, cool me so, let it wash over me, let it ...

(SHE washes her body in Rivkele's hair)

Wait. Let me comb your hair like a bride's, parted in the middle, with two long braids. Would you like that?

RIVKELE: (hypnotized): Yes, Manke.

MANKE: You will be the bride, a lovely bride, on Friday at Shabbes. You're sitting at the Shabbes table with your father and mother. I'm the bridegroom, tall and strong, your bridegroom, coming to see you. Would you like that, Rivkele? Would you?

RIVKELE: Yes, Manke.

MANKE: Wait, wait. No. Your father and mother have gone to bed. Bride and Groom are alone at the table. We're shy and embarrassed. Alright?

RIVKELE: Yes, Manke.

MANKE: Then we overcome our shyness and draw close to each other. You're my bride and I'm your bridegroom. We finally embrace.

(SHE puts her arms around Rivkele, presses her close)

We're pressed together so closely, your flesh and mine, then we kiss each other so shyly, like virgins. Like this.

(THEY kiss)

MANKE: We blush, we're embarrassed. We've never been left alone before, never tasted such a sweet kiss ... It's good so far, isn't it?

RIVKELE: Yes, Manke.

MANKE (back in her "role," whispering in Rivkele's ear):   Then we go to sleep in the same bed. Our two bodies lying there, side by side. No one sees. No one knows. Just the two of us, lying there like this. Like two children who are without sin. But we're not children, are we? (SHE pulls Rivkele close)   Would you like to sleep the whole night with me, Rivkele, in the same bed?

RIVKELE: Yes, Manke. I would.

MANKE: Come along.

(MANKE helps Rivkele up, THEY start toward her cubicle)

RIVKELE (stops):   I'm afraid of my father. What if he gets up?

MANKE: Wait. What if I took you away from here? We could be together all day and night. No one would scold you or hit you. It would be such fun.

RIVKELE: Wouldn't Papa find out?

MANKE (shakes her head):   We'll run off tonight, now, with Hindl. She has a place. She and Shloyme. We'll be alone the whole day. We'll dress up like officers and ride around on our horses. Wouldn't you like that?

RIVKELE: Papa will hear us.

MANKE: He won't. He's sleeping so soundly. Can't you hear him snoring?

(MANKE runs to Hindl's cubicle, pulls HINDL out into the open)

MANKE: You do have a place, don't you?

(HINDL throws Rivkele a dress to wear)

HINDL: Quickly, to Shloyme's. He'll take us there.

MANKE (dressing Rivkele):   You'll see how good it will be. How much fun.

(MANKE and HINDL each throw on a coat, THEY all start to leave. At the door, THEY run into REYZL and BASHA, who have been washing their hair.)

REYZL: Where are you going?

HINDL (tries to seem casual):   We're going out for something to drink. Don't tell anyone.

(HINDL, MANKE, and RIVKELE exit into the night)

REYZL: I don't like it.

BASHA: Me either.

REYZL: Something's going on. It's none of our business. We don't know a thing.

(REYZL turns down the lamp. The GIRLS go to their cubicles.
The stage is half-dark now. A few moments pass.)

REYZL: Boy, was my granny right. Who said it was an old wives' tale?

(BASHA runs from her cubicle with a sob. REYZL looks out.)

REYZL: What's the matter?

BASHA: I keep seeing my mother with the briars and thorns. She's walking around my room.

REYZL: I don't like this. There are bad spirits in the air, the Torah Scroll is no good now ...

BASHA: Don't say that, Reyzl! How will I ever get to sleep?

(A terrible noise is heard upstairs: YANKEL and SORE screaming O.S., furniture flying around the room, etc.)

YANKEL (shouting O.S.): Rivkele? Rivkele? Where are you?

REYZL (To Basha):   Remember, we don't know a thing.

(BASHA nods. BASHA and REYZL go back to bed.

YANKEL enters, storming around wildly. HE pushes back the cubicle curtains, rousing REYZL and BASHA.)

229

YANKEL: Where is Rivkele? Where is my daughter?

BASHA (rubbing her eyes):   What?

REYZL: How should we know?

YANKEL: You don't know? You didn't hear anything? Basha?
    (HE grabs Basha and shakes her)
Basha, where is she? Where is she?

    (REYZL tries to get in between Yankel and Basha)

REYZL: Get off her! Get away!

    (YANKEL pushes Reyzl away)

BASHA: I don't know. I don't know anything.

YANKEL (shaking Basha):   Where is my daughter? Tell me!

REYZL: She's gone.

YANKEL: What?

REYZL: She went off with Hindl and Manke.

    (YANKEL lets go of Basha, turns to Reyzl)

YANKEL: And you didn't stop her?

REYZL: What could I do?

YANKEL: You could have stopped her!

REYZL: I couldn't.

YANKEL: Where is she?

REYZL: They went off with Hindl. I heard them talking about a place.

YANKEL: Where is this place?

REYZL: I don't know. Really. But I'm sure that it's not far away.

YANKEL (To Basha):   What about you?

BASHA: I don't know either. I swear. (Pause)

YANKEL (yelling upstairs):   Sore! Sore!

    (HE runs out wildly, scrambling back up the O.S. stairs. HE emerges into the
    upstairs set, throwing furniture and clothing around, while shaking SORE.)

YANKEL (upstairs, screams out):   Your daughter! Your daughter! Where is your
daughter?

ACT III

(The next morning. Lights up on Yankel's living quarters. Clothing and
underwear are strewn around, the room is in disarray.

SORE, disheveled, picks up scattered garments and puts them into piles, preparing to pack her suitcase, then stopping, unsure.

YANKEL sits in a chair, unmoving.

A gray light seeps in through the closed shutters.)

SORE (picking up garments):   Look at him: just sitting there thinking, thinking, thinking about his precious Torah Scroll. What's there to think about? If you're in trouble, then do something, while there's still time. Go out and take care of the bastard. Yankel? (SHE approaches him)   Why don't you say something? Say something! Please. (SHE sits on a bundle)   Do you want me to leave? If you want me to leave, Yankel, I'll leave. It's all the same to me. I'll earn my bread somehow.

(SHE stands, begins packing)

YANKEL: I'll go ... You'll go ... Rivkele will go ... Everything down to the house.

SORE: Yankel, what's wrong with you? Just think what you're doing. We've had some bad luck. Alright. Who doesn't? But there's still time. (Pause) Come, let's find Shloyme. We'll give him some money, and he'll give us our child back. Come on! Why sit around doing nothing?

YANKEL (speaks in a monotone, walks aimlessly around the room):   It doesn't matter. Nothing will help. God is against it.

(HE stops at the window and looks through the shutters)

SORE (mimicking him):   "God is against it." "God is against it." Stop dreaming! It's you who's against it. Do you love your child? (SHE pulls at his clothes, shaking him)   Wake up, Yankel! Wake up. He could be taking her somewhere right now. Let's go over to his place. Why stand around? (pause) I sent for Reb Elye. Let's hear what he has to say. (Pause) What are you looking at? Say something for heaven's sake, Yankel! Why don't you speak?

YANKEL: No more daughter. A whore, just like her mother. (Pause) Down to the house. Everything down to the house.

SORE: You can sit on your hands if you want to. Not me. (stands) I'll give Shloyme my diamond earrings. (SHE takes these out) And this gold chain, I'll throw that in too. (SHE puts this in her pocket) I own some things too. If the bloodsucker won't hand her over, I'll throw in a hundred. (SHE searches through Yankel's pockets, removes money) You watch: in fifteen minutes I'll have Rivkele back here.

(SHE throws on a shawl and leaves, slamming the door)

YANKEL (wandering):   No more daughter ... No more Torah Scroll. Everything down to the house.

(REYZL knocks, then pokes her head in the front door)

REYZL: Reb Elye is here. Madame sent me to bring him.

YANKEL: What can he do?

REYZL: She was such a good girl too. It's a pity. (Pause: YANKEL looks at her) Madame asked me to wait here until she gets back.

YANKEL: I haven't gone mad yet, don't worry.

(REB ELYE enters, carrying a lantern)

REB ELYE: What's happened? It's almost daybreak. I have to get back for prayers.

YANKEL: The Torah Scroll has been defiled.

REB ELYE: Do you know what you're saying? God help us! Was it dropped to the ground? The whole city will have to fast!

YANKEL: Worse than that, Reb Elye. Much worse.

REB ELYE (To Reyzl):   What in God's name is he saying?

REYZL: His daughter Rivkele's gone, sir. The Torah Scroll is unharmed. In there.
     (SHE points to Rivkele's room)

REB ELYE: Thank God! You're sure it's unharmed? What a scare! (HE spits. To Yankel) What kind of nonsense was that? This is nothing to joke about.

YANKEL: For me, my daughter is holier than a Torah Scroll.

REB ELYE: That's enough babbling. So has anyone gone to look for your daughter?

REYZL: The Madame went after her, sir.

REB ELYE: Then what's all the fuss about? You don't even need me. (Pause) Just keep this quiet, you understand? Let the young man's father find out, it'll cost you a few hundred extra right off.

YANKEL (shrugs):   I don't care anymore. No more daughter. No more Torah Scroll. Everything down to the house.

REB ELYE: What's gotten into you? You're really going too far. (Pause) So what if you've had some misfortune? Trust in God and the troubles will pass. The main thing is to just keep it quiet. You hear? (Pause) Now I saw a certain young man's father . . .

     (HE sees Reyzl, motions for her to go. REYZL exits)

REB ELYE: I spoke with the father at synagogue between afternoon and evening prayers. He is close to agreeing. Even though I made it clear that the bride doesn't come from the best of families. Another hundred more for the dowry—it's worth it in the end, don't you think? The most important thing is that no one must ever find out. It's in both of our interests, you see? (Pause) Let me know as soon as the girl is returned. Right away. Alright? (HE starts to leave, turns) Right away. (Continues going)

YANKEL (grabs Reb Elye's hand):   Please, Reb Elye. Take your Torah Scroll with you. I don't want it here.

REB ELYE: What are you talking about? Are you crazy?

YANKEL: The Torah Scroll has been defiled. God is punishing me.

REB ELYE: Get a hold of yourself!

YANKEL: Why couldn't He have broken my legs, or sent me to an early grave? What did he want of my daughter?

REB ELYE: Stop it right now! You mustn't talk against God.

YANKEL: I may be Yankel Chapchovich, owner of a house, but even I can tell God the truth. I'm not afraid. He can strike me dead right here and now. I am ready. (Pause. To Reb Elye) I came to you in the synagogue. You said to have a Torah Scroll written. I put it there, in her room. Night after night I stood before it and said: "You are God. You know what I've done. If you want to punish me, do it. Go ahead, punish my wife. But not my daughter. Have pity. She's only a child.

REB ELYE: Nothing final has happened. Your daughter will still make a good Jewish wife.

YANKEL: If she had died, Reb Elye, I would have said nothing. I would have known that I buried a chaste Jewish girl. But now what am I worth in this world? We're corrupted ourselves, and we leave behind a corrupt generation. Our corruption is passed from one age to the next.

REB ELYE: How dare you talk that way! Remember, my friend, you're a Jew. Better to trust in God and to say: what was done has been done for a reason.

YANKEL: God is against it. That is the only reason. But why? Why did He have to do this? It was me, Yankel the Sinner, who was trying to pull himself out of the swamp. Why did He have to pull down my daughter?

(YANKEL goes into the other room, returns with Torah Scroll, holds it aloft)

YANKEL (to Scroll): You are a mighty God! I, Yankel Chapchovich, humble myself before you! I am the sinner! Me! Send down a fire to burn me! Crack the earth open and swallow me up! But don't hurt my child. Please God. Protect her from harm ...

REB ELYE: Do you have any idea what you're doing? What you've already done?

YANKEL (beseeching the Scroll): You have the power of miracles ... Send her back to me pure, as chaste as she was. You are a mighty God! Do it! (Pause) And if you don't, then You're no God at all. I, Yankel Chapchovich, will renounce You! Because You will have shown Yourself to be vengeful, a God of Vengeance, and no better than me!

REB ELYE: Put that down now! I command you!

(REB ELYE grabs the Torah Scroll out of Yankel's hands.
REB ELYE clutches the Scroll, kissing it.)

REB ELYE (To Yankel): Come here and beg His forgiveness!

YANKEL: God Himself can be told the truth to His face. Even I, a sinner, can tell Him. (Pause) If He is a great and merciful God, then I ask Him to show it!

REB ELYE (recites prayers in an undertone; To Yankel): Come, let's put the Torah Scroll back and pray together. God will help you, you'll see. If you truly repent, He'll have mercy.

(REB ELYE carries the Scroll O.S. to Rivkele's room. YANKEL follows.

SORE comes in the front door, excited. SHE straightens her hair in front of the mirror, catching a glimpse of Yankel and Reb Elye praying in the other room. SHE stealthily closes that door, locks it)

SORE: Come in, Shloyme. Come in. Why stand outside?

SHLOYME (in the doorway): Is Yankel in there?

SORE: Not to worry.

SHLOYME (enters warily): Just tell him I don't hold any grudge, even if he did insult me.

(SORE pockets the key to Rivkele's room, ushers SHLOYME into the room)

233

SORE: We'll leave him alone. Lately he's found religion, you know. Likes to hang around with Rebbes and students. (SHE locks the front door)
Good. We're alone now. (SHE comes toward him, coquettish, teasing)
How could you attach yourself to such a pest? A strong man like you.
I bet she follows you back here. (SHE smiles coyly)

SHLOYME: What if she does? Who cares?

SORE: A handsome fellow like you ... What do you need with a low-class whore?

SHLOYME: Didn't I tell you we're finished? If Shloyme says it, he means it. I'm a man of my word.

SORE: Oh yes? Then show me. (SHE kisses him on the lips) You know you can deal with me, Shloyme. Haven't I always been straight with you?

SHLOYME: You haven't been very nice to me lately.

SORE: I haven't?

SHLOYME: You've been going around with your nose in the air.

SORE: This is still Sore, isn't it? You can talk to me.

(SORE points coyly to her nose. SHLOYME smiles and kisses it)

SHLOYME: You don't think I would have married that bitch? My mother, God protect her, would have cursed every bone in my body. Not to mention my sister.

SORE: (smiles): That's what I thought. (SHE opens her hand, shows diamond earrings) Here, take these, and here's a hundred besides. (SHE gives these to him) Now tell me where my Rivkele is.

SHLOYME: So that's your game, is it? (HE pockets the earrings and the money) You were once a very good woman. Then you got spoiled.

SORE: Where is she, Shloyme? You promised.

SHLOYME: You've got a very good girl there. A really sweet child. You could make lots of money.

SORE: You know such talk doesn't scare me. It takes a lot more than that. (Pause) Have you taken her somewhere? Is that it?

SHLOYME: You were a good woman, Sore. You were the best.

(HE initiates the kiss this time, but SORE more than matches him, taking control. SHE grabs Shloyme by the hair and pulls his head back.)

SORE: Where have you taken her, Shloyme? I want to know now.

SHLOYME: This is why I always liked you.

SORE: I'm not playing around!

SHLOYME (smiling): She's not far from here, not very far. I'll take you to her.

SORE: That's better. (SHE lets him go.) Whenever you're ready ...

SHLOYME: You've got spirit, Sore. I like that.

(The sound of fists are heard beating on the front door)

HINDL (O.S., calling): Don't tell her anything! You don't know a thing! Shloyme!

SORE (to Shloyme): Let her beat her head against the wall. Maybe she'll get some sense.

SHLOYME (to Sore):   Open the door.

SORE: You don't need her. I'll get you a better girl, you'll see.

HINDL (O.S.):   Shloyme, don't trust her!

SHLOYME (to Sore):   You'll get your daughter, don't worry. Now open the door.

(SORE shrugs and unlocks the door. HINDL rushes onstage)

HINDL: You didn't tell her our secret, did you? You swore on your father's grave.

SORE: What a dog!

HINDL (taking Shloyme aside):   We can still go to Lodz and get married. With two girls like that! We'll be rich.

SORE: Go on, Shloyme, go with her. But don't forget your good Jewish mother. And your father was a pious man too. What would he think of such garbage?

SHLOYME (nodding):   A promise is a promise. I'm a man of my word.

(SHLOYME and SORE head for the door. HINDL runs to the door, blocks it)

HINDL: What about your promise to me? You swore to me, Shloyme.

SHLOYME: You're old news. (HE pushes her away. To Sore) Let's go.

SORE: Just wait a minute. (SHE hurries to Rivkele's room, unlocks door. To Yankel:)   Rivkele's coming back! She'll be home soon!

SHLOYME: I'll be outside.

(SHLOYME exits, HINDL follows him out)

HINDL (O.S.): You can't do this to me! I won't let you!

SORE: I'm coming, Shloyme!

(SHE exits. REB ELYE and YANKEL enter)

REB ELYE: God be praised! God be praised! (To Yankel, who paces the room) You see? God did help you, even though you spoke blasphemy to Him. He punishes us with sickness, but He also sends us a cure. From now on, though, you must be more careful. Come to the synagogue more. Learn what the Torah Scroll means.

(Pause: HE watches Yankel pace back and forth.)

REB ELYE: I'll go over and see the bridegroom's father. We'll work out the details. Just remember: don't haggle. A hundred or so more's not too bad. Just pay him right away and don't make any trouble. You're lucky you have me to help. Are you listening?

YANKEL: I want to ask her one thing. Just one thing ... Let her tell me the truth.

REB ELYE: Don't make things any worse. You're a fortunate man.

YANKEL: Just yes or no. Let her tell me.

REB ELYE: Let God worry about the truth, my friend. You look after your daughter. And tell your wife to clean this place up.

(REB ELYE exits)

YANKEL (pacing):   All I want is the truth. Just the truth. Let her tell me.

(Pause: YANKEL paces.

SORE opens the front door, enters.)

SORE (to O.S.): Come in. Come in. Your father won't hurt you. (Pause) It won't help anything, standing out in the hall ...

(RIVKELE enters slowly, a shawl pulled over her head.
SHE stands in the doorway, looking in, grim and defiant)

SORE: Come in already, our daughter who has made us so proud. Go on, comb your hair. Put on a dress. We have company coming. (To Yankel) Reb Elye agreed that he'll bring the groom's father here. The sooner we do this ... (SHE starts cleaning up)

(YANKEL goes to RIVKELE, leads her by the hand to the table)

YANKEL: Don't be afraid. I won't hit you. (HE sits) Sit down.

RIVKELE (hiding her face): I can stand just as well.

YANKEL: I said to sit down.

(HE walks over and forces HER to sit. HE sits again.)

YANKEL: Rivkele, you are my daughter and I am your father ... Don't be afraid of me.

RIVKELE: What should I be afraid of?

YANKEL: Tell me the truth, child, the whole truth. There's nothing to be ashamed of. I know that you're not to blame, the sins are mine and your mother's.

SORE: Let her go and get dressed! The bridegroom's father will be here any minute.

YANKEL: I am warning you now, get away!

SORE: What' the matter with you? (SHE turns away) He's gone mad!

(YANKEL seats RIVKELE down again)

YANKEL: I won't hurt you. (HE strokes her hair)
Rivkele, Rivkele ... I gave you my life.

RIVKELE: What about my life? What kind of life did you give me?

YANKEL: I gave you the world!

RIVKELE: Trying to make a rabbi's wife out of me, when all along ...

YANKEL: I wanted to protect you.

RIVKELE: Protect me from what?

YANKEL: Your mother and I—

RIVKELE: What about Mama? Why didn't Mama marry as young?

SORE: Just listen to her!

RIVKELE: Don't worry, I know. I know everything.

YANKEL: What do you know? (Pause) Tell me! I want to hear it.

SORE: Leave the girl alone, will you?

YANKEL: No one's talking to you. Alright, enough of this.
(HE rises, takes Rivkele's hand)
Tell me the truth. Are you still as pure as when you left here? Are you still a chaste girl?

(RIVKELE looks away)

Look me in the eye! In the eye. Are you still the same as when you left here? Tell me the truth.

RIVKELE: I don't know.

YANKEL: You don't know? What does that mean? Were you with a man, yes or no?

(RIVKELE tears away from her father's grip, stands up)

RIVKELE: What difference does it make? I'm just like the other girls now. The ones who work for you.

(YANKEL raises his hand to strike her)

RIVKELE: Go ahead. Hit me. I'm just like you. Now I'm really your daughter. (Pause)

(SORE steps in between them)

SORE: Yankel, stop now! Rivkele can still get married. We'll say nothing happened. (Pause) Put on your jacket. They're coming ...

(SORE helps YANKEL put on his jacket, etc.)

SORE: We'll just make the effort, alright?

(REB ELYE enters with the bridegroom's FATHER in tow.
SORE, the hostess, pushes her stray hairs beneath her wig.)

SORE: Welcome, welcome. Please come inside.

(SORE offers REB ELYE and FATHER chairs to sit in.)

REB ELYE (to Yankel):   So how is the father of the bride?

(Awkward Pause)

SORE (prompting):   Yankel.

(SORE signals YANKEL to get moving. YANKEL walks over and shakes hands. THEY all sit)

REB ELYE: Let's get right down to business. (To Father, referring to Yankel) This man wants to arrange a match. His daughter is a chaste Jewish maiden, an ideal wife for a scholar such as your son. He has agreed to support them both for the rest of their lives.

FATHER: Very good.

YANKEL (muttering):   A chaste Jewish maiden ... a chaste ...

REB ELYE (hurrying along):   This man will pay 500 cash at the engagement. He'll treat your son like his own child.

FATHER: No need for me to boast about what I've got. He's a real prize. Two more years of study and he'll be a rabbi.

REB ELYE: Fine, fine. We know that. This man will treasure him more than his own life. He'll be able to sit and study here all day and night.

YANKEL (points to Rivkele's room):   Yes, in there he can study the holy Torah. (Pause) I have a good girl, so innocent. Pure ...

(YANKEL suddenly stands and goes into Rivkele's room, drags RIVKELE out by the arm. SHE is half-dressed, her hair is disheveled, etc.)

237

YANKEL: Here she is. Look at her. Here. The flesh of my flesh.

SORE: Yankel!

FATHER: What's going on?

REB ELYE: This is unseemly. Take her inside.

YANKEL: I wanted to show you my child. Isn't she a beautiful whore?

FATHER: What in God's name ...? (HE stands) This man is crazy.

REB ELYE (standing):   I'm as astonished as you are. How could I know?

(REB ELYE runs after the FATHER, but FATHER has already exited.

YANKEL grabs hold of REB ELYE)

YANKEL: Take your Torah Scroll with you. I don't want it here.

(REB ELYE shakes his head, enraged.

YANKEL runs into Rivkele's room, comes back holding the Scroll.)

YANKEL: Take it out of my house!

(REB ELYE takes the scroll from him)

REB ELYE: What were you thinking? You've ruined us all!

(REB ELYE leaves hurriedly, carefully carrying the Scroll)

YANKEL moves Downstage and sits down heavily. Pause.

Then RIVKELE grabs her shawl and walks out the front door.)

SORE: Rivkele!

YANKEL: Let her go.

SORE: Rivkele!

YANKEL: Down to the house. Everything down to the house.

(Lights fade slowly to black.

END OF PLAY)

Index

239

Stephen Fife's plays have been produced in NYC at Jewish Rep, Playhouse 91, Primary Stages, Circle Rep Lab, La Mama, Theater for the New City, the Samuel Beckett Theater, and many other venues. *Break of Day*, his play about van Gogh's early career, was given a Hollywood production that prompted one critic to write, "It leads lovers of theater to have hope that there is a future for brilliant writers." (That makes two of us.) His work has also been done at 7 Stages in Atlanta, and other regional and college theaters.

Fife is a graduate of Sarah Lawrence College and Columbia's School of the Arts, and his writing has appeared in the *New York Times*, *Village Voice*, and *New Republic*. He has received several grants and awards, including a Federal writing grant, which seemed like a big deal at the time. He is currently at work on several new projects, including an 11-book cycle called *A Short History Of a People Who Can't Remember a Thing About Their History*.